A *NEW YORK TIMES* NOTABLE BOOK

BLOODS

Black Veterans of the Vietnam War: An Oral History

"Simply the most powerful and moving book that has emerged on this topic."
—United Press International

D0030094

WALLACE TERRY

"Terry's oral history captures the very essence of war, at both its best and worst. . . . [He] has done a great service for all Americans with *Bloods*."
—*The Washington Post Book World*

"More than just a black view of the Vietnam conflict . . . If your eyes don't mist during one of the chapters, your tear ducts don't work."
—*Los Angeles Times*

"An invaluable addition to the expanding legion of histories about the Vietnam War."
—*Chicago Sun-Times*

"Almost any glowing adjective—or group of adjectives, for that matter—can be used to describe *Bloods*."
—*Detroit Free Press*

Ballantine / Del Rey /
Presidio Press /
One World

ISBN 978-0-345-31197-9

U.S.A. $8.99 CANADA $11.99

9 780345 311979

50899

EAN

"A portrait not just of warfare and warriors but of beleaguered patriotism and pride. The violence recalled in *Bloods* is chilling. . . . On most of its pages hope prevails. Some of these men have witnessed the very worst that people can inflict on one another. . . . Their experience finally transcends race; their dramatic monologues bear witness to humanity."

—*Time*

"Terry's oral history captures the very essence of war, at both its best and worst. . . . Wallace Terry . . . has done a great service for all Americans with *Bloods*. Future historians will find his case studies extremely useful, and they will be hard pressed to ignore the role of blacks, as too often has been the case in past wars."

—*The Washington Post Book World*

"Wallace Terry set out to write an oral history of American blacks who fought for their country in Vietnam, but he did better than that. He wrote a compelling portrait of Americans in combat, and used his words so that the reader—black or white—knows the soldiers as men and Americans, their race overshadowed by the larger humanity Terry conveys. . . . This is not light reading, but it is literature with the ring of truth that shows the reader worlds through the eyes of others. You can't ask much more from a book than that."

—Associated Press

"This is an invaluable addition to the expanding legion of histories about the Vietnam War. . . . A graphically illuminating but disquieting collection of twenty personal accounts reflecting the black military experience in Vietnam . . . Through their recollections of the war, we see America's internal racial strife set against a major conflict."
—*Chicago Sun-Times*

"The soldiers' descriptions of the war's ugliness and that of Americans fighting and dying were so dramatically explicit a reader could visualize himself shivering in the monsoon rain, stalking through muddy swamps, and witnessing comrades cut the ears off dead Vietcong rebels to wear on their dog chains. . . . *Bloods* is an attention-keeper. It lets the reader relive the emotions and the turmoil of these men during the war and upon returning home. . . . *Bloods* recovers once-lost pages of the Vietnam War that should never be forgotten again."
—*Nashville Banner*

"Although Bloods are what black soldiers called themselves in Vietnam, the title also suggests the racism, vileness and bloodletting they experienced in America's most unpopular war. . . . But more than just a black view of the Vietnam conflict, the book is an absolute condemnation of war. If your eyes don't mist during one of the chapters, your tear ducts don't work."
—*Los Angeles Times*

BLOODS

Black Veterans of the Vietnam War:
An Oral History

WALLACE TERRY

BALLANTINE BOOKS • NEW YORK

2006 Presidio Press Mass Market Edition

Published in the United States by Presidio Press, an imprint of The Random House Publishing Group, a division of Random House, Inc., New York. Originally published by Random House, an imprint of The Random House Publishing Group, a division of Random House, Inc., in 1984.

PRESIDIO PRESS and colophon are registered trademarks of Random House, Inc.

This edition published by arrangement with Random House, Inc.

ISBN 978-0-345-31197-9

Cover photo courtesy of the U.S. Marine Corps

Printed in the United States of America

www.presidiopress.com

OPM 49 48 47 46 45 44 43

This book is for my wife, Janice,
who did not defer the dream that
it would one day happen.

I have an intuitive feeling that the Negro
servicemen have a better understanding than
whites of what the war is about.
—*General William C. Westmoreland,*
U.S. Army, Saigon, 1967

The Bloods is us.
—*Gene Woodley, Former Combat*
Paratrooper, Baltimore, 1983

 Acknowledgments

Every book is born in debt. In this small way I acknowledge the debt this book and I owe to those who made the birth possible. Without the generous support of those friends of the black Vietnam War veteran and their belief in me, these stories would not have been told here.

I thank them all.

Marc Jaffe welcomed the concept of this book when I brought the idea to Random House. Erroll McDonald, the editor of the book, guided its development and provided invaluable suggestions for its form and shape. Robert Wyatt contributed his gifts as the editor of the Ballantine edition.

Roslyn Targ, my literary agent, never wavered in her belief in the book's importance. She freed me from my doubts and held my hand.

Richard Boone, president, Leslie Dunbar, past president, and The Field Foundation supported my early research into the experience of black Vietnam War veterans.

Franklin Thomas, president, and The Ford Foundation made their support available for the completion of that research in the form of this book.

John Quinn and John Seigenthaler granted me a leave of absence from the editorial staff of *USA Today* in order to complete the interviewing and editing.

Ronald H. Brown, chairman of the board of trustees, Robert L. Green, president, and the community of the University of the District of Columbia made me feel at home at the university during that time.

I found some of the veterans included in this book through the assistance of the Veterans Administration's Vet Center Program. Especially helpful were Dr. Arthur Blank, the program director, Elaine Alvarez, Harold Doughty, Husher Harris, Tom Harris, Michael Jackson, George Knight, Edward Lord, Erqin Parson, Leonard Porter, Robert G. Smith and Arto Woods.

In the military community I received the wise advice and counsel of B/Gen. Richard Abel USAF, M/Gen. Harry Brooks, Jr., USA (ret.), Cmdr. Carlos C. Campbell USNR, Capt. Kenneth Norman USA (ret.), M/Gen. Frank Petersen USMC, Maj. Gilford Robinson USMC, and CMSGT James H. Smith USAF (ret.).

Many members of my family shared their love, support, and, most of all, patience, during the research and writing. I am especially grateful to Gus and Betty Hamilton, Billye and Cedric Jessup, and my children, Wallace III, Lisa and David.

Wally, the oldest, was virtually a second editor of the book. He devoted several months to the research and preparation of the stories. He was a veritable sounding board, for I had at my side a young man of the approximate age and with similar thoughts and feelings as those GIs who fought the war. His opinions gave the book a special grace.

During the time that I was covering the Vietnam War for *Time* magazine, my wife, Janice, made eighteen trips to visit me in Saigon. Each time she would go upcountry to visit an aid station, hospital or base camp to help boost the morale of black fighting men. They were her "heroes." And to them, she was "Soul Sister No. 1." She gave this book and its author the same mothering care.

For reasons best known to them I am also grateful to: Sallie Blake, Don Brandt, John Britton, Kristin Clark, Marsh and Pippa Clark, Rep. Ron Dellums, Shearon Dishman, Eugene C. Dorsey, Ted Van Dyk, Murray Gart, Michelle Gundy, Charles Harris, Carl Holman, Mary Jane Hunter, Bruce Jessup, Gayle Jessup, Larry L. King, Stephen Lane, Bernard Lang, Carl McCarden, Dan Martin, William Mayo, Frank McCulloch, Nancy Nelson, Michelle Nielsen, Anne Elizabeth Oliver, Ed Pfeiffer, Pat Reis, Sandra Roberts, Pat Smith, John and Bunny Sanders, Gerald Sass, Jack A. Scott, Dick and Germaine Swanson, Wallace Terry, Sr., Raphael Tisdale, Ron Townsend and Patricia Woodlin.

The twenty veterans whose stories comprise this book opened their hearts and homes, minds and memories to me, often on several occasions, sometimes across a dozen years or more. They shared more than time and friendship; they shared their spirit and soul. And that is what I tried to capture in the telling of their stories for posterity. They and their families have my special appreciation for their gifts to this book.

 **Contents**

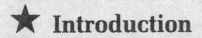 # Introduction

In early 1967, while at the Washington bureau of *Time* magazine, I received a telephone call from Richard Clurman, then chief of correspondents. Clurman wanted me to fly to Saigon to help report a cover story on the role of the black soldier in the Vietnam War. Already the war was dividing the Nation deeply. In the black community, highly popular figures such as Martin Luther King, Jr., and Cassius Clay were speaking out against it.

I gladly accepted the assignment.

The attention President Lyndon Johnson was giving to the Great Society and civil rights progress, which I was covering at the time, was being eroded by his increasing preoccupation with the war. The war was destroying the bright promises for social and economic change in the black community. I was losing a great story on the home-front to a greater story on the battlefront.

At that moment the Armed Forces seemed to represent the most integrated institution in American society. For

the first time blacks were fully integrated in combat and
fruitfully employed in positions of leadership. The Pentagon was praising the gallant, hard-fighting black soldier,
who was dying at a greater rate, proportionately, than
American soldiers of other races. In the early years of
the fighting, blacks made up 23 percent of the fatalities.
In Vietnam, Uncle Sam was an equal opportunity employer. That, too, made Vietnam a compelling story.

And finally, Vietnam was, as I told my worried wife
who was concerned about my safety, the war of my generation.

In May of 1967 I reported in *Time* that I found most
black soldiers in Vietnam supported the war effort, because they believed America was guaranteeing the sov-
ereignty of a democratically constituted government in
South Vietnam and halting the spread of communism in
Southeast Asia. President Johnson called me to the White
House to hear that assessment first-hand; he was pleased
by my briefing.

Later that year I returned to Vietnam for a two-year
assignment that ended when I witnessed the withdrawal
of the first American forces in 1969. Black combat fatalities had dropped to 14 percent, still proportionately higher
than the 11 percent which blacks represented in the American population. But by that same year a new black soldier
had appeared. The war had used up the professionals who
found in military service fuller and fairer employment
opportunities than blacks could find in civilian society,
and who found in uniform a supreme test of their black
manhood. Replacing the careerists were black draftees,
many just steps removed from marching in the Civil Rights
Movement or rioting in the rebellions that swept the urban
ghettos from Harlem to Watts. All were filled with a new
sense of black pride and purpose. They spoke loudest
against the discrimination they encountered on the battlefield in decorations, promotion and duty assignments.
They chose not to overlook the racial insults, cross-
burnings and Confederate flags of their white comrades.
They called for unity among black brothers on the battlefield to protest these indignities and provide mutual
support. And they called themselves "Bloods."

In the last years of the American presence, both black

soldier and white fought to survive a war they knew they would never win in the conventional sense. And, often, they fought each other. The war, which had bitterly divided America like no other issue since the Civil War, had become a double battleground, pitting American soldier against American soldier. The spirit of foxhole brotherhood I found in 1967 had evaporated.

In the years since the collapse of the Saigon government to the victorious Communist forces, I have believed that America owed the black veterans of the war a special debt. There were no flags waving or drums beating upon the return of any Vietnam veterans, who were blamed by the right in our society for losing the war, and by the left for being the killers of the innocent. But what can be said about the dysfunction of Vietnam veterans in general can be doubled in its impact upon most blacks; they hoped to come home to more than they had before; they came home to less. Black unemployment among black veterans is more than double the rate for white veterans. The doors to the Great Society had been shut.

Among the 20 men who portray their war and postwar experiences in this book, I sought a representative cross-section of the black combat force. Enlisted men, noncommissioned officers, and commissioned officers. Soldiers, sailors, airmen and Marines. Those with urban backgrounds, and those from rural areas. Those for whom the war had a devastating impact, and those for whom the war basically was an opportunity to advance in a career dedicated to protecting American interests. All of them had won a badge of courage in combat, whether on a patrol boat or in a POW camp, on a night ambush or in the skies above North Vietnam, as medics and platoon leaders, as fighters pilots and grunts.

These stories are not to be found in the expanding body of Vietnam literature; they deservedly belong in the forefront because of the unique experience of the black Vietnam veteran. He fought at a time when his sisters and brothers were fighting and dying at home for equal rights and greater opportunities, for a color-blind nation promised to him in the Constitution he swore to defend. He fought at a time when some of his leaders chastised him for waging war against a people of color, and when his

Communist foe appealed to him to take up arms instead against the forces of racism in America. The loyalty of the black Vietnam War veteran stood a greater test on the battleground than did the loyalty of any other American soldier in Vietnam; his patriotism begs a special salute at home.

Above all, his experience requires the special notice of history, as it judges and continues to judge the Vietnam saga. In any black soldier of Vietnam can be found the darkness that is at the heart of all wars. What the black veteran illuminates in these pages of his own humanity as well as racial perception will help complete the missing pages of the American experience, and add to the pages of universal understanding of man's most terrible occupation.

When my youngest child, David, was still a baby, I learned about the death of the youngest American soldier who would die in combat in Vietnam. I was visiting Hoi An. The soldier was a sixteen-year-old black Marine from a poor and broken family in Brooklyn. He had lied about his age to join the Marines and thereby earn money to help support his mother. I vowed then that one day I would see between the covers of a book the story of the sacrifice of such young black men and others in the rice paddies of Vietnam—10,000 miles from the heartbreak of American poverty and discrimination and injustice. This is that book.

And now, as I write these words, that youngest child of mine is himself sixteen.

—Wallace Terry
Washington, D.C.
January 1, 1984

**Private First Class
Reginald "Malik" Edwards
Phoenix, Louisiana**

Rifleman
9th Regiment
U.S. Marine Corps
Danang
June 1965–March 1966

I'm in the Amtrac with Morley Safer, right? The whole thing is getting ready to go down. At Cam Ne. The whole bit that all America will see on the *CBS Evening News,* right? Marines burning down some huts. Brought to you by Morley Safer. Your man on the scene. August 5, 1965.

When we were getting ready for Cam Ne, the helicopters flew in first and told them to get out of the village 'cause the Marines are looking for VC. If you're left there, you're considered VC.

They told us if you receive one round from the village, you level it. So we was coming into the village, crossing over the hedges. It's like a little ditch, then you go through these bushes and jump across, and start kickin' ass, right?

Not only did we receive one round, three Marines got wounded right off. Not only that, but one of the Marines was our favorite Marine, Sergeant Bradford. This brother that everybody loved got shot in the groin. So you know how we felt.

The first thing happened to me, I looked out and here's a bamboo snake. That little short snake, the one that bites you and you're through bookin'. What do you do when a bamboo snake comin' at you? You drop your rifle with one hand, and shoot his head off. You don't think you can do this, but you do it. So I'm so rough with this snake, everybody thinks, well, Edwards is shootin' his ass off today.

So then this old man runs by. This other sergeant says, "Get him, Edwards." But I missed the old man. Now I just shot the head off a snake. You dig what I'm sayin'? Damn near with one hand. M-14. But all of a sudden, I missed this old man. 'Cause I really couldn't shoot him.

So Brooks—he's got the grenade launcher—fired. Caught my man as he was comin' through the door. But what happened was it was a room full of children. Like a schoolroom. And he was runnin' back to warn the kids that the Marines were coming. And that's who got hurt. All those little kids and people.

Everybody wanted to see what had happened, 'cause it was so fucked up. But the officers wouldn't let us go up there and look at what shit they were in. I never got the count, but a lot of people got screwed up. I was telling Morley Safer and his crew what was happening, but they thought I was trippin', this Marine acting crazy, just talking shit. 'Cause they didn't want to know what was going on.

So I'm going on through the village. Like the way you go in, you sweep, right? You fire at the top of the hut in case somebody's hangin' in the rafters. And if they hit the ground, you immediately fire along the ground, waist high, to catch them on the run. That's the way I had it worked out, or the way the Marines taught me. That's the process.

All of a sudden, this Vietnamese came runnin' after me, telling me not to shoot: "Don't shoot. Don't shoot." See, we didn't go in the village and look. We would just shoot first. Like you didn't go into a room to see who was in there first. You fired and go in. So in case there was somebody there, you want to kill them first. And we was just gonna run in, shoot through the walls. 'Cause it was nothin' to shoot through the walls of a bamboo hut.

You could actually set them on fire if you had tracers. That used to be a fun thing to do. Set hootches on fire with tracers.

So he ran out in front of me. I mean he's runnin' into my line of fire. I almost killed him. But I'm thinking, what the hell is wrong? So then we went into the hut, and it was all these women and children huddled together. I was gettin' ready to wipe them off the planet. In this one hut. I tell you, man, my knees got weak. I dropped down, and that's when I cried. First time I cried in the 'Nam. I realized what I would have done. I almost killed all them people. That was the first time I had actually had the experience of weak knees.

Safer didn't tell them to burn the huts down with they lighters. He just photographed it. He could have got a picture of me burning a hut, too. It was just the way they did it. When you say level a village, you don't use torches. It's not like in the 1800s. You use a Zippo. Now you would use a Bic. That's just the way we did it. You went in there with your Zippos. Everybody. That's why people bought Zippos. Everybody had a Zippo. It was for burnin' shit down.

I was a Hollywood Marine. I went to San Diego, but it was worse in Parris Island. Like you've heard the horror stories of Parris Island—people be marchin' into the swamps. So you were happy to be in San Diego. Of course, you're in a lot of sand, but it was always warm.

At San Diego, they had this way of driving you into this base. It's all dark. Back roads. All of a sudden you come to this little adobe-looking place. All of a sudden, the lights are on, and all you see are these guys with these Smokey the Bear hats and big hands on their hips. The light is behind them, shining through at you. You all happy to be with the Marines. And they say, "Better knock that shit off, boy. I don't want to hear a goddamn word out of your mouth." And everybody starts cursing and yelling and screaming at you.

My initial instinct was to laugh. But then they get right up in your face. That's when I started getting scared. When you're 117 pounds, 150 look like a monster. He would just come screaming down your back, "What the hell are you looking at, shit turd?" I remembered the time where you cursed, but you didn't let anybody adult hear it. You were usually doing it just to be funny or trying to be bold. But these people were actually serious about cursing your ass out.

Then here it is. Six o'clock in the morning. People come in bangin' on trash cans, hittin' my bed with night sticks. That's when you get really scared, 'cause you realize I'm not at home anymore. It doesn't look like you're in the Marine Corps either. It looks like you're in jail. It's like you woke up in a prison camp somewhere in the South. And the whole process was not to allow you to be yourself.

I grew up in a family that was fair. I was brought up on the Robin Hood ethic, and John Wayne came to save people. So I could not understand that if these guys were supposed to be the good guys, why were they treating each other like this?

I grew up in Plaquemines Parish. My folks were poor, but I was never hungry. My stepfather worked with steel on buildings. My mother worked wherever she could. In the fields, pickin' beans. In the factories, the shrimp factories, oyster factories. And she was a housekeeper.

I was the first person in my family to finish high school. This was 1963. I knew I couldn't go to college because my folks couldn't afford it. I only weighed 117 pounds, and nobody's gonna hire me to work for them. So the only thing left to do was go into the service. I didn't want to go into the Army, 'cause everybody went into the Army. Plus the Army didn't seem like it did anything. The Navy I did not like 'cause of the uniforms. The Air Force, too. But the Marines was bad. The Marine Corps built men. Plus just before I went in, they had all these John Wayne movies on every night. Plus the Marines went to the Orient.

Everybody laughed at me. Little, skinny boy can't work in the field going in the Marine Corps. So I passed the test. My mother, she signed for me 'cause I was seventeen.

There was only two black guys in my platoon in boot camp. So I hung with the Mexicans, too, because in them days we never hang with white people. You didn't have white friends. White people was the aliens to me. This is

'63. You don't have integration really in the South. You expected them to treat you bad. But somehow in the Marine Corps you hoping all that's gonna change. Of course, I found out this was not true, because the Marine Corps was the last service to integrate. And I had an Indian for a platoon commander who hated Indians. He used to call Indians blanket ass. And then we had a Southerner from Arkansas that liked to call you chocolate bunny and Brillo head. That kind of shit.

I went to jail in boot camp. What happened was I was afraid to jump this ditch on the obstacle course. Every time I would hit my shin. So a white lieutenant called me a nigger. And, of course, I jumped the ditch farther than I'd ever jumped before. Now I can't run. My leg is really messed up. I'm hoppin'. So it's pretty clear I can't do this. So I tell the drill instructor, "Man, I can't fucking go on." He said, "You said what?" I said it again. He said, "Get out." I said, "Fuck you." This to a drill instructor in 1963. I mean you just don't say that. I did seven days for disrespect. When I got out of the brig, they put me in a recon. The toughest unit.

We trained in guerrilla warfare for two years at Camp Pendleton. When I first got there, they was doing Cuban stuff. Cuba was the aggressor. It was easy to do Cuba because you had a lot of Mexicans. You could always let them be Castro. We even had Cuban targets. Targets you shoot at. So then they changed the silhouettes to Vietnamese. Everything to Vietnam. Getting people ready for the little gooks. And, of course, if there were any Hawaiians and Asian-Americans in the unit, they played the roles of aggressors in the war games.

Then we are going over to Okinawa, thinking we're going on a regular cruise. But the rumors are that we're probably going to the 'Nam. In Okinawa we was trained as raiders. Serious, intense jungle-warfare training. I'm gonna tell you, it was some good training. The best thing about the Marine Corps, I can say for me, is that they teach you personal endurance, how much of it you can stand.

The only thing they told us about the Viet Cong was they were gooks. They were to be killed. Nobody sits around and gives you their historical and cultural background. They're the enemy. Kill, kill, kill. That's what we got in practice. Kill, kill, kill. I remember a survey they did in the mess hall where we had to say how we felt about the war. The thing was, get out of Vietnam or fight. What we were hearing was Vietnamese was killing Americans. I felt that if people were killing Americans, we should fight them. As a black person, there wasn't no problem fightin' the enemy. I knew Americans were prejudiced, were racist and all that, but, basically, I believed in America 'cause I was an American.

I went over with the original 1st Battalion 9th Marines. When we got there, it was nothing like you expect a war to be. We had seen a little footage of the war on TV. But we was on the ship dreaming about landing on this beach like they did in World War II. Then we pulled into this area like a harbor almost and just walked off the ship.

And the first Vietnamese that spoke to me was a little kid up to my knee. He said, "You give me cigarette. You give me cigarette." That really freaked me out. This little bitty kid smokin' cigarettes. That is my first memory of Vietnam. I thought little kids smokin' was the most horrible thing that you could do. So the first Vietnamese words I learned was *Toi khong hut thuoc lo.* "I don't smoke cigarettes." And *Thuoc la co hai cho suc khoe.* "Cigarettes are bad for your health."

Remember, we were in the beginning of the war. We wasn't dealing with the regular army from the North. We was still fightin' the Viet Cong. The NVA was moving in, but they really hadn't made their super move yet. So we were basically runnin' patrols out of Danang. We were basically with the same orders that the Marines went into Lebanon with. I mean we couldn't even put rounds in the chambers at first.

It was weird. The first person that died in each battalion of the 9th Marines that landed was black. And they were killed by our own people. Comin' back into them lines was the most dangerous thing then. It was more fun sneakin' into Ho Chi Minh's house than comin' back into the lines of Danang. Suppose the idiot is sleeping on watch and he wake up. All of a sudden he sees people. That's all he sees. There was a runnin' joke around Vietnam that we was killing more of our people than the Vietnamese were. Like we were told to kill any Vietnamese in black. We didn't know that the ARVN had some black uniforms, too. And you could have a platoon commander calling the air strikes, and he's actually calling on your position. It was easy to get killed by an American.

They called me a shitbird, because I would stay in trouble. Minor shit, really. But they put me on point anyway. I spent most of my time in Vietnam runnin'. I ran through Vietnam 'cause I was always on point, and points got to run. They can't walk like everybody else. Specially when you hit them open areas. Nobody walked through an open area. After a while, you develop a way to handle it. You learned that the point usually survived. It was the people behind you who got killed.

And another thing. It's none of that shit, well, if they start shootin' at you, now all of a sudden we gonna run in there and outshoot them. The motherfuckers hit, you call in some air. Bring in some heavy artillery, whatever you need to cool them down. You wipe that area up. You soften it up. Then you lay to see if you receive any fire. An *then* you go on in.

I remember the first night we had went out on patrol. About 50 people shot this old guy. Everybody claimed they shot him. He got shot 'cause he started running. It was an old man running to tell his family. See, it wasn't s'posed to be nobody out at night but the Marines. Any Vietnamese out at night was the enemy. And we had guys who were frustrated from Korea with us. Guys who were real gung ho, wanted a name for themselves. So a lot of times they ain't tell us shit about who is who. People get out of line, you could basically kill them. So this old man was running like back towards his crib to warn his family. I think people said "Halt," but we didn't know no Vietnamese words.

It was like shootin' water buffaloes. Somebody didn't tell us to do this. We did it anyway. But they had to stop us from doing that. Well, the water buffaloes would actually attack Americans. I guess maybe we smelled different. You would see these little Vietnamese kids carrying around this huge water buffalo. That buffalo would see some Marines and start wantin' to run 'em down. You see the poor little kids tryin' to hold back the water buffalo, because these Marines will kill him. And Marines, man, was like, like we was always lookin' for shit to go wrong. Shit went wrong. That gave us the oppurtunity.

I remember we had went into this village and got pinned down with a Australian officer. When we finally went on through, we caught these two women. They smelled like they had weapons. These were all the people we found. So the Australian dude told us to take the women in. So me and my partner, we sittin' up in this Amtrac with these women. Then these guys who was driving the Amtrac come in there and start unzippin' their pants as if they gonna screw the women. So we say, "Man, get outta here. You can't do it to our prisoners." So they get mad with us. Like they gonna fight us. And we had to actually lock and load to protect the women. They said, "We do this all the time."

One time we had went into this place we had hit. We was takin' prisoners. So this one guy broke and ran. So I chased him. I ran behind him. Everybody say, "Shoot him. Shoot him." 'Cause they was pissed that I was chasin' him. So I hit him. You know I had to do something to him. I knew I couldn't just grab him and bring him back. And his face just crumbled. Then I brought him back, and they said, "You could have got a kill, Edwards."

The first time we thought we saw the enemy in big numbers was one of these operations by Marble Mountain. We had received fire. All of a sudden we could see people in front of us. Instead of waiting for air, we returned the fire, and you could see people fall. I went over to this dude and said, "Hey, man, I saw one fall." Then everyone started yelling, "We can see 'em fall. We can see 'em fall." And they were fallin'. Come to find out it was Bravo Company. What the VC had done was suck Bravo Company in front of us. 'Cause they attacked us and Bravo Company at the same time. They would move back as Bravo Company was in front of us. It was our own people. That's the bodies we saw falling. They figured out what was happening, and then they ceased fire. But the damage is done real fast. I think we shot up maybe

40 guys in Bravo Company. Like I said, it was easy to get killed by an American.

The first time I killed somebody up close was when we was tailing Charlie on a patrol somewhere around Danang. It was night. I was real tired. At that time you had worked so hard during the day, been on so many different details, you were just bombed out.

I thought I saw this dog running. Because that white pajama top they wore at night just blend into that funny-colored night they had over there. All of a sudden, I realized that somebody's runnin'. And before I could say anything to him, he's almost ran up on me. There's nothing I can do but shoot. Somebody get that close, you can't wait to check their ID. He's gonna run into you or stop to shoot you. It's got to be one or the other. I shot him a bunch of times. I had a 20-round clip, and when he hit the ground, I had nothing. I had to reload. That's how many times he was shot.

Then the sergeant came over and took out the flashlight and said, "Goddamn. This is fucking beautiful. This is fucking beautiful."

This guy was really out of it. He was like moanin'. I said, "Let me kill him." I couldn't stand the sound he was makin'. So I said, "Back off, man. Let me put this guy out of his misery." So I shot him again. In the head.

He had a grenade in his hand. I guess he was committing suicide. He was just runnin' up to us, pullin' a grenade kind of thing. I caught him just in time.

Everybody was comin' congratulatin' me, saying what a great thing it was. I'm tryin' to be cool, but I'm really freakin' out. So then I start walking away, and they told me I had to carry the body back to base camp. We had a real kill. We had one we could prove. We didn't have to make this one up.

So then I start draggin' this body by the feet. And his arm fell off. So I had to go back and get his arm. I had to stick it down his pants. It was a long haul.

And I started thinkin'. You think about how it feels, the weight. It was rainin'. You think about the mist and the smells the rain brings out. All of a sudden I realize this guy is a person, has got a family. All of a sudden it wasn't like I was carrying a gook. I was actually carrying a human being. I started feeling guilty. I just started feeling really badly.

I don't feel like we got beat in Vietnam. We never really fought the war. People saying that America couldn't have won that war is crazy.

The only way we could actually win the war was to fight every day. You couldn't fight only when you felt like it. Or change officers every month. Troops would learn the language, learn the people, learn the areas. If you're gonna be fighting in an area, you get to know everybody in the area and you stay there. You can't go rotate your troops every 12 months. You always got new people coming in. Plus they may not get to learn anything. They may die the first day. If you take a guy on patrol and he gets killed the first day, what good is he? See, if you have seasoned troops, you can move in and out of the bush at will. You get the smell of the country on you. You start to eat the food. You start to smell like it. You don't have that fresh smell so they can smell you when you're comin'. Then you can fight a war. Then you can just start from one tip of South Vietnam and work your way to the top. To China. Of course, if we had used the full might of the military, we'd be there now. We could never give the country back up. Plus we'd have to kill millions of Vietnamese. Do we want to do that? What had they done to us to deserve all that? So to do it would have been wrong. All we did was give our officers the first combat training they had since Korea. It was more like a big training ground. If it was a real war, you either would have come out in a body bag or you would have come out when the war was over.

Sometimes I think we would have done a lot better by getting them hooked on our life-style than by trying to do it with guns. Give them credit cards. Make them dependent on television and sugar. Blue jeans works better than bombs. You can take blue jeans and rock 'n' roll records and win over more countries than you can with soldiers.

When I went home, they put me in supply, probably the lowest job you can have in the Marines. But they saw me drawing one day and they said, "Edwards can draw." They sent me over to the training-aids library, and I became an illustrator. I reenlisted and made sergeant.

When I went to Quantico, my being black, they gave me the black squad, the squad with most of the blacks, especially the militant blacks. And they started hippin' me. I mean I was against racism. I didn't even call it racism. I called it prejudice. They hipped me to terms like "exploitation" and "oppression." And by becoming an illustrator, it gave you more time to think. And I was around people who thought. People who read books. I would read black history where the white guys were going off on novels or playing rock music. So then one day, I just told them I was black. I didn't call them *blanco*, they didn't have to call me Negro. That's what started to get me in trouble. I became a target. Somebody to watch.

Well, there was this riot on base, and I got busted. It started over some white guys using a bunch of profanity in front of some sisters. I was found guilty of attack on an unidentified Marine. Five months in jail, five months without pay. And a suspended BCD. In jail they didn't want us to read our books, draw any pictures, or do anything intellectually stimulating or what they thought is black. They would come in my cell and harass me. So one day I was just tired of them, and I hit the duty warden. I ended up with a BCD in 1970. After six years, eight months, and eight days, I was kicked out of the Corps. I don't feel it was fair. If I had been white, I would never have went to jail for fighting. That would have been impossible.

With a BCD, nothing was happenin'. I took to dressin' like the Black Panthers, so even blacks wouldn't hire me. So I went to the Panther office in D.C. and joined. I felt the party was the only organization that was fighting the system.

I liked their independence. The fact that they had no fear of the police. Talking about self-determination. Trying to make Malcolm's message reality. This was the first time black people had stood up to the state since Nat Turner. I mean armed. It was obvious they wasn't gonna give us anything unless we stood up and were willing to die. They obviously didn't care anything about us, 'cause they had killed King.

For me the thought of being killed in the Black Panther

Party by the police and the thought of being killed by Vietnamese was just a qualitative difference. I had left one war and came back and got into another one. Most of the Panthers then were veterans. We figured if we had been over in Vietnam fighting for our country, which at that point wasn't serving us properly, it was only proper that we had to go out and fight for our own cause. We had already fought for the white man in Vietnam. It was clearly his war. If it wasn't, you wouldn't have seen as many Confederate flags as you saw. And the Confederate flags was an insult to any person that's of color on this planet.

I rose up into the ranks. I was an artist immediately for the newspaper. Because of my background in the military, obviously I was able to deal with a lot of things of a security nature. And eventually I took over the D.C. chapter.

At this time, Huey Newton and Bobby Seale were in jail and people sort of idealized them. The party didn't actually fall apart until those two were released, and then the real leader, David Hilliard, was locked up. Spiro Agnew had a lot to do with the deterioration when he said take the Panthers out of the newspapers and then they will go away. And the FBI was harassing us, and we started turning on each other because of what they were spreading. And the power structure started to build up the poverty programs. Nobody was going to follow the Panthers if they could go down to the poverty program and get a check and say they are going to school.

We just didn't understand the times. All we wanted to do was kick whitey's ass. We didn't think about buying property or gaining economic independence. We were, in the end, just showing off.

I think the big trip America put us on was to convince us that having money was somehow harmful. That building businesses and securing our economic future, and buying and controlling areas for our group, our family, our friends like everybody else does, was wrong. Doing that doesn't make you antiwhite. I think white people would even like us better if we had more money. They like Richard Pryor. And Sammy Davis. And Jabbar.

Economically, black folks in America have more money than Canada or Mexico. It's obvious that we are doing something wrong. When people say we're illiterate, that doesn't bother me as much. Literacy means I can't read these books. Well neither does a Korean or a Vietnamese. But where they're not illiterate is in the area of economics. Sure, we're great artists, great singers, play great basketball. But we're not great managers yet. It's pretty obvious that you don't have to have guns to get power. People get things out of this country and they don't stick up America to do it. Look at the Vietnamese refugees running stores now in the black community where I live.

Right now, I'm an unemployed artist, drawing unemployment. I spent time at a community center helping kids, encouraging kids to draw.

I work for the nuclear-freeze movement, trying to convince people nuclear war is insane. Even when I was in the Marine Corps, I was against nuclear war. When I was a child, I was against nuclear weapons, because I thought what they did to Hiroshima and Nagasaki was totally cold. There's nothing any human being is doing on the planet that I could want to destroy the planet for future generations. I think we should confine war to our century and our times. Not to leave the residue around for future generations. The residue of hate is a horrible thing to leave behind. The residue of nuclear holocaust is far worse.

I went to see *Apocalypse Now*, because a friend paid my way. I don't like movies about Vietnam 'cause I don't think that they are prepared to tell the truth. *Apocalypse Now* didn't tell the truth. It wasn't real. I guess it was a great thing for the country to get off on, but it didn't remind me of anything I saw. I can't understand how you would have a bridge lit up like a Christmas tree. A USO show at night? Guys attacking the women on stage. That made no sense. I never saw us reach the point where nobody is in charge in a unit. That's out of the question. If you don't know anything, you know the chain of command. And the helicopter attack on the village? Fuckin' ridiculous. You couldn't hear music comin' out of a helicopter. And attacking a beach in helicopters was just out of the question. The planes and the napalm would go in first. Then, the helicopters would have eased in after the fact. That was wild.

By making us look insane, the people who made that movie was somehow relieving themselves of what they asked us to do over there. But we were not insane. We were not insane. We were not ignorant. We knew what we were doing.

I mean we were crazy, but it's built into the culture. It's like institutionalized insanity. When you're in combat, you can do basically what you want as long as you don't get caught. You can get away with murder. And the beautiful thing about the military is there's always somebody that can serve up as a scapegoat. Like Calley. I wondered why they didn't get Delta Company 1-9 because of Cam Ne. We were real scared. But President Johnson came out and defended us. But like that was before My Lai. When they did My Lai, I got nervous again. I said my God, and they have us on film.

I was in Washington during the National Vietnam Veterans Memorial in 1982. But I didn't participate. I saw all these veterans runnin' around there with all these jungle boots on, all these uniforms. I didn't want to do that. It just gave me a bad feeling. Plus some of them were braggin' about the war. Like it was hip. See, I don't think the war was a good thing. And there's no memorial to Cam Ne, to My Lai. To all those children that was napalmed and villages that were burned unnecessarily.

I used to think that I wasn't affected by Vietnam, but I been livin' with Vietnam ever since I left. You just can't get rid of it. It's like that painting of what Dali did of melting clocks. It's a persistent memory.

I remember most how hard it was to just shoot people.

I remember one time when three of our people got killed by a sniper from this village. We went over to burn the village down. I was afraid that there was going to be shootin' people that day, so I just kind of dealt with the animals. You know, shoot the chickens. I mean I just couldn't shoot no people.

I don't know how many chickens I shot. But it was a little pig that freaked me out more than the chickens. You think you gonna be shootin' a little pig, it's just gonna fall over and die. Well, no. His little guts be hangin' out. He just be squiggling around and freakin' you out.

See, you got to shoot animals in the head. If we shoot you in your stomach, you may just fall over and die. But an animal, you got to shoot them in the head. They don't understand that they supposed to fall over and die.

Specialist 5
Harold "Light Bulb" Bryant
East St. Louis, Illinois

Combat Engineer
1st Cavalry Division
U.S. Army
An Khe
February 1966–February 1967

We were in a fire fight one morning. We had our mad minute at six o'clock. We received some fire, and so we just started shooting. I guess maybe about eight o'clock a dust-off came in to take out a wounded guy. And they came and asked for me, and they told me that I was rotating. Going home right in the middle of the fire fight. I hadn't kept up with my days. I didn't have a short-time calendar. So I was a little surprised. So they took me back to An Khe for me to clear base camp.

I went downtown and bought a few trinkets to give people. A opium pipe. Four or five of those little jackets that said on the back, "I know I'm goin' to heaven, 'cause I done spent my time in hell." I grabbed my stuff out of the connex and put it in two of those Air Vietnam suit-cases and my two duffel bags. And I went to the airstrip for the Caribou that would fly me into Pleiku.

When I got to Pleiku, I guess it was about 4 P.M. They

said the plane was gonna be comin' in about seven. Then
Pleiku started gettin' hit, and the plane didn't come in.
And they had us in a secure area with no weapons while
Pleiku was being mortared. So we had to spend the night.

The plane to take us to Japan got there the next morning. And it picked up two rounds as we were leaving. And
this white guy got hit. Killed. And he was rotating home,
too. And his body, it stayed on the plane until we got to
Japan.

From Japan, they flew us to Oakland. Then they gave
us uniforms, 'cause when I left 'Nam I was still in jungle
fatigues. And I took a shower, put on my Class A's, got
my records. Finally they let us go, and I caught a bus
over to the San Francisco airport and got home about
three o'clock that morning.

My mother didn't keep up with my days left either, so
she was surprised when I called from San Francisco. She
met the plane. I said, "Mom, I'm happy to be home."
And she said, "I'm happy to see you here with everything.
It's God's blessing that you didn't get hurt." My father
wasn't there 'cause he worked at night, driving eighteen-
wheelers.

I went right out into the streets in my uniform and
partied. Matter fact, got drunk.

I wasn't sleepy. I was still hyped up. And East St.
Louis is a city that never closes. So I went to a place
called Mother's, which was the latest jazz joint in town.

A lot of people knew me, so everybody was buying
me drinks. Nobody was asking me how Vietnam was,
what Vietnam was all about. They just was saying, "Hey,
happy to see you back. Get you a drink?" They were
happy I made it back, because a lot of my friends who
had been over there from my city had came home dead
in boxes, or disabled.

Finally, I got guys that asked me what it was really
like. And when I was trying to explain it, after a while,
I saw that they got disinterested. So I just didn't talk about
it anymore. I was just saying, "I'm happy to be home. I
hope I'll never have to go back."

I had six more months to go, so they sent me to Fort
Carson in Colorado. There weren't any more airborne
soldiers on post but me and maybe five or six. We either

had come back from Vietnam or were getting ready to go.

Well, I ran into this officer. Second lieutenant. Just got out of OCS. He asked me if I was authorized to wear a combat infantryman's badge and jump wings. I told him, "You damn right. I earned them." He didn't like that answer. So I said, "You can harass me now, sir, but you can't go over in Vietnam and do that shit." So he ended up giving me a Article 15 for disrespect. And I got busted one rank and fined $25.

That was just another nail in the coffin to keep me from reuping. I didn't want career military nohow.

I told him taking my stripe away from me wasn't shit. And he couldn't do nothing to me, 'cause they couldn't send me back to Vietnam. He didn't enjoy that, so he tried to make it hard for me until *he* got shipped out. And when I heard he had orders for 'Nam, I went and found him and laughed at him and told him that he wasn't gon' make it back.

"Somebody's gon' kill you," I said. "One of your own men is gon' kill you."

I enlisted in the Army to stay out of the Marines. I had went to college for a semester at Southern Illinois University at Edwardsville. But the expenses had gotten too much for my family, so I went and got me a job at McDonnell Aircraft as a sheet-metal assembler. About eight months later, two guys I went to high school with got drafted by the Marines. So I joined the Army so I could get a choice.

It was August of '65. I was twenty.

My father was not too hot about it. He was in World War II, in France and Germany. He was a truck driver on the Red Ball Express, gettin' gas to Patton's tanks. He resented the Army because of how they treated black soldiers over there, segregated and not with the same support for white soldiers.

My left ear was pierced when I was nine just like my father's left ear was pierced when he was nine. Grandmother said all the male warriors in her mother's tribe in Africa had their ears pierced. Her mother was born in Africa. You can imagine the teasing I got in high school for wearing an earring. But I felt in this small way I carry

on the African tradition. I would go in the Army wearing
the mark of the African warriors I descend from.

I did my basic and my AIT at Fort Leonardwood,
Missouri. "Lost in the Woods," yeah. Trained for combat
engineer to build bridges, mountain roads. But we didn't
build too many bridges. Cleared a lot of LZs. Did a lot
of demolition work.

I was sent to An Khe, 8th Engineers Battalion, and
attached to the 1st of the 9th of the Cav. It was in February, after the first battle of the Ia Drang Valley, when
300 Cav troops got wiped out in the first real fight anybody
had with the NVA. I was one of those replacements.

We probed for mines, blew up mines, disarmed and
blew up booby traps. If you saw a trip wire, you could
take a look at what was happening. You could see where
the booby trap was, then throw a grenade at the beginning
of the booby trap. Or shoot up the trail to make 'em go
off. The land mines, ones you had to dig up, was the big
problem, 'cause they could have another one planted
somewhere next to it.

And you had to worry about crimping right and taking
your time. You squeeze the blasting cap and the fuse
together so they won't come apart. Crimping, right. But
if you don't crimp right, like an inch high from the bottom
of the cap, it will blow you up. And you can't be rushed
by some second lieutenant, telling you, "Hurry up, hurry
up, so we can move on." If you rush, something wrong
would happen. We lost three guys from rushing or crimping wrong.

One time I had to get a guy off a mine. It looked like
it was impossible.

This infantry unit was on a little trail, west of Pleiku,
makin' a sweep towards the Ia Drang Valley. This white
dude had stepped on a mine. And knew it. He felt the
plunger go down. Everybody moved away from him, about
20 meters. So they called for the engineers, and somebody
asked for Light Bulb.

I have a nickname from the streets of East St. Louis.
Light Bulb. Came from a friend of mine when we were
growing up, 'cause he said I was always full of ideas.

When I got there on the chopper, he's been standin'
there for over an hour. He really wasn't in any panic. He

was very calm. He knew if he alleviated any of the pressure, both of us would have got destroyed.

I dug all around the mine with my bayonet and found out that it was a Bouncin' Betty. I told him I was gonna try to diffuse it. But the three-prong primer on the Bouncin' Betty had gotten in between the cleats on his jungle boots, so there wasn't any way I could deal with it. So I said let's see if we could kind of change the pressure by him takin' his foot out of his boot and me keepin' the pressure by holding his boot down. That way he could get out uninjured. But when he started doin' that, I thought I was seein' the plunger rise, so I told him to stop.

I guess maybe I'd been working with him for maybe an hour now.

Then I got the idea. I knew when the plunger would depress, the Bouncin' Betty would bounce up about 3 feet and then explode. So I got the other members of his team together, and I tied a rope around his waist. And everybody, including me, moved off about 20 yards from the mine and him. And when I counted to three, everyone would pull on the rope and snatch him about 15 feet off the mine. And it would bounce up its 3 feet and then explode. And it did that. And the only damage that he received was the heel of his jungle boot was blown off. No damage to him.

This was somethin' that they never taught us in school.

This guy thanked me for saving his life and the life of his squad. And whenever we were back in base camp, I would always go with them. And since a platoon would always carry three or four combat engineers with them in the bush, I would always go with them.

When I came to Vietnam, I thought we were helping another country to develop a nation. About three or four months later I found out that wasn't the case. In high school and in the papers I had been hearing about Indochina, but I couldn't find Indochina on the map. I didn't know anything about the country, about the people. Those kinds of things I had to learn on myself while I was there.

We had a Vietnamese interpreter attached to us. I would always be asking him questions. He had told me this war in Vietnam had been going on for hundreds of years. Before the Americans, they had been fighting for hundreds

of years against the Chinese aggressors. I thought we had
got into the beginning of a war. But I found out that we
were just in another phase of their civil wars.

And we weren't gaining any ground. We would fight
for a hill all day, spend two days or two nights there, and
then abandon the hill. Then maybe two, three months
later, we would have to come back and retake the same
piece of territory. Like this Special Forces camp outside
Dak To. The camp was attacked one evening. Maybe two
or three platoons flew up to give them some assistance.
Then somehow headquarters decided we should close
down that camp. So they ended up closing down. Two
or three months later, we went back to the same area to
retake it. We lost 20 men the first time saving it, 30 or 40
men the next time retaking it.

And they had a habit of exaggerating a body count. If
we killed 7, by the time it would get back to base camp,
it would have gotten to 28. Then by the time it got down
to Westmoreland's office in Saigon, it done went up to
54. And by the time it left from Saigon going to Washington, it had went up to about 125. To prove we were
really out there doing our jobs, doing, really, more than
what we were doing.

I remember a place called the Ashau Valley. The 7th
went in there and got cut up real bad. They had under-
estimated the enemy's power. So they sent in the 9th, and
we cleared the Ashau Valley out. All we was doing was
making contact, letting the gunships know where they
were, and then we would draw back. We had 25 gunships
circling around, and jet strikes coming in to drop napalm.
We did that all day, and the next day we didn't receive
any other fire.

Stars and Stripes said we had a body count of 260
something. But I don't think it was true.

By then I had killed my first VC. It was two or three
o'clock in the afternoon, somewhere in the Central Highlands. I was point man. I was blazing my own trail. I was
maybe 40 meters in front of the rest of the squad. And I
just walked up on him. He just stepped out of the bush.
I didn't see him until he moved. I'd say maybe 50 meters.
And then he saw me. We both had a look of surprise. And
I cracked him, because it just ran through my mind it

would be either him or me. I just fired from the hip. And he hadn't even brought his weapon down from port arms.

But what really got to me from the beginning was not really having any information, not knowing what I was gonna be doin' next. We might be pullin' guard for some artillery one night. Then the next day some choppers would come and get us. We would never know where we were going until in the air. Then we would get word that we were going to the LZ that was really hot. Or something ignorant, like the time we went over in Cambodia to pull guard on a helicopter that had been shot down. And we got stuck there.

It was in the latter part of '66, late in the afternoon. I think it got shot down probably in 'Nam and just ended up in Cambodia. So they sent out a squad of us combat engineers to cut around the shaft so a Chinook could come in, hook up, and pull it out. We didn't get there until six or seven, and it was getting dark. So the Chinook couldn't come in, so we had to stay there all night. The chopper had one door gunner and two pilots, and they were all dead. It wasn't from any rounds. They died from the impact of the chopper falling. I thought it made a lot more sense for us to get out of there and bring the bodies back with us.

When it got dark, we could see a fire maybe half a mile from us. We knew it had to be a VC camp. In the bamboo thicket right up on us we kept hearing this movement, these small noises. We thought if we fired, whoever was out there would attack us. We were so quiet that none of us moved all night. Matter of fact, one of the guy's hair turned stone gray. Because of the fear. He was just nineteen. He was a blond-headed kid when the sun went down, and when the sunlight came up, his hair was white.

We didn't find out they were monkeys until that morning.

That was about as crazy as the time we tryin' to take a shower in a monsoon rain. We had no shower for maybe ten days in the bush. We was standin' out there in the middle of a rice paddy, soapin' up. By the time all of us got soaped up, it stopped rainin'. So we had to lay down and roll around in the rice paddy to get the soap off of us. We never did call that a shower.

It seems like a lot of green guys got killed just coming in country by making a mistake. I remember this white guy from Oklahoma. We got to callin' him Okie. He said that the reason he had volunteered to come over to Vietnam was because he wanted to kill gooks. He was a typical example of a John Wayne complex.

It was a week after he had just gotten there that we got into any action. He was just itching to get into some. We went out and got pinned down by machine guns. They were on our right flank. He saw where the machine-gun net was, and he tried to do the John Wayne thing. He got up, trying to circle around the machine-gun net. Charge the machine gun. And never made it. Whoever was firing saw him move and turned the machine gun on him. We stayed down till we could call in some gunships. Then we moved back.

There was another guy in our unit who had made it known that he was a card-carrying Ku Klux Klan member. That pissed a lot of us off, 'cause we had gotten real tight. We didn't have racial incidents like what was happening in the rear area, 'cause we had to depend on each other. We were always in the bush.

Well, we got out into a fire fight, and Mr. Ku Klux Klan got his little ass trapped. We were goin' across the rice paddies, and Charlie just start shootin'. And he jumped in the rice paddy while everybody else kind of back-tracked.

So we laid down a base of fire to cover him. But he was just immobile. He froze. And a brother went out there and got him and dragged him back. Later on, he said that action had changed his perception of what black people were about.

But I got to find out that white people weren't as tough, weren't the number one race and all them other perceptions that they had tried to ingrain in my head. I found out they got scared like I did. I found out a lot of them were a lot more cowardly than I expected. I found out some of them were more animalistic than any black people I knew. I found out that they really didn't have their shit together.

At that time we would carry our dog tags on a chain and tie it through the buttonholes of our fatigue jacket.

Wearing them around our necks would cause a rash. Also, they would make noise unless you had 'em taped around your neck.

Well, these white guys would sometimes take the dog-tag chain and fill that up with ears. For different reasons. They would take the ear off to make sure the VC was dead. And to confirm that they had a kill. And to put some notches on they guns.

If we were movin' through the jungle, they'd just put the bloody ear on the chain and stick the ear in their pocket and keep on going. Wouldn't take time to dry it off. Then when we get back, they would nail 'em up on the walls to our hootch, you know, as a trophy. They was rotten and stinkin' after a while, and finally we make 'em take 'em down.

These two guys that I can specifically think of had about 12. I thought it was stupid. And spiritually, I was lookin' at it as damaging a dead body. After a while, I told them, "Hey, man, that's sick. Don't be around me with the ears hangin' on you."

One time after a fire fight, we went for a body count. We wiped part of them out, and the rest of them took off. There were five known dead. And these two other guys be moanin'. One of them was trying to get to his weapon. One of the guys saw that and popped him. Then another guy went by and popped the other one to make sure that he was dead. Then this guy—one of the white guys—cut off the VC's dick and stuck it in his mouth as a reminder that the 1st Cavs had been through there. And he left the ace of spades on the body.

That happened all the time.

So did burnin' villages.

Sometimes we would get to villages, and fires would still be burnin', food still be cookin', but nobody was there. The commanding officer, this major, would say if no one is there in the village, then the village must not belong to anybody, so destroy it. But the people had probably ran off because they knew we were comin'.

If we didn't want people further down the road, like the VC, to know we were comin', we wouldn't fire the village. Or if we were movin' too fast, we wouldn't. Otherwise, you would strike your lighter. Torch it. All of 'em were thatched huts anyway. I looked at the major's orders as something he knew more about than I did.

And the villagers caught hell if they were suspect, too. I remember at this LZ. We could sit on our bunkers and look across the road at the POW compound. The MPs had them surrounded by barbed wire. We would see MPs go in there and get them and take 'em to another bunker. Then we'd hear the Vietnamese hollerin' and shit. The MPs would take the telephone wires and wrap it around the Vietnamese fingers and crank the phone so the charge would go through the wires. Papa san, mama san, would start talkin'. And then we'd see the MPs carry 'em back into the camp.

One day at the LZ we saw a chopper maybe a mile away, high up in the air. Maybe 300 feet. And we'd see something come out. I didn't think it was a body until I talked to the other guys. I had thought maybe the chopper had banked and then somebody had rolled out. That was a fear that we always had when we were ridin' in choppers 'cause there weren't any seat belts in the choppers at that time.

What happened was they were interrogating somebody. And the interrogation was over with.

Outside An Khe, the 1st Cav built an area for soldiers to go relieve theirselves. Bars, whorehouses. It would open at nine in the morning. We called it Sin City. And it had soul bars. A group of us would walk around to find a joint that would be playin' some soul music, some Temptations, Supremes, Sam and Dave. I would want to do my drinking somewhere where I'd hear music that I liked rather than hillbilly. But a lot of gray guys who wasn't racially hung up would also be there.

The women were much more friendly there. We had heard that was because they thought of the black man as bein' more stronger, more powerful, because Buddha was black. Take a good look at a Buddha. You'll see that he has thick lips and has a very broad nose and very kinky hair. But I didn't know that until I got in country.

We would go to a Class 6 store and get two half-gallons of Gilby's gin for a $1.65 each. We take a bottle to papa

san. Buy a girl for $5 or $10. Whatever came by, or whatever I liked. And still have a half a gallon of gin. We would
have to leave the area at six o'clock.

Another good thing about the girls in Sin City was that
the medical personnel in the camp would always go and
check 'em once a week. And if they got disease, they'd
get shots and wouldn't be able to work until they were
clear. Nobody used rubbers because all the girls in Sin
City were clean.

But the people got abused anyway. Like a lot of guys
would have Vietnamese give them haircuts. And after
papa san got through cuttin' the hair, this guy would tell
him that he wouldn't like it and would walk off. He
wouldn't pay papa san. And the haircut cost no more than
thirty cents.

And it seemed the Vietnamese were always hung up
on menthol cigarettes. Kools and things. And they knew
brothers all smoked Kools. And they would always ask
us for a cigarette. So a lot of guys would start givin' 'em
loaded cigarettes to stop 'em from always askin' us. One
of the guy's brothers had mailed him some loads from a
trick shop. You take out some of the tobacco, then put
in a small load of gunpowder. When the Vietnamese smokin' it, it just blow up in his face, and he wouldn't go back
to that GI and ask him for a cigarette 'cause he was scared
he'd get another loaded cigarette.

One night I saw a drunk GI just pull out his .45 and
pop papa san. Papa san was irritatin' him or botherin'
him or something. Right downtown in Sin City. After he
fired, the MPs and a lot of soldiers grabbed him. They
took him to the camp, and he got put up on some charges.

You could find plenty of women out in the field, too.
We would set up our perimeter, and all of a sudden a little
Coke girl would show up with Coca-Cola. And also some
broads would show. We would set up lean-tos, or we'd
put up bunkers. A guy would go outside the wire, take
the broad through the wire to the bunker, knock her off,
and take her back outside the wire. Normally, those kinds
of deals was a C-ration deal. Or a couple of dollars. We
would give the girl a C-ration meal. Ham and lima beans,
'cause nobody in the squad would want to eat ham and

lima beans. You would never give up spaghetti and meat-balls.

One morning, we were sweepin' a highway near Phu Cat. Four of us in a jeep with two M-60 machine guns mounted on the back. We were coming down the road, and we looked off on to a spur and we saw three black pajama bodies start runnin' away from us. So one of the two white guys turned his gun on automatic and knocked all three down. The three of them ran over there to see what was happening and found out that two of them were women, maybe eighteen or nineteen, and one of them was a man. I stayed with the Quad 60, just pullin' guard to make sure there might have been some more VC in the area.

As I was watching, I noticed one of the white guys take his pants down and just start having sex. That kind of freaked me out, 'cause I thought the broad was dead. The brother was just standin' guard watchin'. It kind of surprised him to see this guy get off. After about 20 minutes, I ended up saying, "Hey, man. Come on. Let's go."

When they got back in the jeep, they start tellin' me what was happenin'. They had told me that they had confirmed three KIA. And the brother asked the dude what was wrong with him, why did he fuck a dead woman. And he said he just wanted to get his rocks off. And that was the end of it.

Today I'm constantly thinking about the war. I walk down streets different. I look at places where individuals could hide. Maybe assault me or rob me or just harass me. I hear things that other people can't hear. My wife, she had a habit at one time of buying cheap watches and leaving them on top of the dresser. I could hear it ticking, so she would put it in a drawer. I could still hear it ticking. And I dream of helicopters coming over my house, comin' to pick me up to take me to a fire fight. And when we get to the fire fight, they were dropping napalm on our own men. And I have to shoot our own soldiers to put them out of their misery. After my discharge, I lived off my unemployment until it ran out, which was about 18 months. Then I decided to go back to school. I went two years, and then I got involved in veterans affairs. I was noticing that in my city, which is 95 percent black, that there were a lot of black combat veterans coming back not able to find any employment because of bad discharges, or killing theirselves or dopin' up. We started the Wasted Men Project at the university, and I have been counseling at veterans centers ever since.

In 1982 I transferred to the Vet Center in Tucson because I wanted to do some research on the Buffalo Soldiers. In 'Nam I didn't know they were part of the original 9th Cav. These are black boys who had just received their freedom from the United States government, and they had to go to the West and suppress the freedom from another race of people who were the Indians. I think they won 13 or 14 Congressional Medals of Honor. But they were really policing other people, just like we were in Vietnam.

When my son, Ronnie, turned sixteen, I had him sit down and watch all thirteen hours of this film documentary about the Vietnam War so he could have an understanding of what war really was about. He had asked had I did any killing. I told him, "Yes. I had to do it. I had to do it to keep myself alive."

I wouldn't want him to go and fight an unpopular war like I did. I wouldn't want him to go down to El Salvador. And if that means that I would have to pick up me and my family baggage and move somewhere out of the country, then I would do that.

America should have won the war. But they wouldn't free us to fight. With all the American GIs that were in Vietnam, they could have put us all shoulder to shoulder and had us march from Saigon all the way up to the DMZ. Just make a sweep. We had enough GIs, enough equipment to do that.

When I came to Washington to see the Vietnam Veterans Memorial, I looked through the book and there were about 15 guys from my hometown who were killed. And six of them I knew.

But I looked up the memorial for James Plummer first.

Plummer was a black guy from Cincinnati. We were the same age. Twenty. We were at Camp Alpha together. That's where they assign you when you first come to 'Nam. I was in C Company, a line company. He was a truck driver, so he was in Headquarters Company, where they had all the heavy equipment.

I liked Plummer's style. He was just so easygoing. We'd sit down and just rap. Rap about music, the girls, what was happening in the world. Get high. Plummer was a John Coltrane fan. And I'm bein' a Miles Davis fan, we just automatically fell in with each other.

He was my best friend.

One day we were at the airfield at the LZ. Plummer was out of the truck, over by the ammo dump. And the ammo dump received a mortar round. It blew him up.

It freaked me out. I mean that here I saw him, and five minutes later he's instantaneously dead.

Me and two other guys ran and grabbed what we could. We pulled on the jungle fatigues, which was full of blood. It looked like maybe a dog after it crossed the street and got hit by a truck. His head was gone, both his legs from about the knee down were both gone. One arm was gone. The other was a stump left. We finally got his trunk together. The rest of it we really couldn't find, 'cause that one mortar round, it started the ammo dump to steady exploding. It constantly blew up for about an hour.

What we found was probably sent back to the States. They probably had a closed-casket funeral.

I kind of cried. I was sayin' to myself that this was such a waste because we weren't really doin' anything at the time. And him just being such a nice fella, why did he have to go this way? Go in pieces?

Everybody knew that me and him was tight, so a couple of guys took me up over to a bunker and we rapped about him all night. 'Cause we were out in the bush, I really couldn't get no booze. But when I did get back, I bought me a half gallon of gin, and I knocked it off. And that didn't make me feel any better.

When I got back, I called his mother. His mother knew me from him writing to her. I told her I was close by when he did get killed. I just told her a ammo dump blew up. I'm pretty sure she didn't have no idea what that was.

Every year I send her a Christmas card. I just sign my name.

When I saw Plummer on the memorial, I kind of cried again.

I guess deep down in my head now I can't really believe
in God like I did because I can't really see why God would
let something like this happen. Specially like to my friend
Plummer. Why He would take such a good individual
away from here.

Before I went to Vietnam, I was very active in the
church, because of my mother's influence. She sent me
a Bible, and I carried it in my pocket everywhere I went.
When I couldn't find any *Playboy*s or something like that,
I would read it. Matter of fact, I read it from cover to
cover, starting from Genesis.

I guess I got kind of really unreligious because of my
Vietnam experience. Oh, I went to church once in my
uniform to please my mother. But I haven't been back
since except for a funeral. I've talked to chaplains, talked
to preachers about Vietnam. And no one could give me
a satisfactory explanation of what happened overseas.

But each year since I've been back I have read the
Bible from cover to cover. I keep looking for the explanation.

I can't find it. I can't find it.

Specialist 4
Richard J. Ford III
Washington, D.C.

LURP
25th Infantry Division
U.S. Army
Hill 54
June 1967–July 1968

I should have felt happy I was goin' home when I got on that plane in Cam Ranh Bay to leave. But I didn't exactly. I felt—I felt—I felt very insecure 'cause I didn't have a weapon. I had one of them long knives, like a big hacksaw knife. I had that. And had my cane. And I had a couple of grenades in my bag. They took them from me when I got to Washington, right? And I felt insecure. I just felt real bad.

You know, my parents never had a weapon in the house. Rifle, shotgun, pistol, nothing. Never had one. Never seen my father with one. And I needed a weapon. 'Cause of that insecurity. I never got over it.

It was Saturday evening when we landed. Nineteen sixty-eight. I caught a cab from Dulles and went straight to my church. The Way of the Cross Church. It's a Pentacostal holiest church. I really wasn't active in the church before I went overseas. But a lot of people from the church wrote me, saying things like "I'm praying for you." There was a couple of peoples around there. They had a choir rehearsal. And they said they were glad to see me. But I went to the altar and stayed there from seven o'clock to about eleven-thirty. I just wanted to be by myself and pray. At the altar.

I was glad to be home. Just to be stateside. I was thankful that I made it. But I felt bad because I had to leave some friends over there. I left Davis there. I couldn't say a prayer for people that was already gone. But I said a prayer for them guys to come back home safely. For Davis. Yeah, for Davis.

The first nights I came home I couldn't sleep. My room was the back room of my parents' house. I couldn't sleep in the bed, so I had to get on the floor. I woke up in the middle of the night, and looking out my back window, all you see is trees. So I see all these trees, and I'm thinkin' I'm still in Vietnam. And I can't find my weapon. And I can't find Davis. I can't find nobody. And I guess I scared my mother and father half to death 'cause I got to hollering, "Come on, where are you? Where are you? Davis. Davis. SIR DAVIS." I thought I had got captured or something.

The first thing I did Monday was went to the store and bought me a .38. And bought me a .22.

It was right after the Fourth of July, and kids were still throwing firecrackers. I couldn't deal with it. Hear the noise, I hit the ground. I was down on 7th and F, downtown. I had this little .22. A kid threw firecrackers, and I was trying to duck. And some guys laughed at me, right? So I fired the pistol back at them and watched them duck. I said, "It's not funny now, is it?" I didn't go out of my way to mess with nobody, but I demanded respect.

One day, me and my mother and my wife were coming home from church, up Illinois Avenue. I made a left turn, and four white guys in a car cut in front of me and blew the horn. They had been drinking. They gave me the finger. And, man, I forgot all about my mother and wife was in the car. I took off after them. I had the .22 and was firing out the window at them. I just forgot where—and Vietnam does that to you—you forget where you are. It was open season. I'm shooting out the window. My mother said, "Oh, my God. Please, please help him."

Got home and it was, "You need help. You need help." But I was like that. I just couldn't adjust to it. Couldn't adjust to coming back home, and people think you dirty 'cause you went to Vietnam.

The Army sent me to Walter Reed Hospital for therapy. For two weeks. It was for guys who had been involved in a lot of combat. They said that I was hyper. And they pumped me up with a whole bunch of tranquilizers.

I'll never forget this goddamn officer. I'm looking at him. He's got a Good Conduct ribbon on. He's a major. He's reading my jacket, and he's looking with his glasses at me. I'm just sitting there. So he says, "Ford, you were very lucky. I see you got these commendations. You were very lucky to come back." So I told him, "No, I'm not lucky. You're lucky. You didn't go. You sitting there with a Good Conduct Medal on your chest and haven't been outside the States. You volunteered for service. You should have went. I didn't volunteer for Vietnam. They made me go."

There was 12 guys in the therapy session up there at Walter Reed. It was six white, and it was six black. I was the only combat person up there in the class. These guys were having flashbacks and had no combat experience. I can relate to it now, but at that point I couldn't understand. I said, "What y'all talking 'bout? You was in artillery. At the base camp. You fired guns from five miles away and talking 'bout flashbacks?" Other guys was truck drivers or supply. Nobody done hand-to-hand combat. I said, "You bring me somebody in here with a CIB. We can sit down and talk. But I can't talk to none of y'all 'cause y'all wasn't there."

You know, they decorated me in Vietnam. Two Bronze Stars. The whiteys did. I was wounded three times. The officers, the generals, and whoever came out to the hospital to see you. They respected you and pat you on the back. They said, "You brave. And you courageous. You America's finest. America's best." Back in the States the same officers that pat me on the back wouldn't even speak to me. They wanted that salute, that attention, 'til they holler at ease. I didn't get the respect that I thought I was gonna get.

I had six months to go. So now they trying to figure

out where they can put me for six months. They said my time was too short to qualify for school. Then up pop my medical record. The one they couldn't find when they sent me to 'Nam. The one say I shouldn't even be runnin', my knees so bad. They tell me I can't learn no skill. Drive no jeep. 'Cause of my knees. So they put me in charge of the poolroom at Fort Meade.

They lost my medical records when they wanted to. Now they got 'em back when they wanted to. They just wanted another black in the field. Uncle Sam, he didn't give me no justice. You had a job to do, you did it, you home. Back where you started. They didn't even ask me to reenlist.

I graduated from Roosevelt High School in 1966 and was working for the Food and Drug Administration as a lab technician when I was drafted. My father was administrator of a halfway house for Lorton, and my mother was on the Board of Elections in D.C. I was nineteen, and they took me to Fort Bragg. Airborne.

We were really earmarked for Vietnam. Even the drill sergeant and the first sergeant in basic told us that we was going to Vietnam. From basic we went straight to jungle warfare AIT in South Carolina. Before I went to Vietnam, three medical doctors at Fort Dix examined my knees. They trained us so hard in Fort Bragg the cartilages were roughed up. The doctors signed the medical record. It was a permanent profile. Said they would find something in the rear for you. A little desk job, clerk, or medic aid. But they didn't. I was sent straight to the infantry.

I really thought Vietnam was really a civil war between that country, and we had no business in there. But it seems that by the Russians getting involved and supplying so many weapons to the North Vietnamese that the United States should send troops in.

When I stepped off the plane in Tan Son Nhut, that heat that was coming from the ground hit me in the face. And the odor from the climate was so strong. It hit me. I said, Goddamn, where am I? What is this?

While we was walking off the plane, guys were coming toward the plane. And guys said, "Happy Birthday, Merry Christmas, Happy Easter. I'll write your mom." They kept going. In other words, you gon' have Easter here, gonna have a birthday here, and you gonna have Christmas here. And good luck.

It was in June 1967. My MOS was mortarman, but they made me be a rifleman first and sent me to Company C, 3rd Brigade, 25th Infantry Division. We was operating in Chu Lai, but we was a floatin' battalion.

It was really weird how the old guys would ask you what you want to carry. It wasn't a thing where you get assigned an M-14, M-16. If you want to carry an M-16, they say how many rounds of ammo do you want to carry? If you want to carry 2,000, we got it for you. How many grenades do you want? It was really something. We were so in the spirit that we hurt ourself. Guys would want to look like John Wayne. The dudes would just get in the country and say, "I want a .45. I want eight grenades. I want a bandolier. I want a thousand rounds ammo. I want ten clips. I want the works, right?" We never knew what the weight of this ammo is gon' be.

A lot of times guys be walkin' them hills, choppin' through them mountains, and the grenades start gettin' heavy. And you start throwin' your grenades under bushes and takin' your bandoliers off. It wasn't ever questioned. We got back in the rear, and it wasn't questioned if you felt like goin' to get the same thing again next time.

Once I threw away about 200 rounds of ammo. They designated me to carry ammo for the M-60 machine gun. We was going through a stream above Chu Lai. I'm carrying my C rations, my air mattress, poncho, five quarts of water, everything that you own. The ammo was just too heavy. I threw away the ammo going through the river. I said it got lost. The terrain was so terrible, so thick, nobody could question that you lost it.

I come from a very religious family. So I'm carrying my sister's Bible, too. All my letters that I saved. And a little bottle of olive oil that my pastor gave me. Blessed olive oil. But I found it was a lot of guys in basic with me that were atheist. When we got to Vietnam there were no atheist. There was not one atheist in my unit. When we got hit, everybody hollered, "Oh, God, please help, please." And everybody want to wear a cross. Put a cross on their helmet. Something to psych you up.

Black guys would wear sunglasses, too. We would put

on sunglasses walking in the jungle. Think about it, now.
It was ridiculous. But we want to show how bad we are.
How we're not scared. We be saying, "The Communists
haven't made a bullet that can kill me." We had this attitude that I don't give a damn. That made us more aggressive, more ruthless, more careless. And a little more
luckier than the person that was scared.

I guess that's why I volunteered for the LURPs and
they brought me into Nha Trang. And it was six other
black fellas to go to this school at the 5th Special Forces.
And we would always be together in the field. Sometimes
it would be Captain Park, this Korean, with us. Most of
the time it was us, five or six black dudes making our
own war, doing our thing alone.

There was Larry Hill from New York. Garland from
Baltimore. Holmes from Georgia. Louis Ford from New
Orleans. Moon from Detroit, too. They called him Sir
Drawers, 'cause he wouldn't wear underwear. Said it gave
him a rash. And this guy from Baton Rouge named Albert
Davis. He was only 5 feet 9. Only 120 pounds. He was a
terrific soldier. A lot of guts, a lot of heart. He was Sir
Davis. I was Sir Ford. Like Knights of the Round Table.
We be immortal. No one can kill us.

I didn't believe Nha Trang was still part of Vietnam,
because they had barracks, hot water, had mess halls with
three hot meals and air conditioning. Nha Trang was like
a beach, a resort. They was ridin' around on paved streets.
They be playing football and basketball. Nobody walked
around with weapons. They were white. And that's what
really freaked me out. All these white guys in the rear.

They told us we had to take our weapons to the armory
and lock 'em up. We said naw. So they decided to let us
keep our weapons till we went to this show.

It was a big club. Looked like 80 or 90 guys. Almost
everybody is white. They had girls dancing and groups
singin'. They reacted like we was some kind of animals,
like we these guys from the boonies. They a little off. I
don't know if I was paranoid or what. But they stare at
you when you first come in. All of us got drunk and
carryin' on. I didn't get drunk, 'cause I didn't drink. And
we started firin' the weapons at the ceiling. Telling everybody to get out. "Y'all not in the war." We was frustrated

because all these whites were in the back having a big show. And they were clerks. Next thing I know, about a hundred MPs all around the club. Well, they took our weapons. That was all.

The next day Davis got in trouble 'cause he wouldn't salute this little second lieutenant. See, we weren't allowed to salute anybody in the field. Officers didn't want you to. A sniper might blow his head off. The captain wanted to be average. He say, "I'm just like you, brother." When we got in the rear, it was hard for us to adjust to salutin' automatically.

When we got to be LURPs, we operated from Hill 54. Then they'd bring us in for like three days. They'd give you steak, all the beer you could drink. They know it's your last time. Some of us not coming back. We'd eat half the steaks, throw 'em away, have a ball. Go into town, and tear the town up.

Davis couldn't make no rank 'cause he got court-martialed for somethin' we do in town. We stole a jeep. Went to town. Tuy Hoa was off limits. Davis turned the jeep over comin' around one of them curves. But Davis was a born leader. He went back to the unit and got some more fools to get another jeep to push this jeep up. But he got court-martialed for stealin' the jeep. And for having United States currency.

Davis would take American money into town. Somebody send him $50, he get 3 to 1. Black market. First chance we go to town, he go get some cash. 'Cause he stayed high all the time. Smokin' marijuana, hashish. At mama san's house.

And some guys used to play this game. They would smoke this opium. They'd put a plastic bag over their head. Smoke all this smoke. See how long you could hold it. Lot of guys would pass out.

In the field most of the guys stayed high. Lot of them couldn't face it. In a sense, if you was high, it seemed like a game you was in. You didn't take it serious. It stopped a lot of nervous breakdown.

See, the thing about the field that was so bad was this. If I'm working on the job with you stateside and you're my friend, if you get killed, there's a compassion. My boss say, "Well, you better take a couple of days off. Get yourself together." But in the field, we can be the best of friends and you get blown away. They put a poncho around you and send you back. They tell 'em to keep moving.

We had a medic that give us a shot of morphine anytime you want one. I'm not talkin' about for wounded. I'm talkin' about when you want to just get high. So you can face it.

In the rear sometimes we get a grenade, dump the gunpowder out, break the firing pin. Then you'll go inside one of them little bourgeois clubs. Or go in the barracks where the supply guys are, sitting around playing bid whist and doing nothing. We act real crazy. Yell out, "Kill all y'all motherfuckers." Pull the pin and throw the grenade. And everybody would haul ass and get out. It would make a little pop sound. And we would laugh. You didn't see anybody jumpin' on them grenades.

One time in the field, though, I saw a white boy jump on a grenade. But I believe he was pushed. It ain't kill him. He lost both his legs.

The racial incidents didn't happen in the field. Just when we went to the back. It wasn't so much that they were against us. It was just that we felt that we were being taken advantage of, 'cause it seemed like more blacks in the field than in the rear.

In the rear we saw a bunch of rebel flags. They didn't mean nothing by the rebel flag. It was just saying we for the South. It didn't mean that they hated blacks. But after you in the field, you took the flags very personally.

One time we saw these flags in Nha Trang on the MP barracks. They was playing hillbilly music. Had their shoes off dancing. Had nice, pretty bunks. Mosquito nets over top the bunks. And had the nerve to have this camouflaged covers. Air conditioning. Cement floors. We just came out the jungles. We dirty, we smelly, hadn't shaved. We just went off. Said, "Y'all the real enemy. We stayin' here." We turned the bunks over, started tearing up the stereo. They just ran out. Next morning, they shipped us back up.

In the field, we had the utmost respect for each other, because when a fire fight is going on and everybody is facing north, you don't want to see nobody looking around south. If you was a member of the Ku Klux Klan, you didn't tell nobody.

Take them guys from West Virginia, Kentucky. First time they ever seen blacks was when they went in the service. One of them told me that the only thing he hate about the service was he had to leave his sheep. He said he used to never wear boots or shoes. He tell us how he cut a stump, put the sheep across the stump, and he would rape the sheep. Those guys were dumb, strong, but with no problems about us blacks. Matter of fact, the whites catered to the blacks in the infantry in the field.

Captain one time asked Davis what kind of car he gonna have when he get back in the States. Davis told him, "I'm not gonna get a car, sir. I'm gonna get me a Exxon station and give gas away to the brothers. Let them finish burnin' down what they leave." It wasn't funny if he said it in the stateside. But all of 'em bust out laughing.

We used to bathe in the stream. Shave and everything. Captain was telling Davis he had some Ivory soap. Davis said, "I don't take baths. Water rusts iron and put knots on the alligator's back." Creole talk. Everybody laugh. They know he don't bathe, but he was a terrific soldier. Small fella. He had one of the Napoleon complexes. Always had to prove something. He wasn't scared. He had more heart than anybody. They respected him, and they knew if you need fire cover or need help, he right there.

Right after Tet, the mail chopper got shot down. We moved to Tam Ky. We didn't have any mail in about three weeks. Then this lady by the name of Hanoi Helen come on the radio. She had a letter belong to Sir Drawers. From the chopper that was shot down. She read the letter from his wife about how she miss him. But that didn't unsettle the brothers as much as when she got on the air after Martin Luther King died, and they was rioting back home. She was saying, "Soul brothers, go home. Whitey raping your mothers and your daughters, burning down your homes. What you over here for? This is not your war. The war is a trick of the Capitalist empire to get rid of the blacks." I really thought—I really started believing it, because it was too many blacks than there should be in infantry.

And take the Montagnards, the brothers considered them brothers because they were dark. They had some of the prettiest ladies, pretty complexion, long hair, and they didn't wear no tops. Breasts would be exposed. And the Montagnard be walking with his water buffalo, his family, his crossbow. You waved at them, kept on walking. The people in Saigon didn't have anything to do with Montagnards. It was almost like white people in the States didn't have anything to do with blacks in the ghetto. So we would compare them with us.

I remember when we was stealing bananas in Pleiku and here come a bunch of Montagnards. Some white guys were talking about them: "Now I'd like to bang one of them." I remember Davis said, "Yeah. But you get that thought out your mind, 'cause I'll blow your brains out just for thinking it."

In the field, I wasn't about to do nothing crazy. Not like Davis. I got two Bronze Stars for valor by accident. It wasn't intentional.

The first time, it was really weird. We hadn't had any activity for about three weeks. Not even a sniper round. We was sitting at the bottom of this hill, sitting around joking. Some guys smoking, eating C-rations, talking about their homes. I saw this little animal run into this bush about 50 yards away. I told everybody, "Quiet. I saw a gook." Everybody grabbed their weapons, got quiet.

Well, I knew it wasn't no dink. I had the machine gun. I was just gon' play with the guys. I'ma get this little fox, little weasel, whatever, and bring him back down the hill. So I gets up to where I saw him runnin' in this real thick terrain. So I opened up with this M-60. About 20 rounds. Goddamn if three dinks ain't jump up. They was hiding in the terrain. I'm shooting at them on the joke, right? When they jumped up, I fell all the way back down the hill 'cause they scared me half to death. Then the rest of us moved on up. The dinks had about 100 rounds of ammo, 'bout 12 grenades. I had killed all three of them.

Anyway, the commendation read how I crawled 100 yards to attack three enemy scouts and killed them single-handedly. I joke about it, 'cause if I knew they was up there, I wouldn't have went up there by myself. Naw, everybody was going, and I'd be in the rear, 'cause I didn't walk point.

When I got the second Bronze Star, it was almost similar. I took some guys out on a listening post. At that time, Charlie would throw rocks at listening posts to find out where your location is and make you open up. He would find your claymore mines, turn them around to face you, for you to blow your own self away. I told the men, "If y'all hear something, y'all wake me up."

It was getting close to day, and this guy say he heard somethin'. I said to myself I know what it was. It was a water buffalo. That's what's messing with the trip wires. But I decided to have some fun, play with the captain. I told them to radio back we got activity, they coming toward us. And I just said, "Shit, I'ma have me a mad minute."

I saw the buffalo. And I opened up the M-60. I sprayed the area, threw a couple of grenades, and I got a couple of NVAs. I didn't know they were there either.

Davis wasn't scared even when he was hit. He would just go on encouragin' you.

I remember we was up in Chu Lai, going on an assault in this hot LZ. You got 30 choppers, and the first chopper got hit. It don't turn around 'cause the other choppers waitin' for you. We was in the first chopper. When he got to treetop level, the chopper gunner tell you hit it. If you not out, he'll throw you out. We was jumping out, and Davis got shot in the tail. He never paid it any mind. He was bleeding bad. No question. He was hard.

Another guy named Taylor got hit at the same time. Taylor cried like a baby. This black guy. Davis told him, "You cryin' 'cause you gettin' ready to die. You dying, and you know you dying. You might as well come on and take some of these gooks with us."

Taylor said, "I'm not gonna die."

He said, "Why you sittin' there crying if you not gon' die? You cryin' cause you a big faggot, and you gettin' ready to die."

And he put the spunk back in Taylor. Davis would intimidate you into not dying.

So Taylor got to fightin' until the medevac carried both

of them back. Matter of fact, all of us went back. I got
hit in the head. Five steps off the chopper. Trying to be
cool, I had took my helmet off, put my soft cap on. It
knocked me down. I saw this blood. It was burning. I
said, "I'll be damned."

The weird thing, after we always have a little jive assault, these majors and these idiots in the back would say
they want a body count. Go back out there and find the
bodies. After we found the body count, then we had to
bury them. Geneva Convention says we have to bury 'em.
And I said, "What the hell y'all talkin' 'bout the Geneva
Convention? We're not in a war."

I remember February 20. Twentieth of February. We
went to this village outside Duc Pho. Search and destroy.
It was suppose to have been VC sympathizers. They sent
fliers to the people telling them to get out. Anybody else
there, you have to consider them as a VC.

It was a little straw-hut village. Had a little church at
the end with this big Buddha. We didn't see anybody in
the village. But I heard movement in the rear of this hut.
I just opened up the machine gun. You ain't wanna open
the door, and then you get blown away. Or maybe they
booby-trapped.

Anyway, this little girl screamed. I went inside the
door. I'd done already shot her, and she was on top of
the old man. She was trying to shield the old man. He
looked like he could have been about eighty years old.
She was about seven. Both of them was dead. I killed an
old man and a little girl in the hut by accident.

I started feeling funny. I wanted to explain to someone.
But everybody was there, justifying my actions, saying,
"It ain't your fault. They had no business there." But I
just—I ain't wanna hear it. I wanted to go home then.

It bothers me now. But so many things happened after
that, you really couldn't lay on one thing. You had to keep
going.

The flame throwers came in, and we burnt the hamlet.
Burnt up everything. They had a lot of rice. We opened
the bags, just throw it all over the street. Look for tunnels.
Killing animals. Killing all the livestock. Guys would carry
chemicals that they would put in the well. Poison the

water so they couldn't use it. So they wouldn't come back
to use it, right? And it was trifling.

They killed some more people there. Maybe 12 or 14
more. Old people and little kids that wouldn't leave. I
guess their grandparents. See, people that were old in
Vietnam couldn't leave their village. It was like a ritual.
They figured that this'll pass. We'll come and move on.

Sometimes we went in a village, and we found a lot of
weapons stashed, little tunnels. On the twentieth of February we found nothing.

You know, it was a little boy used to hang around the
base camp. Around Hill 54. Wasn't no more than about
eight years old. Spoke good English, a little French. Very
sharp. His mother and father got killed by mortar attack
on his village. I thought about that little girl. And I wanted
to adopt him. A bunch of us wanted to. And we went out
to the field, and then came back and he was gone.

We went in town looking for him, and we see these
ARVNs pull up. We thought they was chasing Viet Congs.
So the lieutenant and these two sergeants opened fire on
these three guys running. Find out they weren't Viet Cong.
They were draft dodgers. ARVNs would come to the city
and snatch you if you eighteen, sixteen, fifteen, or however old you are. Put you in uniform. So a lots of mothers
would hide their sons from the ARVNs. These guys looked
like they wasn't no more than about fifteen. They killed
all three of them. And Davis went up to the lieutenant
and said, "Man, you fucked up again. Y'all can't do nothin'
right."

We never found that boy.

Davis, this little guy. He was a private 'cause he kept
gettin' court-martialed. But he was the leader with the
LURPs. We was best friends, but I felt a little threatened.
'Cause he would always argue about who killed the last
Viet Cong. "You got the last one, this one—these two
are mine. I'ma jump 'em." Sometimes he would carry me.

Our main function was to try to see can we find any
type of enemy element. They gave us a position, a area,
and tell us to go out there and do the recon. We alone—
these six black guys—roamin' miles from the base camp.
We find them. We radio helicopter pick us up, take us to

the rear. We go and bring the battalion out and wipe 'em
out. You don't fire your weapon. That's the worse thing
you do if you a LURP. Because if it's a large unit and it's
just six of y'all, you fire your weapon and you by yourself.
You try to kill 'em without firing your weapon. This is
what they taught us in Nha Trang. Different ways of killing
a person without using your weapon. Use your weapon,
it give you away.

I wasn't suppose to carry a M-60 as a LURP. But I
told them the hell with that. I'm carrying the firepower.
Davis carried a shotgun. We would lay back, and then
we'll jump one or two. Bust them upside the head, take
their weapons.

Davis would do little crazy things. If they had gold in
their mouth, he'd knock the gold out 'cause he saved gold.
He saved a little collection of gold teeth. Maybe 50 or 60
in a little box. And he went and had about 100 pictures
made of himself. And he used to leave one in the field.
Where he got the gook.

One day we saw two gooks no more than 50 yards
away. They was rolling cigarettes. Eating. Davis said,
"They mine. Y'all just stay here and watch." He sneaked
up on 'em real fast, and in one swing he had them. Hit
one with the bayonet, hit the other one with the machete.

Wherever he would see a gook, he would go after 'em.
He was good.

The second time I got wounded was with the LURPs.
We got trapped. Near Duc Pho.

We saw a couple of Viet Congs. We dropped our packs,
and chased them. The terrain was so thick there that we
lost them. It was jungle. It was the wait-a-minute vines
that grab you, tangles you as you move in the jungle. Start
gettin' kind of dark, so we go on back to where we had
dropped our packs.

And that's where they were.

All of a sudden, something said boop. I said I hope
this is a rock. It didn't go off. Then three or four more
hit. They were poppin' grenades. About ten. One knocked
me down. Then I just sprayed the area, and Davis start
hittin' with the shotgun. We called for the medevac, and
they picked me up. We didn't see if we killed anybody.
Only three grenades exploded. The good thing about the

Viet Congs was that a lot of their equipment didn't go off.

I told them to give me a local anesthesia: "I want to watch everything you do on my legs." I don't want them to amputate it. Gung ho shit. But I was okay, and they got the frags out.

Once the NVA shot down a small observation plane, and we were looking for it. We saw these scouts for the NVA. One was a captain. The other was a sergeant. They were sharp. In the blue uniforms. They had the belt with the red star. They were bouncing across the rice fields, and we hidin'. They was walking through there, so we snatched them. Me and Davis.

We radio in, right? They sent the helicopter to pick us up, bring 'em back. Intelligence was shocked. The gooks wasn't in pajamas. They had on uniforms. They were equipped. Intelligence interrogated them, and they got the whole battalion to go out and look for the plane.

In the helicopter one of the gooks spitted in this lieutenant's face.

When we found the plane, it had been stripped. Nothin' but a shell. The pilot was gone.

We told intelligence the prisoners was ours. So finally, they gave them to the company and left.

I was still messing around in the plane when I heard these shots go off. The NVA captain tried to run, and he was shot. Shot about 20 times. They killed him.

So one of our officers looked at the NVA sergeant and just said, "You can have him."

So at that time they had this game called Guts. Guts was where they gave the prisoner to a company and everybody would get in line and do something to him.

We had a lot of new guys in the company that had never seen a dead NVA. And the officer was telling them to get in line. If they didn't do anything, he wanted them to go past and look at him anyway.

That's how you do this game Guts.

So they took the NVA's clothes off and tied him to a tree. Everybody in the unit got in line. At least 200 guys.

The first guy took a bayonet and plucked his eye out. Put the bayonet at the corner of the eye and popped it. And I was amazed how large your eyeball was.

Then he sliced his ear off. And he hit him in the mouth with his .45. Loosened the teeth, pulled them out.

Then they sliced his tongue. They cut him all over. And we put that insect repellent all over him. It would just irritate his body, and his skin would turn white.

Then he finally passed out.

Some guys be laughing and playing around. But a lotta guys, maybe 30, would get sick, just vomit and nauseated and passed out.

The officer be yelling, "That could be your best friend on that tree. That could be you. You ever get captured, this could be you."

I don't know when he died. But most of the time he was alive. He was hollering and cursing. They put water on him and shaking him and bringin' him back. Finally they tortured him to death. Then we had to bury him. Bury both him and the lieutenant.

A couple of days later we found three guys from the 101st that was hung up on a tree, that had been tortured. Hands was tied. Feet was tied. Blood was everywhere. All you saw was a big, bloody body. Just butchered up. That's how they left GIs for us to see.

They didn't have name patch. All we knew was two was white, one black. And the airborne patch. We had to bury 'em.

Before the Tet Offensive, all the fighting was in the jungles. We might search and destroy some hamlet. But Tet Offensive, the snipers went in the cities. And we wasn't used to that street fighting.

We was in Tuy Hoa. And funny thing. Louis got in one of these little bunkers that the French had left on the street, like a pillbox. He was hiding. And we said, "Come on. We got to move out."

Louis said, "Hell, no. I ain't moving out. I'm safe. Nobody know where I'm at."

And we kept on saying, "Man, we gon' leave you here if you don't come on and move out."

And we start moving out.

And Louis said, "What the hell. Y'all can't do nothing without me anyway." And laughed.

Soon as he got out of his crouch behind the pillbox and got up, that's when he got hit. Got shot in the chest, in the head. A sniper. And we had to leave him. We had to leave him right there.

They gave us some half-ass story that they sent him home. They sent boxes home. A lot of times we couldn't get a helicopter in, the terrain was terrible. So we had to bury 'em. By the time the maggots ate them up, what they gon' get out the ground? If they find them.

The night after Louis got killed, Taylor just broke down. I mean just boohoo and cry. Crying is kind of contagious. When one guy start crying, before you know it, you got a whole platoon of guys just sobbing.

And we all knew Louis was suppose to go home in a week.

But Taylor was just messed up. He would keep saying he couldn't take it no more.

He was always singing old hymns. I had him carrying 200 pounds of ammo once, and when I got to the hill to set up for the night, I said, "Taylor, where's my ammo?" He said, "Man, you know that song about loose my shackles and set me free? I had to get free about a mile down the road. I got rid of that stuff in that stream. Them chains of slavery."

This other time we were going through the wood, and this branch hit Taylor across the nose. He passed out, and would not move. Lieutenant told Taylor if he don't get up, I'll shoot you. He said, "You might as well shoot me, 'cause I feel like I'm already dead. I am not moving till I see the Red Cross helicopter come." So they carried Taylor in. The next thing I know, they told me Taylor got caught off limits in the city.

Ferguson was with him. See, they used to do things like getting a tooth pulled. You never tell them you had a toothache and fill it. Say pull it. That's two days in the rear. The doctor told Ferguson there wasn't no cavity. Ferguson said, "I don't care. It hurts. I want it out."

So Ferguson and Taylor suppose to be sick. But Taylor said he fell in love with one of them little dinks, and him and Ferguson was in the hootch with mama san. They fell asleep at night. And that's when the NVA come out, take over the cities. Taylor said a platoon of them was coming down the street. Taylor said, "I was laying there beside my baby. Then I think I couldn't pass for a gook.

So I am ready to run at all times. My eyes was like flashlights. I didn't even blink. We stayed at the window all night."

When the sun came up, they took off. They couldn't get back in time. Top sergeant met them at the gate and said, "If y'all well enough to fuck, y'all well enough to fight." They got some suspended rank for being AWOL and was sent back to the field.

Then one night, Taylor was sitting on a hill trying to convince us that he saw the Statue of Liberty. He had been smoking, and there was a tree way out. He kept saying, "Sir Ford. Sir Ford. Ain't that the bitch?" I said, "What?" He said, "The world moves, right?" I said, "Right." He said, "Well, we getting closer to New York, 'cause I can see the bitch. Goddamn, that's the bitch, man."

They had to come give him tranquilizers.

Before I went home, the company commanders in Bravo and Echo got killed. And rumor said their own men did it. Those companies were pressed because the captains do everything by the book. And the book didn't work for Vietnam. They had this West Point thing about you dug a foxhole at night. Put sandbags around it. You couldn't expect a man to cut through that jungle all day, then dig a hole, fill up the sandbags, then in the morning time dump the sandbags out, fill your foxhole back up, and then cut down another mountain. Guys said the hell with some foxhole. And every time you get in a fire fight, you looking for somebody to cover your back, and he looking around to see where the captain is 'cause he gon' fire a couple rounds at him. See, the thing about Vietnam, your own men could shoot you and no one could tell, because we always left weapons around and the Viet Congs could get them.

The war never got worse than this time in April. The whole battalion was out in the jungles. We got attacked. We got hit bad. This was a NVA unit. This wasn't no Viet Cong. They were soldiers.

They would come on waves. The back unit didn't even have weapons. They would pick up the weapons from the units that sacrificed themselves and keep on coming. It made it look like we had shot this person and he fell and then kept on runnin' instead of somebody comin' behind him. It played a mental thing on you.

That's when we start hollering, "We gon' burn this jungle down. Get Puff out here, and get the mortars and flame throwers." Puff helped. It's a bad warship. It comes in with them rockets and them guns. Puff the Magic Dragon lets you know it's there.

But I was scared of Puff. He wounded about six of our guys. I ain't wanna see Puff. I was scared of Puff.

Then we called in for mortar. And the mortar squad hit about six or seven of us. Rounds dropped too short. Miscalculated or whatever.

Then I saw a guy that just came in country. A little white boy named Irving, came from Kansas City. Real nice fella; used to talk how the cattle comes down the street in Kansas City. He got shot in the head. And I went over and grabbed him. The bullet went through his eye. Real small hole. But I put my hands behind his head, and the whole back of his head came off in my hands. I just froze.

I was scared to drop it. Scared to move. I was just sittin' there. And this is where Davis helped.

Davis screamed, "Nigger, stop half-steppin'. We gotta move."

Then the lieutenant start yelling about hold your position, hold your position. Davis said, "The hell with some position. Move back. Move back."

We were getting hit terribly.

Davis knew it. And Davis was a private. A private.

Davis saved us.

When I got out of the service, I went back to Food and Drug, the lab technician thing. But I was carrying this pistol all the time, so people come up and say, "Why don't you go in the police department?"

I joined in December '69. And because I was a LURP and had these medals, they figured I wasn't scared of anything. So they asked me to work undercover in narcotics. I did it for 19 months. Around 7th and T, 9th and U, all in the area. The worst in D.C. I would try to buy drugs on a small scale, like $25. Heroin and cocaine. Then I gradually go up to where I could buy a spoon, $100. Then I could buy a ounce for a $1,000. I got robbed three times, hit in the head with a gun once. But my investigation was so successful that they didn't lock anybody up until it was all over.

I threw a great big party at the Diplomat Motel. I had 34 arrest warrants. I invited all the guys that I bought dope from. About 20 of them showed up. All dressed up, and everybody had Cadillacs and Mercedes. We had agents everywhere outside. Then I told them, "I am not a dope pusher like y'all scums." They laughed. I said, "Y'all scums of the earth selling dope to your own. Take the dope up in Georgetown if you want to do something with it. Heroin. Cocaine. Get rid of it." All of them laughed and laughed. And I said, "When I call your name, just raise your hand, 'cause you'll be under arrest for selling these heroins." And they laughed. And I call their names, and they raise their hand. Then these uniforms came in, and it wasn't funny anymore.

But they put out a $25,000 contract on me.

I was in Judge Sirica's court when they brought in the big dealer, Yellow Thompson. He had got a lot of confidence in me. Called me son all the time. He took me to New York and Vegas and showed me his connections in the Mafia and introduced me to some stars. He waved at me, and I waved back. Then they introduced everybody to the jury to make sure nobody in the jury knew any of the government witnesses. When they call on Special Agent Richard Ford, I stood up. And Thompson looked at me and started crying. He had a heart attack right there. I went to see him in the hospital though. I told him, "You cheap son-of-a-bitch. What's this twenty-five-thousand-dollar contract? But first of all, I don't have nothin' personal against you. I can't stand heroin dealers. I got children, and a family. I was on my job, and you wasn't on yours. If you was, you wouldn't have sold a newcomer that heroin." We got along terrific after that. But I had to go see this numbers man, White Top. And he and the man behind him took me down to 9th Street in this Lincoln to this club. Everybody sayin', "There go Rick, that no-good police." But White Top and this dude bought me a drink. They didn't drink nothing. Just said, "This is my son. Whatever he did, it's over with. This is my son." They let me go, because I was not touching the numbers, just the drugs.

I got the gold medal from the police department, and they sent me and my wife to Greece. I got the American Legion Award, too, 'cause I was a Vietnam veteran doing all this good police work. But I left the department, because they wanted me to testify against policemen taking bribes. I said if you want me in internal affairs, make me a sergeant. They said if you want to stay in narcotics, we'll get you in the federal bureau.

I was a federal agent until this thing went down in Jersey. We was working police corruption. This lieutenant was stealing dope out the property office and selling it back on the street. But somethin' told me the investigation just wasn't right. We had a snitch telling us about the lieutenant. But he had all the answers. He knew everything. He knows too much. I think he's playing both ends against the middle. So one night, my partner and me are walking down this street going to meet the lieutenant to buy these heroins. This scout car comes driving down on us, hits us both, and the lieutenant jumps out and shoots me in the head. He knows that even if he didn't sell no dope, we gon' nab him. I didn't have no gun, but I reach like I do from instinct. And the lieutenant took off. He went to jail, and the prisoners tried to rape him, kill him.

I retired on disability, because the wound gives me headaches. I do a little private security work now for lawyers, and I try to keep in touch with Davis and the other guys.

Davis tried to get a job with the New Orleans police, but they said he was too short. When it comes to weapons, Sir Davis is terrific. But he's been in trouble. A drug thing, two assaults. He writes me sometimes. Tells me his light bulb is out. They trained us for one thing. To kill. Where is he gonna get a job? The Mafia don't like blacks.

Hill went home first. Said send him all our grenades. He was on his way to Oakland to join the Panthers. Never heard nothin' about him again.

Fowler got shot through the chest with a BAR. But he got home. He stays in trouble. He's serving 15–45 in Lewisburg for armed robbery.

Holmes got to computer school. He's doing okay in San Diego. I don't know what happened to Ferguson and Taylor.

Sir Drawers came over to see me for the Vietnam Veterans Memorial. He is still out of work. We marched together. When we got to the memorial, I grabbed his hand. Like brothers do. It was all swollen up.

We looked for one name on the memorial. Louis. We found it, and I called his mother. I told her it was nice, and she said she might be able to see it one day.

But I think the memorial is a hole in the ground. It makes me think they ashamed of what we did. You can't see it from the street. A plane flying over it can't see nothing but a hole in the ground.

And it really hurt me to see Westmoreland at the memorial, 'cause he said that we had no intentions of winning the war. What the hell was we over there for then? And the tactical thing was we fought it different from any way we was ever trained to fight in the States. They tell you about flanks, platoons, advance this. It wasn't none of that. It was just jungle warfare. You jumped up and ran where you could run.

We went to church on the Sunday after the memorial thing. I was doing pretty good about Vietnam the last five years, 'cause I was active a whole lot. If I ever sit down and really think about it, it's a different story.

My sister's husband was with me. He got shrapnel in his eye. His vision is messed up. There were 2,000 people in the church. And the pastor gave us space to talk, 'cause we were the only two that went to Vietnam. My brother-in-law is a correction officer at the jail. So we've always been kind of aggressive. Ain't scared that much. But we got up there to talk, and we couldn't do nothing but cry. My wife cried. My children cried. The whole church just cried.

I thought about Louis and all the people that didn't come back. Then people that wasn't even there tell us the war was worthless. That a man lost his life following orders. It was worthless, they be saying.

I really feel used. I feel manipulated. I feel violated.

Specialist 4
Charles Strong
Pompano Beach, Florida

Machine gunner
Americal Division
U.S. Army
Chu Lai
July 1969—July 1970

This dude, Lieutenant Calley, really didn't do nothing, man. I know, because I use to be in the field. He didn't do that on his own to My Lai. He was told to do that. We killed a whole lot of innocent gooks by mistake, because they were not suppose to be there. The GIs would take them out of their home. But dig this, the people's religion is very strong. They can't leave where they live. So I see why they would come back. I didn't kill any civilians personally. But what I know now, maybe I shot a few. When the stuff happened, it happened so fast, most people got killed in the first 15 or 20 seconds. That's how fast a fire fight happened.

The war in Vietnam didn't do nothing but get a whole lot of guys fucked up for some money. There may have been a chance of having a base close to Red China. But actually it was fought for money. And the people in the world didn't want it to stop. That marching to stop the war was a whole lot of bullshit. Because, dig this, I seen this with my own eyes, because my MOS was humping the boonies. We found caches that the North Vietnamese got, full of sardines from Maine and even medical supplies from the U.S.

I wish the people in Washington could have walked through a hospital and seen the guys all fucked up. Seventeen-, eighteen-year-olds got casts from head to toes. This old, damn general might walk in and give them a damn Purple Heart. What in the hell do you do with a damn Purple Heart? Dudes got legs shot off and shit, got half their face gone and shit. Anything that you can mention that would make you throw up, that you can possibly dream of, happened.

Can you imagine walking around policing up someone's body? Picking them up and putting them in a plastic bag? Maybe you find his arm here, his leg over there. Maybe you have to dig up somebody's grave. Maybe he been there for a couple of days, and it will start stinking and shit. You dig graves. You open graves. You are an animal. You be out there so long until you begin to like to kill. You know, I even started doing that. I walked over a body of a North Vietnamese, and said, "That's one motherfucker I don't have to worry about." It made me feel good to see him laying there dead. It made me feel good to see a human life laying down there dead.

I was twenty when I went to 'Nam. My people was from South Carolina. We was migrants. We picked string beans in New York. Strawberries in Florida. When my older brothers started to work in the canneries in Florida, we moved to Pompano Beach. My father, he only went to the fourth grade, but I finished high school. I wanted to go into the field of automation and computers at the time. I had saved some money, and my mother had saved some money. I only needed $27 to take this course in a junior college. I asked my brothers and sisters to loan me $27, and they wouldn't do it. So I got a construction job helping carpenters. Then I had a feeling they were going to draft me, because only one of my brothers had been in the Army. They drafted me 29 days before my twentieth birthday. My boy was born when I was in basic training. I don't think she wanted to get pregnant. I just think that we just got carried away. I married her when I got out in '72.

I really didn't have an opinion of the war at first. I was praying that the war would bypass me. I chose not to evade the draft but to conform to it. I figured it was better to spend two years in the service than five years in prison. And I figured that for nineteen years I had enjoyed a whole lot of fruits of this society. I knew that you don't get anything free in this world.

I first arrived in Chu Lai in July 1969. After a week of orientation, I was assigned to the Americal Division, Alpha Company, 1st of the 96th. My company commander was a very good company commander, because he knew his profession and kept us out of a whole lot of crucial incidents. But the second lieutenant—the platoon leader— he was dumb, because he would volunteer us for all kinds of shit details to get brownie points. We would walk point two or three times a week for the whole company. He was literally the word "stupid," because he couldn't read a map. And he would say, "You don't tell me what to do, because they sent me to officers' training school." When we got one or two sniper fire, he would stop right there and call in artillery to saturate the whole area before you could take another step.

One time we had to check out an area. It was during the monsoon season. It rained 15 days and 15 nights continuously. We stayed wet 15 days. We started catching cramps and charley horses. And guys' feet got messed up. Well, they were trying to get supplies into us. But it was raining so hard, the chopper couldn't get in. After five days, we ran out of supplies. We were so hungry and tired we avoided all contact. We knew where the North Vietnamese were, but we knew that if we got into it, they would probably have wiped a big portion of the company out. We were really dropped there to find the North Vietnamese, and here we was hiding from them. Running because we were hungry. We were so far up in the hills that the place was so thick you didn't have to pull guard at night. You'd have to take a machete to cut even 100 meters. It could take two hours, that's how thick the shit was. We starved for four days. That was the first time I was ever introduced to hunger.

Then we found some kind of path road down into a little village. And we came to a house that had chickens and stuff there. I think the people abandoned it when they saw us coming. I was the machine gunner, so I had to stay where I was and watch the open area while the guys searched the house. They were city guys who didn't know about utilizing the forest or what they were running into. So they started throwing the rice on the ground. They didn't have the experience that I had. When I was younger, I used to go out for miles of distance into the woods and run the snakes. I told my friend Joe to pick up the rice and get the chickens. So Joe got the stuff. I told them not to worry, so I skinned a chicken. I got a whole mess of heat tabs, and put the chicken in my canteen cup and boiled it for a long time. When I thought the chicken was half done, I put in the rice. And a little salt. It was about the only food we had until the bird came in two days after that. Those guys were totally ignorant. They kept calling rice gook food. That's why they threw it on the ground. I told Joe food is food.

It was a good thing that I didn't run in the house. Because I saw something about an eighth of a mile away. It looked like a little scarecrow out there in the rice paddy. It was sort of like a little sign. I looked at it real hard. I stretched my eye to make sure it wasn't nobody. Then I seen another little dark object, and it was moving. So I opened my fire immediately. I think the Viet Cong was trying to get around behind us so he could ambush us. I just happened to recognize him. I cut off maybe 50 rounds, and the CO hollered, "Hold up there, Charles. Don't just burn the gun up." The rest of the company told me I really got him, so that was the only person that I really was told I actually killed.

My feet was all scriggled up. My skin was raw and coming off. I still carry an infection on my feet right now that I have to visit the VA hospital on a regular basis to take treatment for.

Then I started to take drugs to stop the pain in my feet.

When one of our men was killed the next day, it didn't make a whole lot of difference, because I just felt good that it wasn't me. But it gave me a thrill like you take a drink of alcohol or smoke a cigarette to see a Viet Cong laying dead. It was giving me a good feeling. It stimulated my senses. I thought about it, and I really started to love seeing someone dead. And I started doing more drugs. Now I'm afraid that if someone catches me the wrong way, I would do them really bodily harm. It won't be no fight to prove who the best man is, or to prove manhood. Because of 'Nam, I cannot fight, because if I fight now, I'll fight for life. Someone is gonna die immediately.

But it hurt me bad when they got Joe. Joe was an all right guy from Georgia. I don't know his last name. He talked with that "ol' dude" accent. If you were to see him the first time, you would just say that's a redneck, ridge-runnin' cracker. But he was the nicest guy in the world. We used to pitch our tents together. I would give him food. He would share his water. And food and water was more valuable then than paper money. And when we had an opportunity to stand down, he would get sort of drunk and go around the brothers and say, "Hi there, brother man." The brothers would automatically take offense, but I always told them Joe was all right. His accent was just personal.

I remember one night I put my little transistor radio on my pack. We listened to music with the earphones, and he talked about his wife and kids back home on the farm in Georgia. He said he would be glad to see his wife.

The next day he was walking point. I was walking the third man behind him when he hit a booby trap. I think it was a 104 round. It blew him up in the air about 8 feet. He came down, and about an inch of flesh was holding his leg to his body. He rested on his buttocks, and his arms were behind him. He was moaning and crying in agony and pain and stuff. What really got to his mind is when he rose himself up and saw his leg blown completely off except that inch. He said, "Oh, no, not my legs." I really distinctly remember the look on his face. Then he sort of went into semiconsciousness. He died on the way to the hospital. I had to walk up the trail to guard for the medevac to pick him up. And I remember praying to the Lord to let me see some VC—anybody—jump out on that trail.

After six months, it was approaching Christmas, and

we went back through the jungles to the rear area for a stand-down. That was when I made up in my mind that I wasn't going back to the field. The officers were dumb, but besides that, before I went to Vietnam, I had three dreams that showed me places in Vietnam. When we were in this one area, it was just like in the first dream. I felt like I had been there before, but I didn't place much value on it. But when I seen the second place, it dawned on me this was the place in the second dream. I said that in my dream, there's suppose to be a foxhole approximately 15 feet to the left and a little tin can sittin' on it. At the LZ I was in at the time, I walked straight to the place where the foxhole was suppose to be. And there it was. And the can, too. The third dream said that I was going to be crossing a rice paddy, and I was going to get shot in my chest with a sucking wound that I would never recover from. And one of my buddies was holding me in his arms, saying I would be all right until the medevac came in. But it seemed like I never made it out of there. So I wrote my mother and told her that it was time to leave the field, or I would never make it out alive. The first and second dreams came true. It was a sign from the Heavenly Father for me to do something, or the third dream would come true. A Christian never walks into any danger, dumb and blind. Never.

I had three alternatives. One was I could go back to the field. The second was I could go to jail. The third was I could take more time in military service. I chose the third. I enlisted for three years to get out of the field and get trained for welding.

I left the 'Nam the end of July 1970. I had learned my job welding at Lai Khe. Then they transferred me from Fort Dixon to Frankfurt. Germany was good for my readjustment, because I really didn't care nothing about law and all those things. I really didn't have no respect for life. Like I had the power in 'Nam to issue out life or death sentences. If I just wanted to be a real nasty person, then I probably could have just ripped off South Vietnamese civilians for practice. In Germany I learned black people can live together in harmony and that we had to band together in order to make it back to the United States without going to jail.

I got involved in a black study group, and I started reading black history. The racial situation intensified. Then the rioting and fighting broke out all over. They were putting more blacks in jail for the most simple thing. So we tried to get black lawyers from stateside to come over to help us. When I was in the field, they had no room for racism at all. Maybe someone would first come in with it, but after a while, he knew that you were working together as a unit and he needed each man. And besides, common sense would tell you if someone has 200 targets to shoot at, you stand a better chance of living than if he would have 50.

In Germany this first sergeant always hassled me because I had small holes burned in my fatigues from welding. I told the company commander the sergeant was prejudiced, that I might be young but I am a man. The CO told the sergeant to requisition me three more fatigues, and I bought three more with my own money. I would change uniforms twice a day so the sergeant wouldn't hassle me. I didn't take no shortcut. I had the cleanest room in the whole company. The CO usually used my room as a showcase. He was so proud he gave me a bit of furniture. He knew I couldn't stop being a man for a second. You can't go outside the regulations and get anything accomplished. So with a small radius of brothers, we talked to black GIs all over Germany so they would not get fucked up and end up in Mannheim stockade.

I got out in December 1972. The longest day I lived was the day I got out. When I got home, I figured I would lay around a couple of months. I was drinking beer, wine, any kind of alcoholic beverage. That time, too, I started messin' around with some THC. But I really didn't mess around with it for that long, because it makes you feel unsure of yourself. I decided to marry this young lady I was going with for seven years. I wanted to show her I really loved her. That's when the effects of Vietnam really had their toll on me.

I started having flashbacks. When I would lay down and dream at night, my mind would play tricks on me. I still had my jungle boots and fatigues. And when it would rain real hard, I would put them on and go wherever I wanted to go. I would be ducking around in the bushes, crawling around just like you do in actual combat. And I would do silly stuff like breaking out the street lamps, and they put me in jail a couple of times for being disorderly.

But I did a really strange thing. I had this little .22. Something prompted me to turn it into the police department. It was a good thing, too. Because I got real mad at my wife one day. I put on my fatigues, and put this ice pick at my side. When I couldn't find her, I just totally demolished the house. People called the police, but they couldn't find me. I just lightly eased out of the house and went across the street, where there were some high bushes. It was dark and stuff, and I moved just like I learned in Vietnam. I thought I could keep running forever. But after 30 minutes, I cooled off and got out of the bushes and went back over the house. The neighbors said they didn't know what was wrong with me. The police didn't take me to jail but to the hospital, where they put me in the psychiatric ward for four days. And the psychiatrist told me I loved my wife too much. Nothing about Vietnam.

I decided to go live with my mother, because I didn't want to hear my wife nag. I worked at welding for a while, but I kept getting a lot of burns. So I tried construction work, but it got real bad because the housing business went down. So this VA counselor told me to try to enter school, and I started going to Broward Community College to get computers one day like I wanted back before 'Nam.

But the real thing that happened to me was the Lord touched my vision. I found out that I was just not existing. Now I done fell into the real life that I am living. I'm living 24 hours a day, no matter how rough the situation. Within my body I maintain peace and tranquillity. I see I have all I need. I can cope with anything. I lost my fear of death, because I have really accepted life. Although I live in a merchandise society, I don't try to keep up with it. I don't even watch TV unless it is a live sports event or something happening right then. When you watch someone pretend to live life, you wasting your time. And I see many people back here stateside killing as many people as they were killing in Vietnam. Vietnam really gave me a respect for human life. I value people. People make me happy now. And I don't feel inferior anymore. When I was six or seven, I used to wonder why I was born black; I should have been born white. See, I found out from reading about my past before slavery—my ancestors built the pyramids that still stand today. They omitted the small things like the Caesars of Rome studied in a university in Africa before they became Caesars. I learned that as a black man the only problem I had was that I wasn't exposed to things. I feel equal to everyone, and I walk humbly among men. I'm studying to be a computer programmer, but that doesn't make me better than a garbage man.

Most of the nightmares are gone. Except one.

I still think about this North Vietnamese soldier. We took two hours to kill him. This was a brave dude. I'll never forget him. It took a whole platoon to kill him.

He was held up in a tunnel. He knew he had no possible chance of winning whatsoever. And he wasn't really expecting no help. But this was the bravest dude I had ever seen. And I respect this dude.

The "rabbits," they were so crazy they didn't understand nothing, see. We had interpreters to rap to him to give up. If he give up, they would rehabilitate him and shit like that. And he would fight for the regular South Vietnamese army. They rapped and rapped to him. And we started shooting and throwing frags and Willie Peter rounds—white phosphorous grenades that burn through metal and shit.

But the only way we got him was this crazy rabbit jumped down in the hole and beat him to the punch. With a shotgun right through his neck. So when they pulled him out, he was hit badder than an ol' boy. He had a hunk of meat out of his leg, big as that. He had shrapnel all over his body. He had a hole in his side. But he wouldn't give up. Because he really believed in something. This man was willing to die for what he believed in. That was the first time I ran into contact with a real man. I will never forget him.

When I was in Vietnam, it was not important to me where I died. Now it is very important to me. I made a promise in 'Nam that I would never risk my life or limb to protect anybody else's property. I will protect my own.

So this country is not going to tell me to go out again to stop the spread of Communism. In Germany we were buying beef for the GIs that came from Communist countries. They telling us to fight the spread of Communism, but they be helping the Communist economy. I don't walk around blind anymore. If another war breaks out and they want me to go, I'd rather die. I'll fight anyone here in America. But if they come and get me to send to some other country, I'm going to have my gun ready for them.

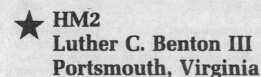

HM2
Luther C. Benton III
Portsmouth, Virginia

Hospital Corpsman
Military Provincial Hospital Assistance
Program Team N-2
U.S. Navy
Hoi An
May 1967–May 1968

Being the only son in my family, I did not have to accept
the orders to Vietnam. I accepted the orders because I
wanted to see what the war was all about. And I thought
that if we were there, then it must be right. We have to
stop Communism before it gets to America. I was just
like all the other dummies.

But it was in Vietnam that I first heard the voice of
God. I didn't know anything about the Bible. I knew it
existed. I believed. I was baptized as a child. But I didn't
have the belief and faith when I went to Vietnam that I
have today.

And there was this one night in particular where God
definitely saved my life. And for a reason, too.

I was a sailor's sailor. I always did my duty and then
some. Perfect military bearing. Immaculate all the time.
On this one ship I worked in the pharmacy, and I was
probably the cleanest person around. When we picked up
the Gemini 10 space capsule, someone said, "We need to

have a medical person open the door." They came and
got me. So I opened the door with all the cameras flashing,
TV and everything. And then I had to escort them to sick
bay, where the doctors would examine them. Another
time I was picked for the surgical team that had been
activated to go right out there on the beach at the Bay
of Pigs. But there was never an invasion even though
everything was in motion for it to happen. And one night,
a friend of mine who was a helicopter pilot crashed in the
water trying to land on the ship. He was, maybe, 50 feet
out. It was nothing wrong with the helicopter. They were
all strapped in and couldn't get out. So I jumped off the
flight deck, swam over to the helicopter, and I unbuckled
two people. The first guy I unbuckled, unbuckled the
other two. They sent a little boat out, and then we all
climbed in and came back. The helicopter had sank in the
ocean. They gave me a bottle of Scotch and told me that
I was makin' Navy history, 'cause whiskey was not allowed on the ship. And they told me those four guys
would've been lost if I hadn't jumped in after them.

The orders I got for Vietnam was to the Military Provincial Hospital Assistance Program Team in Hoi An. Before we went there though, we had to go through special
training at Andrews Air Force Base. 'Bout two months
of Vietnamese language training, Vietnamese custom and
history. We flew into Saigon on a commercial flight in
May of '67. I was to work in this provincial hospital for
a year. Even though they were saying that the mission
was to upgrade the medical standards of the South Vietnamese, I didn't realize at the time that this hospital was
an information-gathering arm of the CIA. We were not
supposed to treat any military people at all. Only treat
civilians. But we did. We were treating the Viet Cong.

In our team there were twelve enlisted men and three
officers. All Navy. We got in a civilian doctor, a doctor
from Turkey, and three nurses from West Germany. There
were three Marines permanently assigned for security.
And we had this one Marine sergeant who lived in a shed
big enough to put a cot in. He was an intelligence officer,
working for the CIA. And there was this one CIA guy
who would come around. He lived some distance away
in this house with Chinese mercenary guards around it.

The first thing I did at this provincial hospital was set up a X-ray unit with Andy Garrett. He was from St. Louis and was the only other black guy there.

Then they took me out of that and made me the medical supply adviser for Quang Nam Province. I issued the Vietnamese medical supplies. I just kept a record of what came in and where it was located. Help them set up a system, just like a warehouse.

A village chief would come in, and he would say to the Vietnamese representative—my counterpart—what he wants. He was not a doctor. He was just the individual who was the head man in that little village. He'd give 'em a list of what he wants. We'd pack it, and he would put it in his cart, and he'd go down the road.

There was no limits established to what they got except those established by the Vietnamese counterpart. They would order all kinds of medical supplies that they liked. Alka Seltzers and aspirins. Even had citrus-flavored Alka Seltzer. I remember I never seen none of them before.

There were all kinds of drugs. Amphetamines. Morphine. Penicillin. Dextrose and saline solution for IV equipment. Anything you could think of, they had it. All the things that you would get for a aid station for individuals who might be injured in war.

I ordered ambulances from America.

I ordered the air conditioners, because they said order 'em. They ain't have no electric power in those villages, but they had air conditioners.

Then they send over rice. I thought it was ridiculous. But after I looked at the countryside and saw that they had napalms on the rice paddies, then I understood why they needed to have rice, 'cause they couldn't grow none.

One day, they said, "Where can we get a pig at?"

Somebody said, "Well, maybe the medical supply adviser can get us a pig."

This USAID man said, "Get a catalog." This would have lists of things in the USAID-sponsored programs. But I found out you just write on an order form you want a pig. Two weeks later, we'd get pigs. They came from America.

These were big pigs. The Vietnamese pigs only get about maybe a foot and a half high. These two things almost look like ponies. And they didn't last a week. They were s'posed to breed them. They ate 'em. They say it's too big to feed. The American pigs ate more food than five or six Vietnamese families, and they were just not gonna feed 'em. So they ate 'em.

It was not my job to find out what they did with any of the stuff. My job was to order what they wanted and get it to 'em.

I lived right next to the hospital. I had built a bunker outside. And right next to it we had a bar and a barbecue pit. At the bar we sold whiskey. We had four slot machines and a jukebox. We would cook steaks, and troops came by and they would have beer. So we had Jim Beam whiskey or whatever they wanted. There were two Vietnamese barmaids and one gentleman that cleaned.

The carbine that they gave me in Saigon before we went to Hoi An didn't have a firing pin in it. They said, "It doesn't make any difference. You're going to a pacified area anyway. You don't need a weapon."

In Hoi An there were Viet Cong throughout the area. Everywhere, really. There was always explosions goin' on. There was always planes flyin' through droppin' bombs. There was always howitzers goin' off, kaboom, kaboom, all the time. There was always somethin' 24 hours a day.

So I had a .38 Smith & Wesson Phantom with a shoulder holster I wore all the time under my clothes not to attract attention. I wore civilian clothes. I bought this .38 from a GI. You could buy anything in Vietnam.

I had a M-4 grease gun, which fires a copper-jacketed .45 round. I had maybe a couple thousand rounds. I had 'em all in clips stashed in certain places in case I needed 'em. I got this gun for a bottle of booze. From this guy goin' through on a tank, because that's normally the weapon the people who rode the tanks had.

Three days earlier we had acquired a .30-caliber machine gun in a trade. We mounted it on top of one of the buildings. I felt it would seem to be a nice piece of equipment to acquire seeing that the individuals who run the area were just doctors and hospital corpsmen. And after being around hospital people for a while, those Marines walking the perimeter were very lackadaisical.

I didn't have a really good friend over there, because I didn't want to. I did not want to have anyone that I got so close to that I would care too much if they become injured or killed.

But the first thing I do when I go into an area that I'm not familiar with is get familiar with the people. I spent a great deal of time discussing the problems of Vietnam with the Vietnamese people, what they felt and what they thought about the Americans and their involvement. I learned right away the war was not the right thing to do from the people's point of view.

I asked a group of young men, "Why aren't y'all fighting for the liberty of your country? Are you crazy?" They rode around on the Suzukis and Hondas all the time.

They said, "You crazy? Our soldiers not trained good enough to fight Viet Cong or NVA."

They said, "Why should we do it anyway if the Americans are gonna do it? If the Marines are gonna come? We really idiotic to do that. And it won't make any difference anyway."

They would tell me that when you don't have anything at all but your life and rice, and the rice the government takes or the Viet Cong takes, it doesn't make any difference which one wins. The country is not gonna change either way no matter who wins. You're gon' have to pay them rice anyway. So the thing to do is let the Viet Cong fight the government.

They said, "We sit and watch and see you win. Whoever win is the one we go with. The Americans are the ones that are crazy, 'cause they not gain anything. They lose their lives and their money here."

So that's what the people felt.

One fascinating thing about the people was that the most reliable information that I ever got was from kids. You had to stay on guard because people would walk up to you with bombs strapped to 'em and just blow up. I didn't wanna be around nothin' like that. But for some reason these kids knew what was goin' on.

There was a couple of kids that I was associated with. A little boy and a little girl. They were orphans. They'd come around, and I'd give 'em soap and food. I'd take 'em downtown in a jeep and buy 'em a pair of shoes. I would fuss at 'em to find out if they went to school.

One time I had been in the jeep by myself. Just drivin'. And I received a couple of gunshots in the vehicle, one through the windshield. But when I drove around with the kids, I never had any problems.

I had been there maybe two months when I went in the marketplace. I was wearing black pajamas. I was real thin then, 116 pounds. And though I was 6 feet, I could be mistaken for them, especially in the dark.

They had a lot of Chinese in the area that were shop owners. And the money people were the Chinese. They were sellin' fish, vegetables, all kinds of stuff.

There were some soldiers walkin' around and some policemen. For some reason I just didn't get into crowds. Well, this guy just walked into this crowd, and he just pulled the string and the thing blew up. And when he blew up, there were other little things on him that flew away that later blew us. Really six different explosions. It was just a mass of mess out there. Blood and guts all over.

I did not travel by land on no convoys either. Little kids come up next to you with little bombs attached to themselves and pull the strings then, too. I traveled from village to village by Air America or helicopter.

There was this one area going down to the river that the kids would not even wave at ya'. The adults would look at you, turn their nose, and walk right away. I knew that this was not a very good place. But the Army would send their younger people down there to practice firing every so often. One Sunday, a whole deuce and a half full of soldiers went down to the river to fire. No minesweep. Nothin'. Dumb. While they were goin' down there, they hit a mine in the road the Viet Cong planted. It was a whole truck load of GIs. Maybe 15, 20 people. And blew it all up. The biggest piece of anything was the chest of this one black soldier and the tailgate of the truck.

The funny thing about the hospital was that working the X-ray, you find people that had bullet wounds. As far as I was concerned, anybody got those kind of injuries was there in the fighting. And it seemed like 99.8 percent of the time it was from weapons that was American. Like from M-16s. Finally, they told us that we were actually

treating the enemy. But they were coming in dressed like
civilians. We had some of them chained to beds. You knew
they were enemies. And the CIA and the Army intelligence would come to the hospital and take them away.
Some were killed. The lucky ones got to POW camps.
We just didn't see people with pneumonia, bed colds, or
some kind of disease. I thought it was a facade. We were
really wastin' our time.

One night the Viet Cong or the NVA must have had
someone in the hospital they really wanted out, 'cause
they went through the hospital. There were some policemen at the hospital. They got shot really fast. We went
over there, and as they were leaving, they fired some
mortars on the hospital. And there were people there that
were blown apart.

I remember this Vietnamese. He was one of the people
who worked at the hospital. He was lying there, you know,
moanin'. I reached down to pick him up, and as I picked
up his back, I discovered all of his back was blown out.
I had actually put my hands on his lungs. I went over and
put him in a stretcher. And I just felt—I just felt—I put
my hands on his lungs. And he died.

Somebody came up with the idea one time that it might
be a good idea to have a medical person around to make
sure that people were not physically injured by the interrogations. Or you could treat them right then if something
happened so they could still be interrogated. I don't know
whose idea that was, but that didn't last long.

So I went over one time for this. They had this young
Vietnamese female, and they had her standing on a little
tiny stool with three legs on it, like a milk stool. They
had taken all her clothes off. She had her hands tied behind her. And there was this ROK Marine doin' the interrogating. There was an American civilian. And a
Vietnamese individual.

The Korean didn't never hit her. But she got really
upset and spit on him.

So what he did was he took a flare and he pushed it
up in her body between her legs. Phosphorous flare. He
stuck it up in her vagina, enough for it to stay there.

And he lit the flare. It burned her legs. Then she just

fell off the stool and flopped around. She moved around. And he just let the flare burn. It burned the inside of her body.

She flopped around.

They just let her burn up like that.

I said, "Hey! This is ridicu— You shouldn't do that."

I walked over to her, and they grabbed me and pulled me out of the room.

I was not allowed to stop it.

She was screamin'. You hear her outside the room. The scream.

When she quit screamin'—when she quit screamin', I knew she was dead.

After that point, I was not privileged to any of that kind of goin's on.

And who was I to report it to? What would've they done? I mean you—you know they're there to kill people anyway. I mean, so what's another person killed?

One evening I was sittin' there on the bunker watching the war. Watching the bombs goin' up. And I heard the voice of God, the Holy Spirit, speak through me.

I hadn't been drinkin' or nothing like that.

It was something that I could not really define, because I'd not heard it before. But I knew that it was God. Because it was not a audible thing. Not nothin' that I heard with my ears. It felt like from the depths within me, within my soul. It felt like something that just caused my entire body to tremor.

All It said was that you are to teach My people.

I said no, no, no, I can't believe this. And I went in the bar. And I sit down. And I start havin' a few drinks. 'Cause I don't believe it.

About a week later, I was down at China Beach. There were some Marines out there havin' a cookout. The German females were there from the German medical team. They were out there splashing around. Just havin' a good time. But I didn't want to swim. I didn't want anything to drink. I remember I didn't want anything to eat. I felt uneasy. I wasn't afraid or frightened or nothin' like that. Just uneasy.

So I started walking up towards the jungle at the edge

of the beach. There was a Catholic nun from the orphanage not very far away. There were kids yellin'. You heard
some of the birds. And the wind was blowin'. And you
heard the weeds were rattlin', the foliage, everything.

And I was walking up there and was just lookin', every-
thing stopped. The bushes quit rattlin'. The birds got quiet.
The kids. Everything got still. There was not a sound.
Nothing moved.

And I heard It again. It said, "You must."

And I said, "Well, Lord, when I get out of the Navy,
I'll do what You want me to do." That's what I said.

Then came the twenty-seventh of August '67. 'Round
about two o'clock in the morning, we were attacked. I
woke up, and there were people runnin' all over the place.
A sapper squad. They were plantin' charges all over. Make
you think you got a lot of incoming mortar.

They were actually in the building that I lived in. And
I am hearing all this stuff. Most of the time I wore sandals.
I didn't wear combat boots. And when you walk across
the floor with a boot on, it doesn't make the same noise
when you wear sandals. I just had on a pair of swimming
trunks. Being so thin, I probably looked just like one of
them to them, runnin' in the night.

I went right past them with the M-4, came out the
building, around the corner, and into the bunker.

A white guy I worked with named Peter Gillis was
sittin' on top of the bunker. I guess the bunker was maybe
6 feet high.

Gillis said, "You better not go in there."

I said, "Why not?"

"Well, they'll know you're in there, and they'll shoot
you in there. Come on up here."

So I got on top of the bunker with him.

Another party of them, maybe 15 or 20, were attacking
the ARVN company to our right. They repaired vehicles
over there. Armored personnel carriers. And the only
thing separating us from the ARVNs was a little chicken-
wire fence. The people the VC were attackin' were yelling
and screaming over there. Then a bunch of 'em put a
Bangalore torpedo down to tear up the wire. And here's
another explosion.

So now there's a really big group of people right inside our compound. Folks right in front of where we had the bar.

Gillis said, "We need to fire on them."

I said, "I don't think we ought to, 'cause we don't know whether they're friendlies or not. You can't go around killing the friendly people, 'cause you get in trouble."

All the Vietnamese looked alike to me. I couldn't tell the good guys from the bad guys. Especially at night.

Well, Gillis had a BAR. So I said, "You fire down in front of the bunker. I'll cover you."

He fired about three rounds down in front of the bunker, and they just opened up on it. They just riddled it with bullets. But they shot inside the bunker. We were sittin' on top of it. And the sandbags just beginnin' to fall away.

Gillis yelled, "They're the enemy. They're the enemy."

I didn't know what to do, because I never been involved in a fire fight before.

I just opened up on a pack of 'em with this M-4 grease gun that shot not only through them but through the building and through the slot machines. Iron slot machines. It just tore them all to pieces. It just blows a hole through you that just can't be imagined.

By now, planes swoop over in the area, 'cause the whole area was under attack. And they dropped in the flares that illuminated the area. Shadows would move across, and I would shoot whatever moved. I shot shadows moving. We had ducks and chickens and dogs. And they were all just shot up. Everything that moved, I engaged in fire.

We had two boxes of grenades. We threw them all out. Just pull the pins, throw the hand grenades. It's like in a mad panic. Throw 'em and throw 'em and throw 'em.

I think I was just makin' it on an animal instinct of survival.

But then I prayed.

I said, "Lord, I know that there's nowhere for me to go. There's nowhere I can run to. There's nowhere I can hide. I have not been such a bad person. I've been good. I always said my Grace and everything. I just got one request that I wanna make to You. That is that when I get shot that I will die instantly. That I won't suffer, and that they won't capture me. I just want to die right away. I don't want to be painin' and yellin' and screamin' and hollerin'. I just want to die right away. And I think that You ought to be able to honor my request."

A moment later, this guy in the command bunker to my right yelled out, "What's going on?"

We did not respond, since we were under direct attack. We knew they would call in artillery on the position. And we, still bein' alive, did not want him to call in anything near out position. The enemy was on top of us. Callin' in artillery when you being overrun was the dumbest thing you could ever think about.

By now, Gillis was hit. He had one bullet in him.

Then some of the enemy came around our rear in a armored personnel carrier. Gillis shot the carrier to death with the BAR. He stopped it. I don't know how he managed to do that, but, you know, the Lord was with us.

I continued to deliver so much fire in the area in front that they could not go back the way they came. They were forced to go in another direction. There was a fence next to the hospital, but they couldn't get through that. Then they climbed up on top of our building to get to the .30-caliber machine gun. They killed one of the Marines and wounded the other. But the sergeant who slept in that little shed got up on the building and engaged them before they could get to the machine gun.

Then they came around the corner again. This time they unloaded this B-40 rocket directly into the bunker. I was facing them. Gillis was covering my back.

We were lifted straight up into the air. The blast blew out his eardrums. They tell me I must've had my mouth open, because all the fillings were blown out of my teeth.

When I fell, I landed on my side and I dropped the weapon. It got so much sand in it that it jammed. I got the sand out. I just took the clip and shook it and shook it. And I started firing. And firing. And firing.

While I was still on the ground, this individual came by. He said, "It's me. It's me."

It was Kelly. The chief hospital corpsman. Short, fat guy. The typical hospital corps chief.

I said, "What are you doing out there?"

I almost had shot him.

I said, "Get out of there. Get out of there."

There were people lying there moanin', cryin', yellin', screamin'. They would scamper around tryin' to find somewhere to hide.

Gillis said, "We ought to do something about them. We're hospital corpsmen."

And I did. I shot 'em. I shot in the direction of the cries and moanin' till I didn't hear 'em anymore.

It just seemed like the thing to do. I didn't want to hear it. That noise. That whining. That groanin'. That moanin'. And I was afraid to go down to administer first aid to someone I shot. They might shoot me even if I'm trying to help them.

I did not stop shooting until daybreak. About five-thirty in the morning.

The Viet Cong had went in and freed all the prisoners in the prison behind us.

The repair company had been destroyed.

We had got no assistance from the police station across the street from us.

Then this CIA civilian guy came down. He said he heard we were gonna be attacked, but he didn't tell us because he didn't believe it would happen.

He started walkin' through the area with Kelly. There were a couple of people badly wounded but still alive. He just killed them. Put a Swedish machine gun to their head.

When the sun came up, they found this one VC in a wood pile. He couldn't get out, and he was afraid to leave. He was taken and interrogated. That's all I know happened to him.

Besides the Marine, one of the corpsmen was dead.

We had to get our wounded out on this deuce and a half that had all the tires shot out. It was a mess. But it would run.

They said I killed 47 of them. I don't really believe it. They always exaggerated the body count. The whole thing in Vietnam was how many people you kill. I saw about 25 bodies in front of my position.

At the time, I thought that I should have at least gotten the Silver Star. But they gave me a Bronze Star. For holding them off even when we were being overrun and for keeping on fighting after the bunker was blown up. Especially me being a sailor. And a hospital corpsman at that.

Everybody said they couldn't believe what I did. I guess because I was black. When you're white and you think that no good can come out of black people, when you think that black men are cowards who run scared, yellin' "Massa save me," then I guess they would be amazed.

The morning after the fight I became acutely aware of the fact that I should stay alive for something. I said, "Wow. Boy. I never thought I'd live through that." Then I thought to myself, If I lived through that, what am I s'posed to do now?

Because of the fight, they moved us to live down at this Army compound. In the evenings I ran the bar there, but I was still the medical supply adviser at the hospital.

There were a couple of people that I did socialize with. They were much older than me. I was twenty-five. There was Andy Garrett. And these two Army brothers. Irvin Nixon from New Jersey. And this other guy from Louisiana, who was called Fully Love.

Andy Garrett, Irvin Nixon, and Fully Love were gamblers. They loved to gamble.

We wouldn't have nothin' else to do. So we gambled and we drank and then, when we were shot at, we shot back. And that was it. Until it came time to go home.

We played Monopoly with real money. We'd make up a bank, maybe $500, $600. We get up sometimes to $1,000. And we'd play all day, all night, whenever, until someone took all the money.

Garrett was a compulsive gambler. He would bet on raindrops on a windowpane. That was one of his favorites. When it would be raining, Garrett would stand in front of the window to see the raindrops. Then he would say, "I got fifty dollars that say that this raindrop here will beat any raindrop that you can select." Somebody say, "I'll take this one." Somebody say, "I want ten dollars on this one." Then the raindrops would come down. And when they get down to the bottom, Garrett say, "Okay. You guys pay me." I mean he was lucky.

Nixon was a real good poker player. Fully Love was

a crap shooter. He was so good with the dice that most people would make him blow the dice out of his mouth. Garrett was a very good poker player. Not a great poker player, but very good. He *thought* he was a great crap shooter. Fully Love never played poker. Garrett and Nixon would play the poker, and they would run the game on people. Nixon and Fully Love would run the craps. And they all played together like that. No other way. And they took everybody else's money.

On Saturdays, we'd go to Danang. We'd catch the Black Cat, which was the Army helicopter squadron. Then they'd go in and wipe out Camp Tien Sha, the Navy base. They'd take all the money that was there, and I got 10 percent.

I was the bag man. They allowed me to carry the money because of my temperament. After having been in that fire fight when we were overrun, I would rather shoot than hold a conversation. I think maybe I kind of went off a little bit.

I was playing poker one evening with four other people. And I thought they were cheating. We were all drinking. And I just pulled out a .38. There was a guy right in front of me. I said, "You ought to be ashamed." And I just fired. He moved out of the way. If he hadn't, I would've killed him.

After a while, nobody really wanted to play with me. They said, "You carry the money."

One time I was outside drinkin' beer. These two guys came up and told me to give them the suitcase the money was in. I told them, "Okay. You can have it."

I gave them the suitcase.

Then I just reached in my coat and said, "Now you can take it wherever you want to, after I shoot you."

They put the suitcase down and ran down the road.

Actually I made more than Garrett and the others did. Even though 10 percent wasn't much. I kept it. And I'd lend it to them. If I lent them $100, they had to give me $200. They knew that they had to pay me, because if they didn't, it wouldn't be nothin' for their demise to come during that period of my life.

When we had five days left in Vietnam, we flew into Danang to wait for the flight to Saigon going back to America.

Garrett and Fully Love got into an argument. Garrett always said that he could beat him anytime, but they never gambled against each other. Garrett and Fully Love decided that they gonna have the crap shoot of the century. So they get this room in the Danang Hotel.

Garrett went over to Camp Tien Sha to get all the money he had coming in from dispersing.

Whenever one of them went to the bathroom, they paid somebody to watch the other roll.

Garrett lost his money. So I lent him $500. He lost that. He had two SLR cameras. He had a Colt Cobra. He had two cashmere coats. He had special shoes he had made. He had an enormous amount of suits. Him and Fully Love happened to be the same size. And Fully Love took all of that, too. He even took the diamond ring Garrett had on his hand. Everything Garrett owned. Clothes, cameras, $3,000, and the ring.

Garrett was really hurt.

His pride—everything he had—was lost.

After I got home, I forgot about the voice I heard those two times. I was not the Christian then that I am today. Nowhere near.

But in '75 I was sittin' in a room at the Naval Regional Medical Center in Norfolk. This man opened the door, walked in, and sat down next to me. He was a commissioned officer in the United States Navy. A lieutenant. A white guy. I never saw him before in my life. And he said, "God wants you to get started. God wants you to go to work for Him now."

I said, "Did He tell you what He wanted me to do?"

He said, "No. He just told me to come and tell you that He wanted you to get started."

So I went to Ebenezer Baptist Church in Norfolk and one of the ministers asked me, "Would you be interested in working in a youth program?" I wasn't so sure at first, but we started a Bible study program that was the best the church ever had. It was my first ministry. Then I got transferred, and the program disintegrated.

I heard the voice again on August 1, 1981, the day I retired from the Navy. I was a chief petty officer by then. I was drivin' home from Jacksonville, North Carolina, maybe 20 miles from Norfolk.

I got no physical sound at all. Just the sensation.

He told me to teach His people.

So I went to the National Theological Seminary and College out in Baltimore to finish my bachelor of arts in religion. I was licensed as a minister in the Baptist church, and now I am teaching three Bible study classes as one of the ministers at Ebenezer.

I believe that a man, even a preacher, cannot preach beyond his experience. How can a individual tell you how the Lord helped him to get over the crisis in life if he hasn't had a certain amount of experience in order to be able to relate to the people he's preaching to?

America hurt so many young men by putting them over in Vietnam to be introduced to prostitution, gamblin', drinkin', drugs. To fear. To terror. To killin'. To they own death.

I think God meant for me to overcome those things.

There is no doubt in my mind that He protected me.

When you think that a B-40 rocket blows up underneath you and the only thing you suffer is your fillings falling out of your mouth, you know it is true. And the fillings is the only unnatural thing attached to you. And the other individual who was almost back to back to me sustained all kinds of wounds.

It lets you know what the power of God is really like.

Specialist 5
Emmanuel J. Holloman
Baltimore, Maryland

Interpreter
25th Infantry Division
U.S. Army
Cu Chi
June 1966–June 1969
Long Binh
January 1971–December 1971

I expected the Vietnamese to give me hell sometimes. That came with the job. But some of my own people hated me. Guys would call me gook lover. Sometimes worse. They would call me turncoat or traitor. That was the worst part. You never get over that.

The Army sent me to language school to learn Vietnamese, even though I only finished the eighth grade. Everybody in my class had been to college, but I got my GED by the time I graduated and shipped out to Vietnam.

I went over with the Three Quarter Cav of the 25th Infantry Division in 1966. I was invited to work with other units, but I never left the Cav. I spent part of the time as an interrogator and part of the time in civic action. When we got into combat, I would drive an APC, or I would fly with the spotter, directing artillery. Or I would go down into a battle in a helicopter. And while the helicopter circled around, I would broadcast in Vietnamese for the enemy to give up their arms and come over to our side. That was the *chieu hoi* program.

That's not what made people mad, though. We had a policy of paying out money if we accidentally killed someone or destroyed their home. The Cav was a fighting unit. That's where the tanks were. So they were destroying quite a bit of stuff. Without me, they would make payments only once in a while. But I would go out of my way to let Division hear about anything the Cav did. I would tell them we destroyed this or we killed that, so we must pay it. In one month the whole division paid out 200,000 piasters, but 194,000 of that was for what the Cav did. The Cav didn't like getting that reputation, so the guys blamed me. They thought that all I was doing was helping to build the people right back up.

But if I didn't do it, the people wouldn't get any help for something we did. I passed up promotion three times to stay in the position where I could get those payments. But one time, my commander gave me a promotion anyway. And I extended my tour for six months four times to keep helping those people.

So some guys took it that I was a VC sympathizer. Every morning somebody would have to ask me, "What are you going to do today? Go out and give them gooks more money?"

But when I did make the payment, it made us look cheap. For somebody dead, 4,000 piasters. That's not even $40. If I pushed hard enough, I could get it up to 6,000. If the survivors were real poor, I would push it. But we would get calls down from JAG saying you shouldn't do that. You should only pay 4,000. You better take it easy.

We got 1,000 piasters for a house. The people had to fill out claim papers, and maybe it would come through five months later. That's only about $9. You can't build a house on that. That's not half of what the poorest one costs. Then they would have to scrounge for what they could. It got next to me, really.

Sometimes I would collect food that we didn't eat to take to an orphanage or give to refugees. When I went to the mess hall to get some one day, this first sergeant, a LURP, jumped down on me. He started yelling, "Give them gooks everything. Make 'em fat. Raise 'em up so my kid will have to grow up and come over here to fight 'em, too." But the mess sergeant, who was from Alaska, said, "This is my mess hall. I run it. What I don't eat, I'm giving to him. I take care of this place. You take care of your place."

I got real close to the people. I taught English to the orphans. If a house was destroyed someplace, me and my driver and some Vietnamese would rebuild the building. People got hurt, we'd go there and sit and eat and drink with them. If somebody got killed, it would get real tough, though. I would go to the wake or funeral, and they would all be looking at me. And they're sad, and there's the body in the casket. I would try to make the payment as quickly as possible. They wouldn't refuse it. It became their custom. Sometimes they would say "thank you," but mostly they were very angry.

One time, one of our tanks made a mistake and fired on this woman and her daughter. The daughter got killed. The woman was running from her village because a stray round from another tank had killed her brother. Later on that night, we fired an illumination round over the village. It didn't explode like it was suppose to, and it fell through the roof of this hut and killed an old woman. When I heard about everything that happened, I took some money out to the village. When I got there, the relatives of all three of those people that got killed started beating on me and yelling, "American get out."

The Americans were amazed, you know, at the way I was able to move around. Like I would go places where you couldn't take a tank. The whole time I was there I was only ambushed once. And I thought it was a mistake. The VC had to know who I was and what I did. So I thought maybe these VC didn't know who we were. We were going to take some lumber to rebuild some houses. But nobody got hurt. I was sure it was a mistake, because I could go and come as I pleased.

Not everything we did bad to the people was a mistake. Many times it was on purpose. You see, a lot of GIs felt they shouldn't be there, so they took it out on the people. Like this APC. Every day for a week, it came in town early in the morning, just at market time. Maybe 2,000 people were shopping. And this GI on the APC took tear-gas grenades and threw them into the crowd. Little children passed out. And this old man passed out. We got the guy who did it that time. Reported him to the commanding general, and he was court-martialed. But that type of thing went on all the time.

There was this GI who sat on the bridge from Cu Chi to Phuoc Vinh shooting the people with a slingshot. He used the links that hold .50-caliber rounds together. We also had this MP who sat on that bridge all day and shot the people going to work with his BB gun. I rode behind him once, and he shot at everybody for 5 miles. There was nothing I could do but follow it and watch.

Sometimes a guy would get tired or bored. Then he would want to do something mischievous. I was on a couple of sweeps, and the guys would be checking wallets for IDs. But they would keep the people's pictures, for no good reason.

During the Tet Offensive, they were doing a lot of looting down in Cholon. You could say the ARVNs were looting, too. The Americans were taking TVs. They were taking motorbikes. It was ridiculous. They couldn't keep them. They would drive them for a few blocks and drop them. Mostly they took whiskey, beer, and money. They should have been more disciplined.

A lot of times they raped the women in the villages they were suppose to be protecting. That happened quite a bit, and nobody said anything about it. Even the lieutenant who was in charge of a platoon let it happen. He's about their age, not experienced enough to control them. He goes along with it. He'd be crazy if he went against his own platoon. He doesn't want to criticize his men; he wants one big happy family. So he's right in it. He got his first. It was standard operational procedure. And the Vietnamese police couldn't do anything about it as long as the Americans were there with the women.

But I had one experience I won't forget. One day, after medcap, we passed this big crowd. This jeep had come by with three Americans. They saw this boy sitting there on a water buffalo. They just wanted to scare him, so they just fired a '16 out there. One round ricocheted and hit the boy in the back and came out through his chest.

He looked like he was about ten. We did all we could, and the boy died of shock just right there. I'll never forget that. That was the first time I seen a kid killed for nothin'. And no one could prove anything, because the three Americans would stick together. They were advisers to the Vietnamese. But once they had been drinking and got their heads bad, they would do this sort of thing. It happened everywhere.

Black people seemed to get along better with the Vietnamese, even though they fought the Communists harder than the white GIs. Two or three of the NVAs I interrogated told me they knew when black soldiers were in action, because they would throw everything they could get their hands on—grenades, tear gas, anything. They feared the black soldier more than the white soldier, because the black soldier fought more fiercely, with more abandonment.

But I think blacks got along better with the Vietnamese people, because they knew the hardships the Vietnamese went through. The majority of the people who came over there looked down on the Vietnamese. They considered them ragged, poor, stupid. They just didn't respect them. I could understand poverty. I had five brothers and three sisters. My mother worked, still works, in an old folks' home. An attendant, changing beds and stuff. My father works in a garage in New York. They are separated, and I had to leave school after the eighth grade to work in North Carolina.

Anything blacks got from the Vietnamese, they would pay for. You hardly didn't find a black cursing a Vietnamese. And a black would try to learn some of the words. And try to learn a few of their customs so they wouldn't hurt them. For instance, when you meet a Vietnamese, you're not suppose to reach out and shake his hands. You are suppose to clasp your hands together and put them in front of you and bow. And another thing, you are not suppose to talk to a girl. If you want to, you talk to her mother first. And you can't hold her hand in public. If you see two Vietnamese men holding hands in public, that's considered friendship. That was their custom. But Americans had a different idea. And you keep your hands off a kid's head. And when you sit down, you never cross your legs. And if you do, never have the bottoms of your soles pointed towards the person. People could have taken time to learn just a few customs, not all of them. It wouldn't have hurt. I was very self-conscious around them. I watched myself.

If nobody talked to them first, a Vietnamese would warm right up to a black person even if he had never seen one. I remember I was in the 94th Evac hospital in Long Binh, and this Montagnard girl, about thirteen, had been shot. Her jaw was broken. She didn't speak. She started crying. The first person she grabbed was me. She wouldn't let anybody feed her but me. I sat with her all night holding her hand. Believe me, it surprised me. I took care of her for four days.

In 1968 I got married to a Vietnamese. Her name is Tran Thi Saly, and her father was an ARVN soldier. It was a Vietnamese ceremony, but I guess it didn't count. So I wanted to go to Saigon and do the paper work at the American Embassy for an American ceremony so she could come home with me. The officers kept asking me why did I want to get married. A few blacks, but mostly whites, felt that the Vietnamese weren't equal to us. So they made it real difficult to marry one. I guess, too, the Army didn't want us marrying them and bringing them back and forgetting about them. So the paper work took a long time. And they knew that if you were in a combat unit, you didn't have time to go to Saigon and wait in line from here to there forever. When the paper work did get approved, it was too late. I was shipped home.

A few months after I got back home, our baby was born. A son. I was supposed to be there and give the Vietnamese officials my ID card. And they would have gave him my name. But I wasn't there, and Saly couldn't give my name. So she called him Tran Ban Hung. Tran is her family name.

I would write and send her money. Then, after a while, I didn't hear from her anymore.

It took me to January of 1971 to get shipped back. They took me to a transportation outfit at Long Binh. I said I had to find my wife and baby. They told me I could do what I want to. So I went out to Cu Chi and talked to the people. Saly had been put out by her family, because they thought I had skipped out on her. I thought I would come back quick. I found out that she had gone to Vung Tau. And I said I would find her.

Then this was an accident. I just got to Vung Tau when I met a little girl I had met a long time ago. So I pulled out Saly's picture. The girl said, "Oh, I know her." She said, "I'll go get her." So she got her. I hugged her and all that. She was working at a hotel. She had the baby with her all the time until he died of pneumonia, just a few weeks before I got back. So I gave her some money and told her to go home. So she came back to Cu Chi, and her parents were happy to see her. She was accepted. I bought her the best things, clothing, TV, furniture. She wanted to learn to type, so I got her a typewriter.

I started the paperwork, to get her out again, but it got stalled. And I had to leave in a rush because my brother got sick.

The next year I couldn't get shipped back, because the last Americans were leaving. So I got myself shipped to South Korea so I could take leave to go see her. And just when I got thirty days' leave, I shattered my leg playing touch football. The leave was cancelled, and I was sent home for treatment.

I was still sending her money and still hearing from her. By now our second son was born, Tran Noc Tuan. Then, in 1974, when the Communists took over, our communications got cut off completely. I haven't heard from her since. I didn't want to send a letter over there because she could end up getting hurt. The last thing they were telling me was that girls her age were being indoctrinated into Communism. And I'm told that they mistreat or maybe killed a lot of kids that, you know, were black. I just hope the baby was able to pass for Cambodian. Then she won't have a problem.

I'm married now to a girl I met in Korea. I explained the situation to her. I told her if I could ever get the little boy out, I was going to adopt the baby. And I told her if Saly could come out, I would help her. She said it was all right. We have a daughter of our own now. Her name is Goldie. That's my mother's name.

I had no idea that maybe South Vietnam would fall. I had worked there for such a long time. When we went over, we took over the war. They got in the back of us and did the police action, and we did the fighting. And then, all of a sudden, everybody decided that we were coming out of there. How are you going to take soldiers working behind you and put them on the front lines with new, modern equipment and no advisers at all? The ARVN were good. They had been fighting for 50 years. They lived with war. It was nothing for them. But I didn't feel they could hold it alone. If they had had some hope, somebody to push them along, I think they would have held.

I know we hurt a lot of people over there. But we done good, you know. Look what they got out of it. They got, oh, my gosh, everything. Roads, factories, machinery. They got everything. They never really had advanced this far, you know.

I'd go back the first chance I got. I would go right now, regardless of the situation, because I feel like I belong there. I would like to work as a missionary. Back in the same areas where I worked before. I know right now it is impossible, but I will always be hoping. I liked to work with the Vietnamese people. That can't change.

I guess I'm lucky, when you think about it. I was there more than four years. And half of the 15 guys in my language class were killed there, and the rest got shot.

I took a little shrapnel in my face. My company was sweeping out this area around Bolo Woods. They didn't have a Vietnamese interpreter, so they flew me out with the colonel. Bolo Woods is where the VC was. They controlled the whole area. We took one hit in the chopper on the colonel's side. Then we took another hit. I had my rifle. I was unbuckled. I was used to jumping out of the chopper. As it was coming down, maybe 10 feet off the ground, I jumped. It took another hit just then. I took it in the face. I didn't know I had some in my eyes until about a week later. My eyes started swelling and pus started coming out. I don't know whether they got all the pieces out. Even today, when it gets hot, water just runs from my eyes.

I did contract some type of skin disease, too. I don't know what it is. My skin just peels off. The doctor says the oil just drained out of my skin. But since I left Vietnam, I get up in the morning and the skin is all around. Everywhere. Just my face. All over my face. I can just get up and pull it off like scales. I got a shoe box full of medication. But my face keeps falling off.

Thank God I've tapered off the drinking. I didn't realize it, but I was drinking two quarts of Old Grand-Dad 100 proof everyday in Vietnam. I was buying liquor by the gallon. You drank it, and you just sweat it out. You needed it to keep going, I guess. You got tired, real tired. You saw so much happening. You would do some good, rebuild something. And then you went back tomorrow, and it was torn down, or somebody was hurt or got killed. And nobody thought our program was the greatest. So I was constantly battling people. And I knew that the Vietnamese would be friends by the day, but at night you could find enemies.

Wherever I'm stationed now, I get assigned to drug programs. I have to keep my head together. So I don't drink.

It's funny how nobody has said anything to me about Vietnam. My relatives, my friends, nobody has asked me anything, or said they were glad I'm back or proud that I served.

Sometimes I get angry when I see guys I grew up with just hanging around doing nothing, drinking wine, and talking about how they beat this person up or jumped this old lady for her pocketbook. I say to myself I spent all this time over there so my friends could have a better life. I think about my friends that died that shouldn't have. And there these guys are ready to gang up on a brother or a sister for a few dollars. It makes me angry.

And it's funny, too, when people are trying to beat me getting on the bus. Pushing and shoving to get on the bus. I have had old women shove me and push me. I guess I learned in Vietnam, I guess, nobody can slip behind me. Nobody. I don't want you to sit behind me. I watch you, and I keep thinking that you might do something to me. So many people I see walking around downtown look like they want to do you harm. I'm always ready to take care of myself. But I can't go out and relax in an atmosphere like that. I keep reverting back to Vietnam, when I had to watch all the time. I stayed over there so long if a rocket would fire 10 miles away, I'd be up and out of there and out of reach when the rocket hit because I could hear 10 miles away. I've conditioned myself. I see stuff that other people don't see, so I'm always looking for something. I'm always on guard.

Specialist 4
Haywood T. "The Kid"
Kirkland
(Ari Sesu Merretazon)
Washington, D.C.

Recoilless Rifleman
25th Infantry Division
4th Infantry Division
U.S. Army
Duc Pho
May 1967–April 1968

I never told anyone this. Not even my wife.

When I was twelve years old something very strange happened to me, which has always been with me, even today.

It was 1960. I hadn't never heard the word Vietnam.

It was about eight-thirty in the morning. It was warm for that time of day. It felt like it was about 70 degrees. Something made me want to get out of the house. So I walks down to the poolroom. Of course, it was closed. So I just sits on this two-step-type stoop in front of the building next door.

All this is clear as day right now. It was the most vivid day of my life.

I was sitting there, and it seemed like I had this great vision. I saw two things. I saw myself on this wall, just clear as day. I mean just clear. I saw myself in a war. Then I saw myself in prison for five years. The number was right there. Five years.

It shook me up, but I didn't tell anybody.

I was basically a C-type student in high school. I guess I didn't care much about anything except pool. By the time I was sixteen, I had won a lot of championships at the Boy's Club. But the real competition was at the poolroom.

They only allowed me in the poolroom 'cause I could play so good. A lot of the older brothers used to bet on me. Basically nine-ball, and a little straight pool. One time I made about $300 in one of those type of six-hour sessions. I beat the owner of the poolroom. And then they started calling me the Kid.

My parents came from South Carolina to Washington. My father was a chef in the restaurant at George Washington University, and my mother worked in basically the same type of thing in the cafeteria at the Department of Transportation. They didn't have much money, because they was 11 of us children.

I got drafted on November 22, 1966. I had been working for a book distributor and as a stock boy in some stores coming out of high school. A lot of dudes were trying to do things to get deferments. One of my brothers put some kind of liquid in his eye and said he had an eye problem at the physical. He never went.

I didn't try anything. I knew when I got drafted I was going to Vietnam, no matter what I did. I knew because of the vision I had when I was twelve.

As soon as I hit boot camp in Fort Jackson, South Carolina, they tried to change your total personality. Transform you out of that civilian mentality to a military mind.

Right away they told us not to call them Vietnamese. Call everybody gooks, dinks.

Then they told us when you go over in Vietnam, you gonna be face to face with Charlie, the Viet Cong. They were like animals, or something other than human. They ain't have no regard for life. They'd blow up little babies just to kill one GI. They wouldn't allow you to talk about them as if they were people. They told us they're not to be treated with any type of mercy or apprehension. That's what they engraved into you. That killer instinct. Just go away and do destruction.

Even the chaplains would turn the thing around in the Ten Commandments. They'd say, "Thou shall not murder," instead of "Thou shall not kill." Basically, you had a right to kill, to take and seize territory, or to protect lives of each other. Our conscience was not to bother us once we engaged in that kind of killing. As long as we didn't murder, it was like the chaplain would give you his blessings. But you knew all of that was murder anyway.

On May 15, 1967, I came into Vietnam as a replacement in the 3rd Brigade of the 25th Division. The Cacti Green. It was the task-force brigade that went anywhere there was trouble. The division was down in Cu Chi, but we operated all over II Corps and Eye Corps.

At the time I basically had a gung ho attitude about being a soldier. But could I get in the best situation and not get hurt was a legitimate concern of mine. So I checked out that the line companies—ones making all the heavy contact—are the ones who are getting overran. I thought maybe I should avoid that and volunteer for one of these long-range recon patrols. It was a smaller group, and I had an opportunity to share my ideas and help make some decisions. With a line company, you're really just a pin on the map for sure.

The recon unit was basically to search out the enemy and call in air strikes or a larger military force to engage the enemy. Most of our activities was at night. We was hide by day, and out by night.

The politics of the war just had not set in when I got there. They told us not to fire unless fired upon. But once we enter into a village, we literally did anything that we wanted to do. There was no rules at all. I began to see a lot of the politics.

When I had just got into my squad, Tango squad, I said, "Anybody here from D.C.?"

There was one brother, Richard Streeter, from D.C., who I used to go with his wife in high school. I mean they weren't married when I was in high school.

Then this white brother said, "Say, hey. I'm from D.C."

I said, "Okay. Just soon as I set up we'll get together."

He began to set up, too. He went down to the water hole to fill up his canteen. On his way back, he stepped on a 500-pound bomb that was laid in a tank track.

You don't walk in no tank tracks, because that's where the bombs are usually. Charlie would use the rationale that most tanks would follow their tracks, and they would booby-trap tank tracks.

We didn't see that white brother anymore. All we saw was a big crater, maybe 6 feet deep. And some remains. You know, guts and stuff. And the dirt had just enveloped the stuff. It looked like batter on fish and batter on chicken pieces. His body looked like that.

That freaked me out, but I wasn't scared yet.

It was those times when information was gotten to us that we were in a bad spot and there's no way you can get out—those were the times that was the most fearful times. Times when I began to understand what fear was all about. It's just that anticipation of something happening as opposed to being in the heat of the battle. In the heat of the battle I don't think people think about getting hurt. In the fire fight, the thought of getting hurt never dawned upon me. You think about doing a blow to the person you're fighting.

The most fearful moment was when we got choppered into the wrong area, right on the perimeter of an NVA camp. It was a pretty huge complex. And there was only about 22 of us. You could smell the food and even feel the heat coming up out of the ground where they was cooking right under us. We could hear them, the muffled sounds. We felt their presence. We was ordered not to make a move in no direction. Everything was 100 percent alert. We just couldn't get out till the morning. They said no way in the world they'd come in there with a chopper at night. Everybody felt the pressure. Everybody felt the stress. Only 22 men. We was gonna get overran. That's the fear of any recon platoon.

The choppers came in bright and early.

Another time we heard there was a NVA batallion coming our way. And our directions was not to move, just hold up and wait till morning again. It was near LZ Montezuma. One of our LURP teams had got wiped out, five of them. We was out there to find they bodies. During the monsoon season. And it was raining sheets and sheets of rain. You couldn't even see the next person past up from you. And we was in the rice paddies in the lowlands, and the water just rose and rose. Next thing I know I was sleeping in water up to my chest. Weapons were basically submerged in water. Nothing happened, but the fear, the fear, man.

I remember night movement in that monsoon. I'm trying to grab hold of the man in front of me, trying to find him, 'cause you have to do that in the monsoon at night. I just fell. I fell into a well about 8 feet deep. My heart just fell. It hit rock bottom. And I couldn't signal anyone real loud. All I could say was "Hey," in a little breath-type thing. And when the lightning came on, the E-6, my platoon sergeant, he spotted me. And he pulled me right out with my weapon.

The other thing we mainly did was search and destroy mission. On a search and destroy mission you just clear the village and burn the hootches because the village is suspected of a Viet Cong stronghold or Viet Cong sympathizers. We did not have the capacity as a platoon to take them and hold them. We just cleared them, because we wanted them secure.

If we were doing this combat assault of the village, the CP would set up in the center of the village. The CP would have the platoon leader, the medics, and the air observers. The squads would pass the CP, and we would throw off our big heavy gear and keep our weapons. Then the squads would set up a perimeter around the command post. So the lieutenant really didn't have any idea what was going on in the rest of the village itself.

One time, in a village near Danang, we was making a perimeter. We passed these two black guys raping this woman at the door of the hootch. She was down on her back on this porchlike thing. Nothing more than a little mud slab. They had stripped off her top. She was struggling. They was from another squad. And the protocol of the folks in my squad was just keep moving, not to interfere, everything was all right.

Most of the time we just rounded the women and children up, and they were literally ran out of the village. Then we start putting fire in the holes, throwing grenades inside the hootches, inside of little bunkers, down the wells. Hoping that we could ferret out a couple of VC. Then we burn the village. That was like a standard operation procedure when we went into a village.

My platoon did that to 50 to 75 villages. Like being in Vietnam, there are little villages all over the place.

If we use the figure 50 villages, we found suspects in 12 of them. Maybe 30 suspects in all of them. We very rarely found a real VC.

When a squad caught a suspect, they would put a rope around they neck, kick them in the butt, and knock them out with they fist. Anything short of killing them, 'specially when the lieutenant was aware of the fact that we found someone. Really, it was the squad leader, the E-5, who makes a lot of the decisions about the lives, because most often we were operating about 2 kilometers away from the lieutenant. We would call the CP and say we ran across a dink or two. If it looks like he has no weapons, we would decide to move on. Never telling that we kicked him, knocked him out, or searched him down for drugs.

One time, the VC we found in the village we was going to take back, because we found him with a .50-caliber machine gun—an antiaircraft-type gun—and a lot of ammo. We felt that this man knows something.

This brother and the squad leader, a white dude, for some reason they felt they could interrogate this man. This man wasn't speaking any English. They did not speak any Vietnamese. I could not understand that at all. But they hollerin', "Where you come from? How many you?" And they callin' him everything. Dink. Good. Motherfucker. He couldn't say anything. He was scared.

The next thing I knew, the man was out of the helicopter.

I turned around and I asked the folks what happened to him.

They told me he jumped out.

I said, "Naw, man. The man ain't jumped out."

The brother said, "Yes, he did. He one of those tough VC."

I didn't believe it. The brother was lying to me, really.

I turned around, and the man was gone. I didn't actually see him pushed, but he was gone. It took a long time for me to believe it. I just kept looking where he sat at. And I couldn't deal with it.

There was two white guys I will never forget. This very young lieutenant, straight out of West Point. He had been out in the field a week and already was doin' things that could get you killed. And Studs Armstrong, this gung ho squad leader. He was the first person that I run into that I now know as a mercenary-type soldier in Vietnam.

One time we were chasing a VC, and the VC run into this hole. The lieutenant wanted one of our men to crawl into the hole after him. In fact, he was telling this little brother, Bobby Williams from Philadelphia, because Bobby was the smallest one.

That was ridiculous. Because those tunnels may look like to be a little hole but may end up to be a total complex. Many times the holes are dug in off the entrance. VC go in and crawl into this little slot. If a man crawled in behind them, he were subject to get his head blown off.

I said, "Bobby, don't go in there. You crazy?"

So I said let's throw some fire in the hole as opposed to sending one of our men in that hole. Do that, and we'll pull Bobby out by his ankles and he won't have a head.

Bobby did not go in. And we put fire in the hole. And the VC did not come out.

Studs Armstrong. I'll never forget him. It was the first time I was introduced to what Philadelphia is all about. He always used to talk about South Philly this. South Philly that. I'm livin' in Philadelphia now, and I see how racist it is.

Armstrong was ruthless, man, really ruthless. If there was an ambush to be set, he wanted his squad to be the ones to lead the ambush. At the time I was in his squad, it was because his men had got injured and we had to balance off the squad. I dreaded being there, because he was always going to volunteer me for something, and me and him would have to get into some type of altercation.

Armstrong had reenlisted three time to stay in Vietnam.

One night we set up near Quang Tri, and two VC walked down the trail right upon us. We didn't bury them. We just left them out there in full display with a little card on them showing the cactus. The name of our unit.

Armstrong immediately started cutting ears off and put them in his rucksack. Then he cut one man's neck off, and stuck the whole head inside.

It got so funky the lieutenant told Armstrong to get rid of it.

Armstrong said, "Listen. I do what I want. This is my war."

Like he ran his own show. Three tours in Vietnam. He wasn't going to let any young lieutenant tell him what to do.

The lieutenant had to threaten him with court-martial to make him give up that head, but Armstrong kept his ears. Those was his souvenirs.

I didn't lose a close, close friend towards being killed in Vietnam. But I lost a very close friend in terms of his mental functioning.

His name was Richard Streeter. Like I said, I knew his wife in high school. I had known him then, too. We used to play football on opposite teams. He used to play for the Stonewalls, and I used to play for the Romans. We were like rivalry.

Streeter was in Vietnam about, I think, sixty days before I got there. He received me in the squad. He was a very gung ho individual. Very gung ho. He used to lead fire fights, lead ambushes. That was one of the most impacting things on me. Studs was ruthless. Streeter was brave. Until that particular night at 2 A.M.

We saw two Viet Cong running across the rice paddy through our starlight scopes. So the lieutenant calls in illumination. The VC runs into this village, so the lieutenant tells Whiskey squad to chase them.

They ran right in behind them and got ambushed. The first three men got hit with grenades.

So then the lieutenant hollered Tango squad move in. We dashed into the village and got ambushed, too. We were trapped. They had machine gun fire on us, and we didn't know where it was coming from. All we could feel was it hitting up around us. And they were shooting M-79 grenade launchers at us they got off Whiskey squad. We could tell that they were our weapons, because we know the sound of them. Poop. And then the blast. We could not raise our heads.

Bobby was behind me. A Spanish brother named Martinez was behind Bobby. Streeter, our fire team leader, was in front. Lloyd, the squad leader, and two white dudes was on the side.

Then Bobby screamed, "I got hit." He was shot in the butt.

I moves back for Bobby and said, "Bobby, go up and grab hold of Streeter. Hold Streeter's leg and let him pull you through the hedgerow. Then we can get down behind the dike."

Then they shot Martinez.

So I pushed Bobby up towards Streeter, and Streeter shakes Bobby off. Wouldn't let him grab his leg. Wouldn't help Bobby, right. So I pushed Bobby on up through the hedgerow and went back for Martinez. I was just a pushin' him. But at the time I had an M-72 LAW, which is like an antitank weapon. Very light. You shoot it one time, you discard it. The firing pin is like a cord loop that you just pull out. This cord loop got caught onto one of the bushes. I couldn't raise up because of the machine guns. I feared if I pressed on it, I would blow me and Martinez up. So I had to like squirm out of my web gear and leave that thing hanging.

I finally gets Martinez down behind the dikes, and Streeter is already down there. But he wasn't firing his weapon.

I said, "Return fire, Streeter!"

He said, "I can't fire my weapon. I can't fire my weapon. I can't shoot."

He said, "I'm scared, Kirk. I can't do it. I can't fight." He was crying down behind the dikes.

Then the squad leader kept telling Streeter to return fire. And he would not fire. So the squad leader said, "Streeter, I'm gon' kill you if you don't fire your weapon."

I said, "No, Lloyd. If you kill him, I'm gon' shoot you. So you gonna have to kill the both of us."

I said, "The man is gone. Let him be."

Then I turned to Streeter.

"We in big trouble, man. Bobby's hurt. Martinez's hurt.

Dan just got it. It ain't nothin' but three of us left in this squad. We need to return some fire."

Then this brother in Whiskey squad hollered out his weapon was jammed. Streeter told him, "Here. Take mine."

I said, "No, Streeter. If you don't do a damn thing, don't give up your weapon. I promise you. You're going with the first medevac that we can get in here."

The gunships came in and raked the whole area. Then the medevacs. And they came through a hell of a fire. And we got all the wounded on. Eight of them seriously wounded. A lost eye. A chest shot open. And Streeter. It took a toll on our squad.

We did not seize control of that village until about noon. We found six VC bodies.

Streeter never came back to the field again. He went back to Pleiku to be a supply sergeant and went from E-4 to E-6. Based on him bein' a real top soldier and what have you in the field, it really did something to me. It said any person can go at any moment.

At the time I initially came over to Vietnam they did not have 106 recoilless rifles where I was at. When I was getting short, like three months short, they began to bring them in to secure perimeters. And that was my MOS. So they brought a brother named Sutton from Orlando, Florida, and me into LZ Baldy. We were securing the command post for the entire battalion.

It was the time of Tet. And the VC were making major onslaught.

Me and Sutton were laying around up on the CP, just relaxing, smoking herb, talking, and what have you. Then we heard incoming rounds.

Sutton said, "Kirk, that was incoming rounds."

I said, "No, man. That's something outgoing."

Another came in. "Shhhhh, boom!"

Johnson said, "That's incoming."

I said, "I think you're right. We better get to the guns."

So we grabbed our steel pots, our weapons, and ran to the jeep where the gun was mounted. And this mortar round hit this big 10-foot rock where the jeep was parked. We had to move from bunker to bunker, because the VC was walking the mortars, from side to side, back and forth, making sure they covered the whole perimeter. They knew where our mortar tubes were, where the command post was. They just had us zeroed in. Oh, yes.

We finally pulled the jeep into position and started returning fire. Sutton spotted the flash of their mortar tubes. I was locking and loading. We must have fired 28 rounds that night. We almost burned the barrel off that thing. And it was no one else returning fire in the whole camp but us. They was about 700 of them taking cover in the bunkers.

Reports came in that our rounds was hitting 100 yards away from the mortar tubes. That's very close at nighttime. We was hitting on the money.

That morning me and Sutton rode down in our jeep to the base of the perimeter and saw all that destruction the mortars had done. Well, we was cheered. The men just raved for us and jumped up in the air. 'Cause they knew the only thing they could hear from our perimeter was that 106 with that back blast. Blast from the front. Boom boom from the back.

Sutton got the Bronze Star for being the person who's firing the 106. I got the Army Commendation Medal with V for valor.

We was heroes, but I didn't feel like it for long. You would see the racialism in the base-camp area. Like rednecks flying rebel flags from their jeeps. I would feel insulated, intimated. The brothers they was calling quote unquote troublemakers, they would send to the fields. A lot of brothers who had supply clerk or cook MOS when they came over ended up in the field. And when the brothers who was shot came out of the field, most of them got the jobs burning shit in these 50-gallon drums. Most of the white dudes got jobs as supply clerks or in the mess hall.

So we began to talk to each other, close our ranks, and be more organized amongst ourselfs to deal with some of this stuff. The ones like me from the field would tell the brothers in base camp, "Look, man, you know how to use grenades. If you run into any problems, throw a grenade in their hootch."

When I came home, I really got upset about the way my peers would relate to me. They called me a crazy nigger for going to the war. And I was still dealing with Vietnam in my head.

Well, they sent me to Fort Carson in Colorado to do the six months I had left. I really didn't want to give no more of myself to the Army. So I played crazy.

I told people I ain't know what rank I was. I told them I was busted in Vietnam. I didn't wear no emblems. I was a buck private. I don't know where the papers at.

They made me cut my bush. What I did, I did not get another size hat. So my hat was falling all over my eyes.

Then I convinced the doctor that my feet was bad. I had jungle rot. I couldn't run, couldn't stand for a long time. I couldn't wear boots. All I could do was wear these Ho Chi Minh sandals I had.

And I would fall out in formation in my sandals, my big hat, and my shades.

I rode them right to the point they was about ready to kick me out of the military.

Then on my twenty-first birthday they said they was going to the Democratic convention. Our unit was going to Chicago to be the riot squadron. I told them I'm not going there holding no weapon in front of my brothers and sisters. The captain said, "Kirkland, you going to Chicago if I have to carry you myself." But I went to the doctor and told him I had a relapse of malaria. He said he couldn't really tell me anything. I would have to stay in the hospital for the weekend. He thought he was getting me. I said, "That's fine."

I was successful playing crazy. I got an honorable discharge.

Because I was a veteran with medals and an honorable discharge, Washington city had a job offer for me. The police force or the post office. The police force had too much military connected to it. My whole thing was to get the military out of my system. I chose the post office. Basically I was sitting on a stool sorting mail. Stuffing mail, sorting mail, do it faster. The supervisors were like first sergeants. Six months later I resigned. I just got tired of it.

I was also enrolled in a computer-operations school. They fulfilled out none of their promises. It was a $2,200 rip-off of the VA money I got for school. They folded at the graduation of my class.

Well, I was getting more of a revolutionary, militant attitude. It had begun when I started talking with friends before leaving 'Nam about being a part of the struggle of black people. About contributing in the world since Vietnam was doing nothin' for black people. They killed Dr. King just before I came home. I felt used.

So some associates and me set up a place called the Africa Hut near 14th and U Streets, where the riots almost went downtown to the White House when Martin Luther King was assassinated. It was a cultural place, where people could buy wine and talk political talk.

And then I thought back to when I was in the post office that there was regular monies going from the post office to the Treasury Department to be burned. Old money, they told me. I couldn't understand that money's going to be burnt when people is in need.

I had never did a criminal thing before. But I began to plan how we could commandeer and hijack the mail truck. Set up an ambush.

I still had some friends in the post office that I socialized with. And around October the information started coming to me.

My friend said, "Look. I got a guard who wants to do something."

So I said, "Okay. You go ahead and set it up. I don't want to see the guard. You talk to the guard."

I found out this truck left out of the main post office between three and four in the morning. The first stop was the Federal Home Loan Bank Board, which is right behind the First Police Precinct, the largest precinct in D.C. The truck would pull in like an alley way into a loading-dock area. They would pull up and unload mailbags, then they would move off and head for the Treasury Department. The driver of the truck would not be carrying a pistol, just the guard.

I needed two men. I had this real close friend of mines who was a veteran, too. I'll call him Smith. And through some of my associates at the Hut I met Robert Johnson.

I told them, in setting up the ambush we would stalk

the truck and lay everybody in the proper place. We would use composure, coolness, just like when you set up claymore mines or set up booby traps at night. Everybody would be perfectly still, like when the NVA was right on top of us.

We layed on the ambush for December 23, 1969.

On the twenty-first and twenty-second we followed the truck and layed out our positions.

We decided that the best place to do it was right there at the Home Loan Bank Board, although it was right by the precinct. We said so what, if we do it right. We thought we would draw the least amount of attention there. It was isolated, like off the main street. Very little traffic. The loading-dock area had definite yellow lines the truck moved into. And that time of the morning was perfectly clear.

On the twenty-third my friend in the post office said the guard is going to back out of it. I said we were still going to do it whether the guard is with us or not. We're not backing out of this one after all he told us. And then Smith's wife had a baby, and he couldn't make it. So we needed a substitute. So we got this brother named Calvin Jones I didn't know too good.

That night we painted our faces white so they couldn't focus on who you are. I had a postal uniform on 'cause I would drive the truck. Me and Johnson had pistols—.32s. Jones had a single-shot shotgun.

I knew that if I walk up to the guard at four in the morning, he's not going to think that I am suppose to be there. So I said how am I going to get to him before he sees me. So I decided to lay right down on the parking lines where his side of the truck would be with a drop cloth over me. It was visible. They would see it. So they wouldn't run over it.

Now what happened before the truck came in was a police officer pulled up and walked directly in front of me. I was under the cloth. I had a little peek hole. I said to myself I hope he does not pull this cloth off of me, because the only thing he would see is a flash. I was committed to shoot him. He walked on to the precinct.

Johnson was on the driver's side, lying behind a parking curb, about thirty feet away from the truck. His thing was to move and take care of the driver as soon as he saw me apprehend the guard. Jones was up on the dock beind a loading skid that was leaning against a wall. When I bring the guard around, all he would have to do is come right out and push him into the back of the truck so I could take over the wheel.

Once I made my move, Johnson was right there almost simultaneously. The guard did not know where I came from. It was like I popped up out of thin air.

After I gave the guard to Jones, I drove the truck back down to the post office and parked it on the post office lot about a block and a half away. It was just daybreak. Light was just comin' in.

In the back of the truck, Jones and Johnson was telling the guard and driver that they were not here to harm them. "You can relax. We just want this money."

They asked the guard for the bag going to the Treasury Department. He pointed to the bag, and they grabbed it. Inside was $320,000.

Then Johnson said, "Look. We are going to leave you in the midst of nowhere. You're tied up here. There is no use in hollering for help, because nobody is going to hear you." I think Jones and Johnson made them so comfortable, they did not know they was back at the post office.

I parked the truck, and we all got into our vehicle.

We went to my mother's. Nobody was home. So we went straight into the kitchen to divide up the money.

I'm twenty-two at the time, and I didn't have a great sense of what you're supposed to do once you got the money. We burned a lot of $1,000 bills in the oven broiler because they was old and worn. We said it ain't no use carrying this around. It's easy to spot. The $50 bills were brand new, razor-sharp, uncreased, like even untouched money right off the press. That surprised us, too.

We divided up the money with the instructions that folks lay dead for about three months and not do any spending. But we didn't do that. We didn't do that at all.

The next day we read in the Washington *Post* that we missed the bag with the million dollars. But it was the largest mail robbery in the history of the District of Columbia. And I was glad we gots what we did.

Each of us put up $10,000 to buy a whole lot of food, a whole lot of clothes, a whole lot of toys for the people who lived around the Hut. It was one big Christmas party giveaway on up to New Year's. Children would come in with their parents and pick up some clothes and toys. We even had it laid out in sizes. And we bought medical supplies for a black culture center.

Then we come to find out, Jones he was giving away $100 bills up and down 14th Street. When we went to try to locate him to get him to stop doing it, we found out he had left town.

Jones was the first one to get caught. He had deposited money in various banks, $20,000 in New Mexico, $20,000 in Texas, X amount in Las Vegas, another amount in L.A. The FBI tracked him because the amounts were so big. They arrested him in Berkeley. And Jones told them everything, even about folks that were not even involved in the crime.

Now they had my name and the name of the brother who was cleaning up the money at this business association. The office was right in the building with the stoop I had sat on when I was twelve and seen myself go to war and go to jail.

I was about ready to go on my circuit around the country to visit all my war buddies I had made a commitment to. Let them know I had did my thing. Give them some money if they needed it. "Here I am y'all."

I'm really lookin' forward to this when the brother at the association calls me over at my mother's.

"Hey, Kirk. Could you bring me a little money?"

I said, "Damn, man. I'm getting ready to leave town. I don't actually have access to any of it."

He said, "I really need it bad."

He beseeched me. He begged me.

I told him I would bring it over. So I drove over. I had the money wrapped up in a *Muhammad Speaks* newspaper. But I left it on the seat of the car, and I walked into the association through the door which had the stoop.

I said, "Is everything okay?"

He said, "Yeah. Where's the money?"

"It's in the car."

"Go get it, man. I need it really bad."

He was looking kind of weird, but I didn't really pick it up.

So I go get the money and come back.

I said, "Are you sure everything all right? You seem to be upset."

He said, "Yeah, I am. But some terrible things been happening to me, that's why I need the money. Where is it?"

So I opened the newspaper. And just as I handed the money to him, the FBI man came from under the desk with a pistol and held it to my head.

He said, "You're under arrest. Please don't move."

Then in through a door to the office came another agent.

It was January 16, 1970. They locked me up on $500,000 bail. I couldn't deal with it. I couldn't raise it.

When I went before the judge, I was saying that we took the money because the community was in need. There are people out here hungry, I said. He said that was irrelevant to the crime. He was wounded in World War II. And I don't think he liked me being a veteran doing what I did.

I got sentenced to the maximum ten years on the federal statute of robbery of a mail custodian without putting his life in jeopardy. And I got ten to thirty years under the District of Columbia statute for armed robbery.

Johnson got the same sentence. Jones got three to nine years.

The inmates at Lorton Reformatory in Virginia, they welcomed me with open arms. They were amazed we tried this thing for the community. It was like "power to the people." Heroes, basically.

At first, I got off into a lot of self-study and self-development. Spiritual, mental, and physical. I used to be the first one out on the track and last one in. I was running about 50 miles a week, really. I got into studying ancient Africa and was fascinated with the Eighteenth Dynasty of Egypt. I learned of the oneness of the universe and the single creator which Akhenaton propogated from the throne of Egypt before the time of Moses. And I took the ancient Egyptian name Ari Sesu Merretazon, which is now my legal name. It means "guardian servant chosen to do the will of the Creator."

Then I got into my brothers. Each evening I was organizing. We had set up ALERTS. It would stand for Association Library Educational Research Team for Survival. The concept was that you give us the information, and we will get the education. The prison authorities tried to keep us from publishing an independent inmate paper, but we won a consent decree to publish. Then I organized a residential religious council for those with religious faith to stop the conflict between the orthodox Muslims and the Black Muslims, the Baptists, and the Black Jews, and whatnot. We became the cooks, servers, busboys, and line monitors in the mess hall. And that stopped all the chaos at dinnertime over people fighting for food and eating on dirty tables.

I was looked upon by the men like some type of adviser-counselor. They would come to me to have me write letters to their wives. Or help them with legal problems if I could understand them.

But more and more I started talking to Vietnam veterans. The VA wasn't coming down to the prisons, and they had problems with upgrading discharges, getting benefits, and counseling. We realized that we just had to do it ourselves. So I set up the first veterans affairs office inside a prison. We had our own office space, regular office hours, filing system, typewriters, and people just donated enough equipment for us to do the job. And the VA acknowledged us in the prison.

We called it Incarcerated Veterans Assistance Organization, and I wrote a self-help manual on how to set one up inside a prison. I testified before Senator Alan Cranston. It was the first time ever that Congress heard testimony relating to incarcerated veterans. The administrator for programs at Lorton accompanied me to Chicago to participate in veterans' forums. And I visited the White House with other veterans to meet President Carter.

We got over 500,000 Vietnam era veterans in prison, jail, on parole, probation, or awaiting sentence. Most because of drug problems caused by the war. Or they ain't able to cope when society don't care about them. Over half of them are black veterans. So we keep trying to spread the organization. I'm helping to start a veterans office at Grater Ford Prison near my home in Philadelphia. There are more than 100 across the country today.

Back in January of 1975, I got the ruling from the appeals court saying that the judge errored in sentencing us under both those statutes. It had to be one or the other. So I contacted a lawyer at Antioch Law School to help me put together a petition for reduction of sentence. Besides learning about my good behavior in prison and all my work with veterans, the judge could see a physical change. The turban I wore. The African dress. And he knew about the support systems I had with veterans' organizations outside and how I would keep helping veterans. He said he would give me the benefit of the doubt, and he reduced the minimum sentence under the D.C. statute to six years. That made me eligible for parole that day.

One week later I went before the parole board at nine o'clock in the morning. By noon I was in Washington, D.C. Free.

It was August 25, 1975. I had served five and one half years.

The vision I had seen sitting on that stoop when I was twelve had said the number five.

I have taught a law course at Antioch on the urban mission of developing lawyers who want to represent the poor. I've counseled Vietnam veterans at the Vet Center in Little Rock, Arkansas. At the West Philadelphia Corporation, I am helping neighborhood people reduce their energy cost so they will have money left over for economic development. Maybe to invest in a recreation center or even a business.

I am married, and we have a beautiful baby girl.

Johnson is still in prison in Terre Haute, Indiana. Jones is probably out. The government said it only recovered $60,000 of the money. I told the authorities I gave what I had left to a friend, but he ripped it off when I was in prison. To prove I still have no knowledge of where existing money from that crime may be and that I did not receive no money after I came out of prison, I went on the television show *Lie Detector*. And the result was no. I don't want involvement with that type of experience anymore. The money to me was like blood money. I can make money in legitimate ways.

I still think of Vietnam. I come to realize really that

the purpose of the war was something more than any of the men who were fighting realized at the time. It was like a power play. And the people in charge kept getting overcommitted, overextended, and just didn't know how to pull out. No matter how patriotic we was fighting it, we was like cannon fodder. And I will always be thinkin' that way until the government shows me how we benefited from it.

In Vietnam and in Lorton I was with men at their darkest hour. We listened to Aretha Franklin together in both places. And we cried together, and longed for the World together.

War is prison, too.

About a year ago I saw Streeter on a D.C. transit bus. He was having problems. He would express that he could not find a job. He had lost his wife. He was talking very slow and very deliberate. His speech had slowed down. His whole demeanor had slowed down.

I think that what happened to him in Vietnam was the damagingest thing I seen happen to one person.

I did not know how he felt about me seeing him again back in the World.

I did not know what to say to him.

**First Lieutenant
Archie "Joe" Biggers
Colorado City, Texas**

Platoon Leader
9th Regiment
U.S. Marine Corps
Vandergrift Combat Base
March 1968–April 1969

The first one I killed really got to me. I guess it was his
size. Big guy. Big, broad chest. Stocky legs. He was so
big I thought he was Chinese. I still think he was Chinese.

We were on this trail near the Ashau Valley. I saw him
and hit the ground and came up swinging like Starsky and
Hutch. I shot him with a .45, and I got him pretty good.

He had an AK-47. He was still holding it. He kicked.
He kicked a lot. When you get shot, that stuff you see
on Hoot Gibson doesn't work. When you're hit, you're
hit. You kick. You feel that stuff burning through your
flesh. I know how it feels. I've been hit three times.

That's what really got to me—he was so big. I didn't
expect that.

They were hard core, too. The enemy would do anything to win. You had to respect that. They believed in a
cause. They had the support of the people. That's the key
that we Americans don't understand yet. We can't do

anything in the military ourselves unless we have the support of the people.

Sometimes we would find the enemy tied to trees. They knew they were going to die. I remember one guy tied up with rope and bamboo. We didn't even see him until he shouted at us and started firing. I don't know whether we killed him or some artillery got him.

One time they had a squad of sappers that hit us. It was like suicide. They ran at us so high on marijuana they didn't know what they were doing. You could smell the marijuana on their clothes. Some of the stuff they did was so crazy that they had to be high on something. In the first place, you don't run through concertina wire like that. Nobody in his right mind does. You get too many cuts. Any time you got a cut over there, it was going to turn to gangrene if it didn't get treated. And they knew we had the place covered.

Another time this guy tried to get our attention. I figured he wanted to give up, because otherwise, I figured he undoubtedly wanted to die. We thought he had started to *chu hoi*. And we prepared for him to come in. But before he threw his weapon down, he started firing and we had to shoot him.

And, you know, they would walk through our minefields, blow up, and never even bat their heads. Weird shit.

But I really thought they stunk.

Like the time we were heli-lifted from Vandergrift and had to come down in Dong Ha. There was this kid, maybe two or three years old. He hadn't learned to walk too well yet, but he was running down the street. And a Marine walked over to talk to the kid, touched him, and they both blew up. They didn't move. It was not as if they stepped on something. The kid had to have the explosive around him. It was a known tactic that they wrapped stuff around kids. That Marine was part of the security force around Dong Ha, a lance corporal. He was trying to be friendly.

I think it stinks. If those guys were low enough to use kids to bait Americans or anybody to this kind of violent end, well, I think they should be eliminated. And they would have been if we had fought the war in such a manner

that we could have won the war. I mean total all-out war.
Not nuclear war. We could have done it with land forces.
I would have invaded Hanoi so many times, they would
have thought we were walking on water.

The people in Washington setting policy didn't know
what transpired over there. They were listening to certain
people who didn't really know what we were dealing with.
That's why we had all those stupid restrictions. Don't
fight across this side of the DMZ, don't fire at women
unless they fire at you, don't fire across this area unless
you smile first or unless somebody shoots at you. If they
attack you and run across this area, you could not go back
over there and take them out. If only we could have fought
it in a way that we had been taught to fight.

But personally speaking, to me, we made a dent, even
though the South did fall. Maybe we did not stop the
Communist takeover, but at least I know that I did something to say hey, you bastards, you shouldn't do that. And
personally I feel good about it. People like Jane Fonda
won't buy that, because they went over there and actually
spent time with the people that were killing Americans.
That's why I feel that I shouldn't spend $4 to see her at
the box office. She's a sexy girl and all that other kind of
stuff, but she's not the kind of girl that I'd like to admire.
She was a psychological setdown, and she definitely should
not have been allowed to go to Hanoi.

I learned a lot about people in my platoon. I learned
you have to take a person for what he feels, then try to
mold the individual into the person you would like to be
with. Now my platoon had a lot of Southerners, as well
as some Midwesterners. Southerners at the first sign of
a black officer being in charge of them were somewhat
reluctant. But then, when they found that you know what's
going on and you're trying to keep them alive, then they
tried to be the best damn soldiers you've got. Some of
the black soldiers were the worse I had because they felt
that they had to jive on me. They wanted to let me know,
Hey, man. Take care of me, buddy. You know I'm your
buddy. That's bull.

As long as a black troop knows he's going to take a
few knocks like everybody else, he can go as far as anybody in the Corps. Our biggest problem as a race is a

tendency to say that the only reason something didn't go the way it was programmed to go is because we are black. It may be that you tipped on somebody's toes. We as blacks have gotten to the place now where we want to depend on somebody else doing something for us. And when we don't measure up to what the expectations are— the first thing we want to holler is racial discrimination. My philosophy is, if you can't do the job—move.

Let's face it. We are part of America. Even though there have been some injustices made, there is no reason for us not to be a part of the American system. I don't feel that because my grandfather or grandmother was a slave that I should not lift arms up to support those things that are stated in the Constitution of the United States. Before I went to Vietnam, I saw the "burn, baby, burn" thing because of Martin Luther King. Why should they burn up Washington, D.C., for something that happened in Memphis? They didn't hurt the white man that was doing business down there on 7th Street. They hurt the black man. They should have let their voices be known that there was injustice. That's the American way.

I still dream about Vietnam.

In one dream, everybody has nine lives. I've walked in front of machine guns that didn't go off. When they pulled the trigger, the trigger jammed. I've seen situations where I got shot at, and the round curved and hit the corner. I'd see that if I had not made that one step, I would not be here. I think about the time where a rocket-propelled grenade hit me in the back, and it didn't go off. We were in a clear area and got hit by an enemy force. The RPG hit me. Didn't go off. Didn't explode. We kept walking, and five of us got hit. I got frags in the lower back and right part of the buttocks. I didn't want to go back to the hospital ship, so I just created the impression that I could handle it. But the stuff wouldn't stop bleeding, and they had to pull the frags out. There was this doctor at Quang Tri, Dr. Mitchell, who was from Boston, a super guy. He painted a smile on my rear end. He cut a straight wound into a curve with stitches across so it looks as if I'm smiling. When I drop my trousers, there's a big smile.

I dream about how the kids in my platoon would come to talk to you and say things about their families. Their families would be upset when they heard I was black. But then some guy would give me a picture of his sister. He would say, "She's white, but you'd still like her. Look her up when you get back to the States." And there would be the ones who did not get a letter that day. Or never got a letter their whole tour. In those cases, I would turn around and write them letters and send them back to Vandergrift.

And you dream about those that you lost. You wonder if there was something you could have done to save them. I only lost two kids. Really.

Cripes was a white guy. I think he was from St. Louis. He was a radio operator. You could tell him. "Tell the battalion commander that everything is doing fine." He would say, "Hey, Big Six. Everything is A-okay. We are ready, Freddie." You know, he had to add something to whatever you said. Otherwise, he was a very quiet guy. But one big problem he had was that he wanted to get into everything. He was trying to prove something to himself. If he saw somebody move, he was going to follow him. No matter what you could do to tell him not to fire, he'd fire. One night, after we got out to Fire Support Base Erskine, we got hit. It was about eleven. Cripes got shot. We don't know if he got hit by our fire or their fire. I just know he crawled out there. He must have seen something. Cripes just had a bad habit of being in the wrong place at the wrong time.

Lance Corporal Oliver was a black kid from Memphis. He carried an automatic rifle. He had been with us maybe three months. He was a very scary kid. He was trying to prove a lot of things to himself and to his family, too. So he was always volunteering to be point. It was very difficult to appoint someone as a point man. A lot of times when you had a feeling you were going to be hit, you asked for volunteers. Oliver always volunteered.

We were on Operation Dewey Canyon. In February of 1969. We had been told the NVA was in there that night. One platoon had went out and got hit. And we got the message to go in next. I got the whole platoon together and said, "Listen. I'm going to walk point for you." My troops said, "No, sir, you don't need to walk. We will arrange for someone to walk point." So the next day the

whole platoon got together and said, "Who wants to walk
point today?" Oliver stuck up his hand. I said, "I'll be
the second man."

Now we had this dog to sniff out VC. Normally he
would walk the point with the dog handler. His handler,
Corporal Rome from Baltimore, swore Hobo could smell
the Vietnamese a mile away. If he smelled one, his hair
went straight. You knew something was out there.

One time, when we were walking a trail near Con Thien,
this guy was in this tree. At first we thought he was one
of the local indigenous personnel, like the ARVN. He
turned out to be something else. He had his pajamas on
and his army trousers. He wasn't firing. He was just sitting there. Hobo just ran up in that tree, reached back,
and tore off his uniform. He was armed with an AK-47.
Hobo took that away from him, threw him up in the air,
and grabbed him by the neck and started dragging him.
We learned a lot from that guy. You put a dog on a guy,
and he'll tell you anything you want to know.

Another time at Vandergrift, Hobo started barking in
the officers' hootch. We had sandbags between us. And
Hobo just barked and barked at the bags. Nobody could
figure out what was wrong. Finally I told Hobo to shut
up, and I walked over to the sandbags. There was this
viper, and I took a shotgun and blew its head off.

We used to dress Hobo up with a straw hat on his head
and shades on. All of us had shades. And we used to take
pictures of Hobo. And sit him on the chopper. And he'd
be in the back of the chopper with his shades on and his
hat, and he would smile at us.

We got to the place where we could feed him, and put
our hands in his mouth. We would give him Gravy Train
or Gainsburgers. If we ran out on patrol, we would give
him our C-rations. He really liked beef with spice sauce.

Hobo was so gullible and so lovable that when you had
a problem, you ended up talking to him. You could say,
"Hobo, what the hell am I doing here?" Or, "Hey, man.
We didn't find nothin' today. We walked three miles and
couldn't find nothin'. What the hell are you doing walking
this way?" And he'd look at you and smile, you know, in
his own little manner. And he'd let you know that he
should really be here to understand all this shit we're

putting down. Or he would do things like growl to let you know he really didn't approve of all this bullshit you're talking. It's hard to explain. But after eight months, Hobo was like one of the guys.

Hobo signaled the ambush, but nobody paid any attention. We walked into the ambush. A machine gun hit them. Oliver got shot dead three times in the head, three times in the chest, and six times in the leg. Rome got hit in the leg. Hobo got shot in the side, but even though he was hit, he got on top of Rome. The only person that Hobo allowed to go over there and touch Rome was me.

It never got better. It seemed like every day somebody got hurt. Sometimes I would walk point. Everybody was carrying the wounded. We had 15 wounded in my platoon alone. And the water was gone.

Then on the twelfth day, while we were following this trail through the jungle, the point man came running back. He was all heated up. He said, "I think we got a tank up there." I told him, "I don't have time for no games." The enemy had no tanks in the South.

Then the trail started converging into a really well-camouflaged road, about 12 feet wide and better made than anything I had ever seen in Vietnam. Then I saw the muzzle of this gun. It was as big as anything we had. And all hell broke open. It was like the sun was screaming.

I thought, my God, if I stay here, I'm going to get us all wiped out.

In front of us was a reinforced platoon and two artillery pieces all dug into about 30 real serious bunkers. And we were in trouble in the rear, because a squad of snipers had slipped in between us and the rest of Charlie Company. My flanks were open. All the NVA needed to finish us off was to set up mortars on either side.

Someone told me the snipers had just got Joe. He was my platoon sergeant.

That did it. I passed the word to call in napalm at Danger Close, 50 meters off our position. Then I turned to go after the snipers. And I heard this loud crash. I was thrown to the ground. This grenade had exploded, and the shrapnel had torn into my left arm.

The Phantoms were doing a number. It felt like an earthquake was coming. The ground was just a-rumbling.

Smoke was everywhere, and then the grass caught fire. The napalm explosions had knocked two of my men down who were at the point, but the NVA were running everywhere. The flames were up around my waist. That's when I yelled, "Charge. Kill the gooks. Kill the motherfuckers."

We kept shooting until everything was empty. Then we picked up the guns they dropped and fired them. I brought three down with my .45. In a matter of minutes, the ridge was ours. We had the bunkers, an earth mover, bunches of documents, tons of food supplies. We counted 70 dead NVA. And those big guns, two of them. Russian-made. Like our 122, they had a range of 12 to 15 miles. They were the first ones captured in South Vietnam.

Well, I ordered a perimeter drawn. And since I never ask my men to do something I don't do, I joined the perimeter. Then this sniper got me. Another RPG. I got it in the back. I could barely raise myself up on one elbow. I felt like shit, but I was trying to give a command. The guys just circled around me like they were waiting for me to tell them something. I got to my knees. And it was funny. They had their guns pointed at the sky.

I yelled out, "I can walk. I can walk."

Somebody said, "No, sir. You will *not* walk."

I slumped back. And two guys got on my right side. Two guys got on my left side. One held me under the head. One more lifted my feet. Then they held me high above their shoulders, like I was a Viking or some kind of hero. They formed a perimeter around *me*. They told me feet would never touch ground there again. And they held me high up in the air until the chopper came.

I really don't know what I was put in for. I was told maybe the Navy Cross. Maybe the Medal of Honor. It came down to the Silver Star. One of those guns is at Quantico in the Marine Aviation Museum. And the other is at Fort Sill in Oklahoma. And they look just as horrible today as they did when we attacked them.

Rome lost his leg. From what I'm told, they gave him a puppy sired by Hobo. So Hobo survived Dewey Canyon. They wanted to destroy him at first, but he got back to the kennel. If anybody would've destroyed that dog, it would have been me.

But Hobo didn't get back to the States. Those dogs

that were used in Vietnam were not brought back. The Air Force destroyed all those dogs. They were afraid of what they might do here.

If I had Hobo right now, he wouldn't have to worry about nothing the rest of his life. He was a hell of a dog. He could sense right and wrong. I would have trusted Hobo with my own children. If somebody got wrong or was an enemy of my family, Hobo would have brought his ass to me. There ain't no doubt about it. Yet he was a nice dog. He would give me a kiss on the jaw. I loved that dog.

But the thing that really hurt me more than anything in the world was when I came back to the States and black people considered me as a part of the establishment. Because I am an officer. Here I was, a veteran that just came back from a big conflict. And most of the blacks wouldn't associate with me. You see, blacks are not supposed to be officers. Blacks are supposed to be those guys that take orders, and not necessarily those that give them. If you give orders, it means you had to kiss somebody's rear end to get into that position.

One day I wore my uniform over to Howard University in Washington to help recruit officer candidates. Howard is a black school, like the one I went to in Texas, Jarvis Christian College. I thought I would feel at home. The guys poked fun at me, calling me Uncle Sam's flunky. They would say the Marine Corps sucks. The Army sucks. They would say their brother or uncle got killed, so why was I still in. They would see the Purple Heart and ask me what was I trying to prove. The women wouldn't talk to you either.

I felt bad. I felt cold. I felt like I was completely out of it.

Specialist 4
Stephen A. Howard
Washington, D.C.

Combat Photographer
145th Aviation Battalion
U.S. Army
Bien Hoa
January 1968–August 1969

I was going on nineteen when I got drafted. I had graduated from high school the year before, and I was working as a engineering assistant in this drafting firm. My mother went to the bus station with me to see me off to Fort Bragg for basic training, and she said, "You'll be back a man."

I didn't feel anything about Vietnam one way or the other. When you are black and you grow up in urban America in a low-income family, you don't get to experience a lot—if your parents protect you well. My mother did. My mother raised all four of us. She was a hospital maid, then she went to G. C. Murphy's company. And now she's director of security for the stores in Washington D.C.

Mom is not college educated, so all she knows is what the propaganda situation is. She programmed us to be devoted to duty, to God, state, and country. She said you

got to do all these good things—like military service—
to be a citizen here in America. "You're not white," she
would say, "so you're not as good as they are, but you
got to work hard to strive to be as good as they are." And
that's what you're brought up to believe.

I guess I knew that Martin Luther King was against
the war. But I couldn't relate to what he was doing about
it or even about discrimination because I wasn't old
enough. Nor was my mother in a position to explain to
me what that whole power struggle was all about.

I was just brought up to believe that when the opportunity presents itself to you to stretch yourself out, you
do it. Subconsciously or consciously you're trying to sat-
isfy your mother's dreams even before you even deal with
what you even want to do.

Mom wanted us to be better, to be middle class. She
was looking forward to me being something. To going to
Vietnam. To being a man.

The first white friend I had, I had in Vietnam. We were
really very different, but we thought each other had something going for him that made us special.

I think Rosey was from Georgia. A redneck. That's
why we called him Rosey. He was 6 foot 2. I was somewhat shorter, shall I say, and from the city. It was like I
will show you what rednecks are like, then I'll show you
what niggers are about.

We living next door to each other at the Bien Hoa
helicopter base, but we ended up in each other's room
every night. See, when the rednecks got together and
started to stomp and holler, you either had to go over
there and pour beer on the floor and do your little jumpin'
up and down, or you stay out of it. That was their thing,
and we had our thing. It was good to do it together, 'cause
we were all in the war together.

Rosey and me talked a lot about our personal lives.
Having a girl friend that you really were serious about
marrying. Wanting to have a son one day. What our families was all about. What it was like for him living in
Georgia being a sharecropper's son. Not having some of
the basic things that I knew deep down inside that I had.
He starts talking about being hungry. Mom always had
food on the table. I mean it was constant peanut butter

and jelly 'til Mama came home. Then we ate a lot of roast. Mom was there.

Rosey, he and I had a very tight personal relationship.

Rosey was a pathfinder. By himself he would jump into a hot LZ. His job was to direct the helicopter assault, get the ships on the ground, get the troops right on the ships, get them out of there. Being a photographer, my job was to photograph the landing operation, how they got 'em out. And I got on the last ship. Sometimes when a chopper go down and we lose the people, I had to document the situation. Photograph the remains and do the necessary things to act like we still a civilized race of people, even though we not 'cause we're engaged in war.

Serious war.

Sampan Valley was serious. It was supposed to have been a simple mission. It turned out to be a major operation, 'cause they knew we were comin'. I mean they're not crazy. I mean they weren't a bunch of yahoos out there trying to wage war. They knew we lift at eleven, because they see us in the mess hall. They smell us taking a shower. They can smell our soap. They smell our cologne. They smell us gettin' dressed. And we get prepped up like we gettin' ready to go to a serious party. You comb your hair. I mean you're at war combing your hair.

We lost a lot of good people that night. Good people. Because the hierarchy decided that this is what we going to do. And the Viet Cong know it.

We lost four ships that night, and heavy damage to Puff the Magic Dragon. And when you lose two Cobras, the colonel has to explain, 'cause you don't lose Cobras. And they lost two that night. Two.

The Cobra. When they call in the deadly Cobras, they were awesome. If a call goes in that they need close support, they'll bring in three of 'em. All of a sudden, just out of nowhere, this guy is hovering over you. Once he tips the tail up and drops the nose, you know he's got four seconds. Then in four seconds an unbelievable arsenal of destruction is brought forth. Firing these 2.75-millimeter rockets. After he drops 52 of them, he brings those 40 mike-mikes in. And he's still running two miniguns. And they can roll. Roll in on the target. Come in at completely 90 degrees. At 200 miles an hour. Anytime you need them, they are five minutes away. I mean, they better than the transit system.

The commander of the Cobranet team, he got shot down that night. He got killed. We lost Bobby and Kenny, too. Eric lost his leg. Two warrant officers that was flying Slicks got killed. They were two really rowdy guys, too. I mean they like to drink good liquor. They were the only cognac drinkers in the hootch.

It was so dark. I mean dark. I didn't think we knew where we were going or what we were doing half the time. For the first time, I started thinking what is this all about? I'm tired of this. This is enough.

Then we lost a helicopter in the rain one night. The pilot got lost. He knows I am out here flying in the middle of nowhere. Anybody in any tree can shoot me down. He panicked. He happened to have been about 80 feet off the ground, and he pulled a 180-degree turn. Slammed into the bushes. Took us two weeks to find him. All four of 'em were dead.

I had to photograph finding the remains. And the stink, the stench of death, was—was unbelievable. I had never smelled death before. Not after two weeks. And you just smell 'em from a 100 yards. You know you're walking into the smell of death. They—they—they smell like— if you ever smell it again, you'll know.

And you reach down, and you pick up the flack vest, and there's only a carcass, the shell of a carcass. And maybe the head is gone. I mean when you hit the ground at a 100 miles an hour, I don't care what kind of seat belt you got, it's tearin' your limbs off. You don't have no limbs. And these are people that you know, people that you fly with. Not only dead, but you can't bury all of them. You'll never have all of them again. They will never be whole. Or what we know whole is. Not only dead, but torn apart. And whenever we took fire, I always visualized myself being in that position. And I forgot about all the things that ever mattered, except I want to be a whole body if I go out of here.

Long Binh was adjacent to Bien Hoa. Long Binh was a supply depot. The biggest supply depot in the world.

From a paper clip to a jet, you could get it at Long Binh. All you had to do was have the right requisitioning papers. You could find it at Long Binh.

So they decided to blow up Long Binh's ammo dump. January 31, 1968. And when the ammo dump went up, it was like somebody's introduced nuclear weapons into Vietnam.

We gave them the opportunity. See, in our society we will move on any opportunity that will provide us to have servants. We take advantage of it. And the Army did a good job. It allowed us the fact that we could have a hootch maid. Somebody come in to polish our boots, wash our clothes. Well, they could walk in every day and bring a little plastic explosive in at a time. A little bit. See, they would spend a year working on a project and pull it off. That's something that we never had. Patience.

When the ammo dump went up, we went to war. Cooks, mechanics, detail men, everybody. And we had people in Bien Hoa that never shot a weapon out of basic training. This was the first time they ever witnessed somebody's gonna kill them. And they think I don't believe this shit. I really don't believe that I'm at war. This is not what I was programmed for. I was programmed to move pots and pans, and now I got a M-60 in my hand. And all through Tet there was this fear for them for the first time. I might get killed. I have done everything that I was supposed to do to be in the situation that I wasn't gonna get killed. And now I'm in the situation. Everything has failed. And this is where your buddies came in. The fliers. They knew what it was like to be a perfect target.

The 199th Light Infantry Brigade was suppose to be protecting Long Binh and Bien Hoa. But no one knew where they were at.

Well, the Viet Cong came in. They came in through the main gate of the base dressed as ARVNs. A couple of truckloads. They put a Quad 50 on top of that big water tower. It meant they could shot straight down the flight line. So you can't get a chopper or anything off the ground.

And they were coming across the barbed wire with AK-47s, with old French rifles, crudely made grenades, pitchforks—anything they could use to kill, maim, or wound.

Anything had a slant in their eyes out on the barbed wire that night was in trouble. They were the enemy. They was suppose to be dead.

They left about 400 people on the barbed wire that night. When we pulled the bodies out, there was three people that worked in the kitchen in battalion headquarters. They served the food to the officers. One of the cooks from our mess hall was there. Some of the people that owned the little shops that was just outside the base. Some of the boom-dee-boom girls. Some of the owners of the boom-dee-boom clubs. Some of the guys that you see in the clubs that just seem to come in and just be sitting there. And the people that worked in the barbershop. Two of them. And the girls who polished our shoes and washed our clothes.

In other places the Tet fighting went on for a month. I got stuck in An Khe. You couldn't get out, you couldn't get in. It was a matter of life and death every day. So what you learn is go look for somebody that's gonna be secure. You learn that in 15 minutes. The guy that was like battle-worn.

You say, who here is the most nastiest, the raunchiest. Somebody who is going to go for it. And if you got any sense, you do what he says.

It's like having Fred Biletnikoff, knowing that it's the last play of the game and you need a touchdown. If you watch the Oakland Raiders play for years, when Kenny Stabler threw the ball up, sometimes he might not know where it was going, but Biletnikoff ended up with the ball. And he didn't drop the ball. You looked for somebody that was going to be right there.

He would be a grunt. The officers, you try to stay away from them, 'cause they're dangerous. They'll get you killed. 'Cause they don't know.

He would probably be a redneck. White boy. Probably small, but he just had everything he needed to cover his behind. He would have an M-79 grenade launcher strapped on the bottom of an M-16. He knows what it's all about to tie your clips together. Because he's not gon' be diving to the ground with the clips flyin' around. He knows to take care of his weapon, 'cause that's the only thing that's gonna mean that he's goin' to survive.

And you find somebody that don't have no stripes on their shoulders. Why do I have to advertise who I am? It's like certain companies that don't have to advertise. J. Walter Thompson, you don't hear them advertising. But everybody knows who to go to.

And whether or not you black or white, he will treat you like, Hey, you nothing but a punk here. It's like going to jail. Don't accept no favors from nobody. Don't become friendly with anybody. But by the same token, somebody's gon' have to teach you the ropes or else you will never learn the ropes.

That's what you looked for in a situation where you might die. And there's a difference between I might get hurt and I'm gonna die here. On a little piece of land that's not worth a plug nickel to me.

I found the guy quick. White boy. From North Carolina, Georgia, somewhere down South. He had obedient black guys around him that had been in the bush with him. I don't mean they just worship him as a white boy. They worshipped him because of the fact that he stayed alive. I figure anybody do two tours in the bush there is something wrong with him or he enjoy what he did. And he could smell 'em, just like they could smell us.

We smoked a lot. We talked a lot. He said the service was gon' be his life, because there ain't nothing else for him. He said, "You know, I could give a damn about a nigger. But givin' a damn about a nigger doesn't change any situation here, 'cause y'all are gonna be here as long as I'm here."

When I got back to Bien Hoa, I tell this bunch of cooks, radio operators, "Hey, I just walked out of An Khe. And you're still back here." Somebody said, "You know what's gon' be on TV tonight?"

"No, man. I don't know what's gon' be on TV."

I got shot down three times. It always got worse, because their firepower kept gettin' better.

The first time, the ship got hit outside An Khe. The pilot was good enough to understand autorotation. But it is not a lifesaver. If you can get the ship down, you use your trees. You use everything that keep you from hittin' hard. Because you still got 2,000 pounds of fuel. That's the first thing you gotta worry about. How do you get rid of this fuel. They don't put plugs in, you can't jettison any fuel. So you gotta make sure that you don't have a collision with anything that is immobile, like earth. Biggest object in the world to run into is mother earth. And you get friction. Friction generates a spark. The spark will ignite. Your tanks has always got fumes in it. And you don't ignite the fuel, you ignite the fumes.

We got down. I had a concussion and shrapnel in the wrist and in the arm. They had got us with a radar-controlled antiaircraft 37-millimeter.

The second time, something went wrong. Two companies were supposed to have taken a position, and this second lieutenant popped his smoke and called in air support. The Cobras went in. And then the gunships. But once we got in there, he didn't tell us there was any antiaircraft gun. We got hit by a 37 again, and went down in the river. I got a severe concussion and a lot of water in my lungs. And then I contracted some kind of tropical disease from consumption of the water.

In the spring of 1969 we started to lose a lot of ships, based on the fact that we were getting hit by heat-seeking missiles. This guy in intelligence kept saying he saw elephants around Dong Tam. The elephants were their transport systems being that they ain't have any APCs, no motorized vehicles. So he wanted us to go investigate. At ten o'clock. In the Cobra. Now you never send your daughter out to the store at ten o'clock at night in the ghetto. That's what they did. They sent a daughter out, unescorted, unprotected.

And we got hit. And it was like here we go trees. The blade went. You know, the main rotary. But the pilot knew what to do, and we broke through the trees constantly, constantly. I was in the front seat, and you constantly had trees coming. You sitting there in that little plastic bubble. Something that's 37 inches wide. You sitting in the nose. It's like I wonder if Hughes did this right. If this s'posed to be a single piece. Is there a seam in the middle? Am I going to be going off one way or the other? And the tail hit, and we slid down the side of the tree.

I asked the pilot, "Can you move?"

"No."

I can't get out, so I had to break the canopy because

the lock doesn't work. I got out the side, and laid down. And I thought, Well, goddamn. Let me regroup.

I'm bleeding. Not only am I bleedin', excrement is coming out of the wound, which means that my lower intestines are damaged. It's oozing out. It don't run out. All these little enzymes are just rolling down over your clothes.

I was first concerned that I was gon' bleed to death. My pulse was up, and my body hadn't responded to shock yet. But the main artery wasn't severed. A round took out the left side of my prostate gland, came through my lower intestines, and came out the left hip.

The pilot was bleedin' from the mouth. That meant blood had gotten into his stomach. I thought his ribs had punctured somethin', but he was still breathin'.

I cut him out, got him out the back seat. And dragged him away, 'cause, you know, the fuel can blow anytime.

He can't move his arms. When the turbine had exploded, his seat—the back seat—jerked and his back was gone.

I covered him up to stop the shock and gave him some morphine. I jacked him right up to the ceiling. We ain't had no water.

Then I dropped a grenade in the cockpit to destroy the maps. The fuel blew, and that will take care of the miniguns and the rest of it.

The first thing you do on your way down is turn a little device on that's like a homing device. So somebody knew we were down, but nobody knew where. Of course, the hostile force knew, and you could sense they were out there.

We talked and talked. I had to keep him awake, because he was keeping me awake. And amazingly enough, we talked about screwing. 'Bout all the fine dames we ever knew. We lied about everybody we wished we could have had. We weren't bragging, we were lying. And he talked about what life was like when he was a kid. What it was like for me. And what we doin' out here.

It was 13 hours when they spotted us. They spotted us through an opening in the trees that we made when we fell. A couple of Phantoms came and laid down the firepower to get rid of everybody that was within distance of bein' able to pluck you off. And then the Cobras did their thing. Then they brought in that Chinook, and dropped the basket. And there come Rosey down the ropes. "Goddamn, boy," he says. "Good to see your ass."

The medic came down and said, "I think the war's over for you."

When they operated on me in Japan, I had to be detoxified. I had took so much morphine since the first time I got hit I had a morphine habit.

When I got out, I applied for disability. But they didn't give me 10, 20, 30, 90 percent. Nothin'. They said I was physically fit for service. But for years I had to exercise, exercise to tone back the stomach and pelvic muscles. And even today, if I don't follow a perfect game plan eating proper foods, I get congestion in my intestines. And, at first, sex was a problem, but then it became a mental thing. At least there is no more of that to worry about.

I started to free-lance. And I was rolling in this industrial photography, doing the whole deal when they were building the Washington subway. But the contracts dried up. I am a highly skilled photographer, but I can't get a job. And my art is becoming more and more sophisticated, becomin' computerized. And I'm still on the outside looking in. I know that if I go someplace and I tell this employer I'm a Vietnam vet, it don't mean shit. Pardon the expression.

You know, I was sitting in my apartment with Carolyn. We weren't married yet. And I picked up the Washington *Post*, and it said Saigon had fell. I said, "What the F was I there for?" I mean what was the whole purpose? All of a sudden you—your—your mechanism said, Hey, you don't have to worry about it. It cuts off. You don't think about Vietnam. That's the way it was.

Then about two years ago, one day, I decided that I'm not out to lunch. I'm null and void. I am not getting up today for no reason. And not getting up today for any reason is not justifiable in our society. See, you can't quit our society.

I don't have the flashbacks and the nightmares. It's the depression. And you can't identify what the depression is. Plenty of times I just wouldn't come home. All day, you know. And 30 minutes not coming home in my house is a long time. Or you walk into your house one night, take all the clothes out of your closet, and stack 'em up on the floor.

We came back totally fucked up in the head. But it took ten years for our bodies to catch up to where our heads were. All of a sudden you feel this psychological pain become physical pain. Then if you're lucky, which I was, somebody come up and pull your coat and say, "Hey, you need some help." 'Cause if my old lady hadn't decided I needed some help, I would probably either be dead or in jail today.

I went to Walter Reed first. They put me in a situation with about 34 people in a room. How in the hell are you gonna talk to me about my problems with 34 other problems in your face? I went to the VA hospital in Baltimore, and they gave me two aspirins and told me to go to bed and call in the morning. By my wife havin' a job that she could have Blue Cross and Blue Shield, I got a private shrink gettin' me through the moment. But I don't understand why we gotta pay this guy $90 an hour when I gave you three years, four months, five days, and twelve hours of the best of my life.

This psychological thing, we try to suppress it. But it kills us quicker than if somebody just walked up to you and put a bullet in your head. 'Cause it eats away at your inner being. It eats away at everything that you ever learned in life. Your integrity. Your word. See, that's all you have.

Vietnam taught you to be a liar. To be a thief. To be dishonest. To go against everything you ever learned. It taught you everything you did not need to know, because you were livin' a lie. And the lie was you ain't have no business bein' there in the first place. You wasn't here for democracy. You wasn't protecting your homeland. And that was what wear you down. We were programmed for the fact as American fighting men that we were still fighting a civilized war. And you don't fight a civilized war. It's nothing civilized about—about war.

Like this day, they took this water buffalo from the farmers. Either paid them off or killed them. It didn't matter. Whichever was best.

They lifted it with the Huey about 300 feet. Nobody

paid much attention. 'Cause you on a chopper base. You see helicopters liftin' off with all kinds of strange things.

So he flew the chopper up, just outside Bien Hao. The game plan was to drop it. And when you drop a water buffalo 300 feet, it has a tendency to splatter. So that meant the farmers around knew that you were almighty. That you would take their prized possession. That we'll come and get your shit.

So we dropped it in the middle of a minefield. Set off a whole bunch of 'em.

I know the Vietnamese saw it. They watched everything we did.

I think we were the last generation to believe, you know, in the honor of war. There is no honor in war.

My mama still thinks that I did my part for my country, 'cause she's a very patriotic person.

I don't.

**Captain
Norman Alexander
McDaniel
Fayetteville, North Carolina**

Electronics Warfare Officer
432nd Tactical Reconnaissance Squadron
U.S. Air Force
Takhli, Thailand
March 1966–July 20, 1966
Various Prison Camps, Hanoi
July 20, 1966–February 12, 1973

I could smell the hate.

Some of them had pistols. Some guns. Some shook knives at me, shovels, even hoes. They motioned for me to stand up. Then they inched forward. About 50 of them. Communist militia, like popular forces. And just plain folk, too. All pointing guns at me.

They looked to see what I had and took my .38. They made me strip down to shorts and T-shirt. They took off my boots. They tied my hands behind me.

Then they marched me about a 100 yards, right down this hill to this hut. Then around to the backyard. There was a large hole, like a pit. They motioned for me to get into that. I hesitated. Then they pushed and shoved me into it.

I thought I was going to be executed.

I said to myself, This is it.

I guess I was in a state of shock. I wasn't afraid. I just thought my time had come.

It was July 20, 1966. Just seven days short of my twenty-ninth birthday. I had come a half world away from Fayetteville, North Carolina—the son of sharecroppers—to die in North Vietnam at the hands of peasants.

When I was growing up, Fayetteville was no different from most of the other cities in the South and some in the North. You couldn't go in restaurants. You rode in the back of the bus. And there were separate sections and toilets for the black people in bus stations and train stations. I went to a segregated elementary and high school about 15 miles from our home. There was a bus stop to pick up white students about a block and a half from where I lived, but I would have to walk 5 miles to get the bus for black students. But it didn't bother me to walk 5 miles each way. I would press on to get the education. I just never let the race problem inhibit me from whatever I was trying to accomplish.

I did quite well in high school, but I could not afford to go to college. Initially, I planned to go into the Air Force as an enlisted person, and afterwards take advantage of the GI Bill to go to college. But a couple of my teachers made some calls to North Carolina A & T State University to help me get a part-time job in order to go straight to college. And that's what happened. I worked my way through in the cafeteria.

At the time, every physically fit male had to be part of the ROTC program. I chose Air Force. And I passed the qualifying test for officer training. If you got to serve, it seemed a good thing to be an officer.

I became an electronics warfare officer, or EWO, assigned to the EB-66C electronics reconnaissance airplane. It normally carries a six-man crew—pilot, navigator, and four EWOs like me. Our job is to go up and see what kind of defenses the enemy has in terms of radar and missile sites. Then we warn our bombers and fighters to help them to be successful in their bombing missions.

When I heard we were going to Thailand for combat missions against North Vietnam, I felt good, really proud to be part of it. The Communists were attempting to take over South Vietnam. I felt that we had a good cause. And that feeling has not changed.

We took off early on July 20 from Takhli Air Base. Our

missions normally lasted an hour and a half, maybe two hours. The bombers were going after railroads, bridges, storage depots. Pretty much the standard items.

The EB-66C is not armed, so in the daytime, we had fighter coverage—F-100s, F-104s—to keep the MiGs off. If we flew at night, it was assumed that the MiGs couldn't see us. So we flew alone. We flew alone. And some nights it was kind of interesting. Moonlight nights, boy, it was just about like day. We didn't feel too comfortable.

Just as we were completing our support, we were hit by a surface-to-air missile. We were at about 30,000 feet. The missile was not a direct hit. If it had been, the plane would have just exploded right away, and none of us would have survived. But the missile exploded a little distance from the plane, yet it was close enough for some of the fragments to puncture the fuel tanks. The plane caught on fire immediately and started to disintegrate.

We lost all communications with the front section, where the pilot and the navigator were. Smoke and fumes started filling up our section fast. We didn't even have communications within our compartment with each other.

In our section, I was supposed to eject first. The big question was, are we as bad off as I think we are, or am I jumping the gun. But assessing the situation, I chose to eject.

The history of the EB-66C is such that normally in ejection, those who eject upwards—the pilot and the navigator—survive. Those who eject downward—the EWOs—the survival rate for them is very, very low. Later on, the North Vietnamese said one of the crew members died shortly after he was captured because he was injured severely. I tend to believe them because he was the fourth man out of my compartment. The second guy to go received more severe burns than me. The third guy had a head wound that kept him in and out of consciousness for the first couple of weeks. Probably the fourth guy got banged up far worse than that.

As I was coming down in the chute, I thought I saw the plane burning on the ground. And then I could hear bullets zinging through the air. The Vietnamese were shooting at me as I was descending. I looked up and saw a couple of holes in the chute. I didn't look down at them. I was looking more at where I was going to land.

And this is crazy. At the time, *Look* magazine was being published, and as I came down and all this was happening, I said to myself, Boy, *Look* magazine is really going to be glad to get this story. That was my thought. Crazy. Just plain crazy.

I had to steer my parachute to keep from landing in some water. And I came down on a small hillside. Thirty miles northwest of Hanoi. Unfortunately, there were no trees, nothing to hide in. Just knee to thigh deep grass.

As soon as I touched ground, I tried to hide the chute. It was a big orange and white signal telling the whole world, here's McDaniel. All I could do was get it a little bit out of sight. Then I grabbed my survival radio to try to let our friendlies in the air know that I was down. That took 30 seconds. Then I looked around to find a place to hide. There was just nowhere. And within a minute after I hit the ground, they were on me.

I thought about using my gun, but I said, Well, I'd better just lay low for a moment. All of a sudden, things got kind of quiet, and I thought, Maybe they've gone away. Then I heard some grunts, and as I looked around, they were everywhere, all around me. They had gotten quiet to see if I were going to make a move.

Whatever they were going to do to me in that pit, they stopped when a jeep drove up with four regular army men. The soldiers said something in Vietnamese and motioned for the others to back away. Then they took me out of the pit, blindfolded me, and drove me about a mile away to a little place where they started interrogating.

They asked me if I could speak French. I said, no, no. Then in English they asked me what kind of plane I was flying, who else was in the plane, what targets we were trying to hit, what plans we had next. They wanted any military information that would help them to better defend themselves. I just kept giving them my name, my rank, my service number, and my date of birth.

After they tried that a few times, they tied me up and put me in a little hut. About an hour later, somebody with a white smock on came in to examine my injuries. When

I ejected, I had banged up my ankle and got some face and neck burns. He figured I was going to live whether he did anything or not. So he did nothing. Later, they smocked down the burns with something that remind you of iodine. But that was all.

They took me to the prison camp we called the Hilton first for the first extensive interrogations. That's where they had the torture room and can put the screws to you. When I mentioned the Geneva Convention, they laughed in my face. They said, "You're not qualified to be treated as a prisoner of war. You're a criminal. Black American criminal." And they said that Fred Cherry, who went down before me, and the other black prisoners were the blackest of the black criminals.

After two weeks, they took me to a camp we called the Zoo. And they put me in a concrete cell that was about 6 by 9 feet. You either had a board or a concrete pallet for a bed. And, at first, you were told to sit on it all day. If they saw you moving around, trying to exercise, or trying to communicate with somebody, then they would take you out and beat you.

I kept looking for a break to get out that first evening, but I never got the opportunity. I figured if I could get out of the hut into the jungle, I might have a chance. But I never did. Once they got us to Hanoi, there were several things going against a successful escape. Even though they had guards in towers and barbed wire on the walls, we figured it was possible to scale the walls without being seen. There was something like a moat around the camp. But from there it was people, people, people. There were more people there per square hectare than you can shake a stick at. And, unfortunately, they worked more at night than at daytime because of the bombing raids. Another thing was just our size. And the white guys had a problem with the color of their skin and with their hair. And our features were different enough to the point that a black man would be recognized very, very readily. Even so, we were always planning how to escape, the best route, individually and collectively.

We ate twice a day. A little rice and a little soup made from swamp weed that you would see growing out the window. It tasted a little bit like a very bad-tasting turnip green. Not too bitter, just sort of bland. You would get about a third of a bowl with a few of the greens, but mostly colored water. That was the standard fare.

Sometimes you would get a side dish of a tablespoon of turnips, cauliflower, or carrots that were kind of steamed. Once in a while, they might put a little pork fat in. If they had any chicken, they could chop it up, bones and all. You might get a smathering. But usually it was the pork fat, about the size of your thumbnail. A lot of guys couldn't eat it. It wasn't half clean. It would have hair on it. And it looked bad. So they would throw it away. My philosophy was that no matter what it is, no matter how bad it tastes, if it's going to keep me alive, I'm going to eat it.

I ate it. I ate. I ate. I ate. If it was edible at all, I ate it.

Most of the time I would go to sleep hungry. For the first ten months I never saw a piece of bread. They could make good French bread, but by the time we saw it, it would be old and moldy. In spite of that, you'd eat it.

On their special occasions they would give you about a fourth of a cup of coffee. The Tet holiday, Christmas, and their independence day. A lot of the guys looked forward to that.

We would get two or three cigarettes a day. Some they call Vinh Binh. And of course we called them Done Beens.

I don't smoke or use alcohol. And I was never much of a coffee drinker. The only thing I craved was ice cream. All the time. I wanted vanilla ice cream. Every day I thought of vanilla ice cream.

I think I lost 35 pounds, down from 155. But some of the guys who were shot down were just skeleton and bones because they couldn't eat the food and, in some cases, they wouldn't eat the food. There were guys who had weighed 190 pounds and were down to 100.

It gets pretty cold in North Vietnam in the winter months. And it's terrible if you don't have much clothing. We had two sets of prison clothes—shorts, pants, and shirt. But they would only let you wear one set at a time. The first winter I had no socks, just sandals made from rubber tires. And one blanket. The second winter they gave us a pair of socks and a second blanket. But it was still not enough to keep warm.

They wouldn't let us move around much that first winter, too. I got a circulation problem. My feet and legs would swell up and itch and burn. It got so painful that I thought it might be better that I were dead rather than alive.

At about five-thirty in the morning we would hear them beat on those gongs. And the night shift would go home, and the day people would get up and go to work. We had to sit up. Then maybe around ten you might get to go outside to bathe from ice-cold well water or wash your clothes. They would give you just ten minutes. They issued you a toothbrush, a bar of homemade soap, and a little tube of toothpaste. The toothpaste had to last you four months, so you just took a tiny lick each day to catch the taste. And you had to relieve yourself in the cell. They had buckets for you to urinate and defecate in. We called them honey buckets. Sometimes the lids were half rusted out or fallen off. They would let you empty them once a day unless they didn't like what you were doing or they couldn't get the information out of you they wanted. Around nine at night the gongs would go off again, and you could sleep. But this little dingy light stayed on all night.

You had to keep track of time on your own. And the first couple of weeks, I just couldn't put it all together. The interrogations and beatings came in cells where you couldn't see out. You would get so beat out until you might sleep a few minutes and think you'd been asleep all night. But afterwards, you could keep the days together. Being somewhat accustomed to the Western way, Sunday was not a big workday for them. And then you knew a week had rolled around.

In the first few years they wouldn't give us any reading material, and, of course, no mail. And they never let us learn their language, because they felt that we might hear too much. I only learned the words for "yes" and "no" and the words *lai mau*, meaning "come quick," which would get the camp commander in an emergency.

They didn't want us to communicate, because we could

pass information and keep each other's spirits up. Communicating was one of the quickest ways that you could get tortured.

In the first few days we knocked on walls and made signals if we saw each other. Morse code was too slow. So we put the alphabet in a five by five matrix. The first series of taps located the letter vertically, the next series horizontally. We combined J and K, or we would just use six straight taps for a K. Once in a while you would try to talk very low, but that was very hazardous.

They had a public-address system in the camp that they would pipe into the cell. They would read things in their behalf about the Communist way and downgrading the United States, blah, blah, blah, all the time. They would sanitize the broadcast they pumped to the GIs in the South. Whenever you heard something about how the war was going, my general philosophy was to turn it 180 degrees around and you might get close to the truth.

When Dr. King was assassinated, they called me in for interrogation to see if I would make a statement critical of the United States. I said no, I don't know enough about it. They wanted all of us to make statements they could send abroad or make tapes they could play to the GIs. They wanted me to tell black soldiers not to fight because the United States is waging a war of genocide, using dark-skinned people against dark-skinned people. I would tell them no. This is not a black-white war. We're in Vietnam trying to help the South Vietnamese. It is a matter of helping people who are your friends.

Once they found out they couldn't get anything out of me on the racial front, they would harass me a little harder than my white comrades. They would call me a lackey and an Uncle Tom and say, "You suck your brother's liver. You drink your brother's blood."

My personal feeling is that black people have problems and still have problems in America. But I never told them that, because I had no intention of helping them to defeat us. We deal with our problems within our own country. Some people just do not live up to the great ideals our country stands for. And some blacks don't take advantage of the privileges and opportunities we have. Although black people are kind of behind the power curtain, we have just as much claim to this country as any white man. America is the black man's best hope.

We decided not to see any American delegations that came to Hanoi, except if we were trying to get something out. We knew the North Vietnamese were using American sympathizers like Jane Fonda to promote their cause, and all it would do is prolong the war. We hated to see it happen.

The North Vietnamese would only allow you to say certain things to the delegations. You couldn't tell it like it was. And most of the guys who actually saw delegations were tortured into doing it. Some let it be known they were tortured by sending a signal when their pictures were taken. When that was found out, they were beaten and denied food.

I heard that a few prisoners met the delegations or made statements because they were promised sex with a young girl.

I'm sure they selected the interrogators and guards very carefully. They didn't just take anybody off the street. They were well indoctrinated and very disciplined. When they were told to harass or lay off the prisoner, they could turn it on and off like a light switch. You could tell some really didn't have a desire to really put the screws to you. But others seemed to enjoy it, and you could see they really wanted to get to you if they were told to leave you alone. No one ever tried to help us or be kind to us either. They were afraid of the repercussions.

We never were allowed to learn the Vietnamese names of these people, so we would give them names. We gave a few fairly decent names like the Chief, the Professor. But normally we used animal names because of the way they looked or how they acted. Dog, Cat, Rat, and Rabbit. Rat actually looked like a rat.

Rabbit was an interrogator. He thought he was pretty smart. He was very unfeeling. He enjoyed torture. And when I refused to speak against my country because of the way blacks are treated, he would get my rations cut or keep me from washing up.

Early on, Ho Chi Minh put the word out that if you capture Americans—he called us air pirates—don't kill them but make them suffer. So up to the time he died in

September of 1969, we were treated pretty rough. But they didn't kill us unless they overstepped their bounds on a few cases of torture. By 1969, though, the word had gotten around the world that we were being treated very badly. So the powers that took over after Ho Chi Minh's death decided they were going to improve our treatment. So around Christmas we started to get more food and our first packages and letters from home. Of course, the packages were unwrapped by the guards, and they kept the games, the reading materials, and some of the good food items. All that was left in my first package was a tooth-brush, a little candy, some cookies, and a few cheeses. And they had chopped the cookies into crumbs.

My wife, Carol, and I had a close-knit family. It was one of my constant concerns. In my primary petitions to God, I asked Him to take care of them. When I left, my son was approaching four, and my daughter was almost one. I handled most of the bills and made the decisions. When I found out I was going to Thailand for a year, we made plans for Carol to take care of things for a year.

I did not tell her that I was flying combat missions. So when the Air Force people came to her house saying I was missing in action, she just went out of it. For weeks her face and hands would swell up, and she had to stay on tranquilizers. And she stayed in a state of limbo for three years, because when my plane went down, the fighter cover said they had saw only two chutes. They assumed them to be the pilot and navigator.

Carol kinda had the feeling that I was okay even though there was no word. Our families are very religious. My aunt told her she had a vision that showed that I was actually okay. Carol's mother said she had a dream, and she saw me in a prison cell, talked to me a little bit, and I said, "I'm all right." And there was a blind man in the neighborhood whom people had a lot of faith in because he was very religious. He told Carol not to worry, that I was coming back.

My father died in 1968 without seeing me again. But the family said that before he passed, he told them some-body from France came to see him and said I was okay. The North Vietnamese always tried to get information about your background to pass to their contacts in Eu-

rope. Then they wanted the contacts to try to influence
your family to take antiwar stands that would help their
cause. The contacts would promise we would get good
treatment if they made the statements. But my father said
nothing.

But Carol didn't know for sure that I was alive until
1969. The Air Force showed her pictures taken of me in
the camp, and she said, "My goodness, I'd recognize that
guy anywhere." The pictures were taken for propaganda
purposes at Easter and Christmas. They would let some
of us get together to read Scripture and sing a few songs
to show how good they treated American prisoners. We
gained some benefit, because it was one of the few times
we could pass information and keep morale up.

After United States forces raided the Son Tay prison
camp in 1970, security got a lot tighter. The guards were
fully geared with grenades and everything. And the interrogators said if there was an indication of another raid
going on, we will kill every one of you. And I believe
they would have.

They knew that the United States probably knew where
the camps were located, so they would mount a lot of
their antiaircraft guns close to the prisons, some on the
prison walls. They figured that the United States planes
wouldn't get them. But even from the first, when I was
shot down, our planes would come in and hit close by.
Many times those cell walls would rattle, and plaster would
fall from the ceiling. I never was afraid, because I always
felt that we needed to keep the pressures on them or we
could sit there forever.

From 1968 on, they would give you bits and pieces
about the peace negotiations. When the bombings picked
up in 1972 and the presidential campaign was going on,
we thought something was going to happen. One of the
provisions in the Paris Accords in 1973 was that the prisoners would be notified. So a few days after the peace
agreements were signed, we were called out in a formation, and they announced we would be released soon.

You would think that everybody would have jumped
up and down, and said, "Oh, happy days." Nothing. Not
a sound.

To me it was a feeling of relief. But I wasn't convinced

until we were actually out of there. We just knew we were going to get out after the Tet Offensive because they were getting their ears beat off. And when the incursion took place in Cambodia, we thought so, too.

The North Vietnamese agreed to let American C-141 airplanes into Gia Long airport to pick us up. When I got on the plane, I still thought the Communists could change their minds or the engine might not go. It wasn't until wheels up that I said, "Whoooo, man. We made it."

It was February 12, 1973. Six years, six months, and twenty-three days after my capture.

I think they had some candy and some sodas on the plane. When we got to Clark Air Force Base in the Philippines, we went through the chow hall and, boy, we just tore up the ice cream.

I landed at Andrews Air Force Base near Washington, D.C. The first thing I said to Carol was, "I made it back." She was so excited she just screamed.

Carol did a beautiful job of keeping me alive in the children's minds. When I would put the finger on the son, he responded because he kinda remembered the old days. But the daughter, it was a real trial because she never had a concept of just what a dad does. I guess she supposed that I would be a sugar daddy.

I guess most of us were shocked by how some things had changed. The explicit sex in movies. The openness about homosexuality. The attitude of doing your own thing. The fancy colored pants and wide belts for men. And the high prices!

We really hated that we missed the hot pants and mini-skirts.

For the first couple of years I kept having dreams that you were just about to be released and for some reason you couldn't find your pants or your jacket, and you weren't allowed to leave until you did. But you never could find them. Or one of the interrogators would take you back. Or you would be free, but you would know that in a week you had to go back.

When I was first captured, I was really praying fervently that the Lord would get me and my fellow prisoners out of there right away.

I kinda grew up in the church. At the age of twelve, I

accepted Christ. I was a churchgoer and tried to live right. I had a pretty strong faith at the time I was captured. But one of the things I had to deal with was, Lord, why am I here? Why do you do this to me when I've been trying to do right all this time?

One month passed. Two months passed. Six months passed. A year passed. Old McDaniel's still sitting here, still praying.

After two years, I have to look at this situation. Is the Lord listening to what I'm saying? I am suffering, and nothing's happening. So I had to reconcile myself that it just might be that I'm not to go back in the flesh, alive, to the United States. Then I had a lot more peace of mind, and I was able to continue then to cause that faith to grow.

It says in St. Paul and Romans that if we are children of God, we are not exempted from the trials and tribulations. He's going to give us the strength to go through them. That's in I Corinthians 10:23. So I said even if they take my mortal life, I'm still okay. I never did lose faith.

One of the real pluses from that experience was that I'm a lot closer to God. And a lot of things that might scare a lot of other people in terms of dangers, I can just walk right on through without backing away, shying away, or making compromises that really should not be made.

I've been there.

**Sergeant Major
Edgar A. Huff
Gadsden, Alabama**

Sergeant Major
1st Military Police Battalion
May 1967–July 1968
III Marine Amphibious Force
October 1970–April 1971
U.S. Marine Corps
Danang

We had a grand time. My retirement party on my two-and-one-half-acre home here in Hubert, North Carolina, just down the road from Camp Lejeune. That was 1 October '72. We had some 750 people here on this lawn. All types of people. There was a 12-piece orchestra on the lawn. We had all the barbecue pits going. Four hogs on the spit. My soul pot was in operation with chicken stew. I heard they drank somewhere in the neighborhood of ten barrels of Tom Collins and martinis. The party was supposed to last from three o'clock until six. Apparently they forgot the time, because the last folks left the next morning. I never been to a ball like that in my life. I couldn't stand but one retirement, I'm sure.

When I retired, I had been sergeant major longer than anyone on duty at the time in all the services. I was the senior enlisted man in the whole United States Armed Forces. I could look back to becoming the first black sergeant major in the Marine Corps, serving 19 different generals, and being sergeant major to General Cushman three times, including Vietnam, when it was the largest Marine force ever assembled. After I made sergeant major, it was 12 years before the Marines made another black one.

I guess I heard from two thirds of the generals on active duty at the time I retired, all the way to Okinawa and Japan. General Cushman called me his strong right arm, and President Nixon sent me greetings. But Alabama was somethin'. They made me honorary mayor of my hometown, Gadsden, and gave me the key to the city. Governor Wallace sent his representative, the commander of the National Guard of the state of Alabama, and called to tell me how proud he was of my career and how it stands as an example for others to follow.

That's a long way to come for a boy who come into the Marines so poor he had just a quarter in his pocket, had pasteboard in his shoes to cover the holes, and one pair of drawers with a knot tied in the damn seat to keep them from flappin' around like a dress.

I was six when Daddy died, and it was just me and Mama. He was gassed while serving in Europe in World War I, and I think he never got over the effects. Mama made $3 a week working for white folks, and I used to rake coke from the white people's ashes they threw away so we could get some heat in the fireplace. But when I got to be twelve, Mama wanted me to have a gun and learn how to shoot 'cause Daddy was a soldier boy. So she took in washing for fifty cents a week until she got enough money to buy this gun. It was a single-barrel .22.

When I was fifteen, Mama got sick and needed an operation. So I dropped out of school—I guess it was the eighth grade—and went to work at Republic Steel. By 1942, I was making $1.40 a day and was the first black man to ever operate a overhead crane at the steel company. I was still walking 4 miles to work, too.

Well, one morning, this white man, Mr. Wilcox, who was going to relieve me, had this newspaper, and he showed me a story. "Ed," he said, "here's a new thing starting. If a Negro is qualified, he can join the Marines. That's the greatest outfit that's ever been. I was a Marine. If you join the Marines, you'll go places. It will take

(left to right) "Fast Eddie" Wright, Wallace Terry (author), and Steve Howard before Cobra helicopter at Bien Hoa Airbase South Vietnam, 1969

Norman McDaniel *(standing)* leads captured American pilots in singing Christmas carols at the "Zoo," on the outskirts of Hanoi, North Vietnam, in 1970

Edgar Huff, shortly before his retirement, at Camp Lejeune

Bill Norman *(right)* with then Chief of Naval Operations Admiral Elmo Zumwalt

Joe Anderson *(right)* with then Secretary of State Alexander

Bob Mountain in starting blocks during training in Indianapolis, Indiana

Malik Edwards at work on drawing table

Robert Daniels with daughter, Traci Lynn

Gene Woodley

Bob Holcomb with son,
Christian

Charles Strong with mother at their home in Pompano Beach, Florida

BOB CAMWELL MEDICAL PHOTOGRAPHER VMAC, TUCSON, ARIZONA

"Light Bulb" Bryant before Buffalo Soldier statue at Ft. Huachuca, Arizona

STEPHEN A. HOWARD

Dwyte Brown at work or elevator maintenance job

Joe Biggers before Soviet artillery piece captured by his platoon in South Vietnam, on display at the Quantico, Virginia, Marine base

Manny Holloman with wife, Kwi, and daughter, Goldie

Fred Cherry in Air Force painting on display at the Pentagon

Rick Ford before Vietnam Veterans' Memorial in Washington, D.C.

Luke Benton *(left)* with pastor, the Reverend Dr. Ben A. Beamer, Sr., at Ebenezer Baptist Church in Portsmouth

nothing but a lot of hard work, and you do what you're told."

I heard the Marines were the toughest outfit in the world, and I knew they couldn't be any tougher than what I was going through. So I decided to join.

Mama said, "Son, I don't want you to go into the service, but it was your father's wish. He wanted a soldier boy and a Red Cross girl."

So I walked down to the post office at 6th and Broad. But the Marine recruiter wasn't there. I asked the Army recruiter when he would be back. This Army sergeant said, "Ain't no niggers in the Marine Corps, but we got 'em in the Army. Come on. Let me sign you up." It was a common thing in those days for a white man to talk to you anyway he wanted to. He call you a nigger, it's like, "Hello, James." "Hello, Ed." It wasn't no big thing. And besides, I looked good to him. I was 6 foot 6, and 202 pounds.

I saw the Marine recruiter the next day, and he didn't talk like this Army sergeant. He said, "Boy, can you read?"

I said, "Yes, sir."

"What does that sign say?"

"Walk on in."

"Well, come on in."

Well, I passed the written test, but I needed $1.80 to get the bus to Birmingham and back for the physical examination. I had seven cents. Mama had thirteen cents. Well, Mr. Wilcox loaned me $2, which I paid him back on my first payday in the Marine Corps.

They notified me on June 26, 1942, that I was going into the Marine Corps. One of the first 50 blacks to get accepted.

In September I got my papers, my orders, and train tickets to report to duty in North Carolina. I put on my big apple hat, my triple-E shoes, peg pants, and zoot suit. And went down to the railhead. It was the first time I ever left home. Of course, I never been on a train in my life.

When I got to North Carolina, I felt like a foreigner. It was the first time I ever talked to anybody that wasn't from Alabama.

We got trained at Montford Point, next to Camp Le-

jeune. We had a completely Negro Marine Corps. We had
our own barracks, our own infantry, our own tanks, our
own guns. It couldn't have been more segregated. Of
course, the officers was white.

When I went to bed the first night, I heard this music.
I started crying, wondering what my mama was doing.
So I asked this boy, why in the world is they playing that
song. They told me that was taps. I had never heard a
bugle before in my life. I swear 'fore God.

When I went to dinner the next day, I tried a little piece
of this ham. It was the toughest ham I ever ate in my life.
So I wrote to Mama to send me some pieces of ham out
the smokehouse. Later on, they put that ham out there
again, and this friend of mine said, "Ed, that ain't no
ham."

I said, "The hell it ain't."

"That's corned beef."

And that's the first I ever knew they had corned beef.

In December I had just finished boot camp when Colonel Woods called me in. "Got a telegram. Your mother is
real sick. They want you to come home. At once." See,
I don't have a brother or sister or nobody. Just my mother
and myself. And I said, "I can't. I don't have no money
to go home." We wasn't getting but $30 a month, and I
had me an allotment out to my mother. He said, "I tell
you what. I am going to give you fifteen dollars so you
can go home to see your mama." I said, "Yes, sir." You
don't ask him no question. You do what the hell you told.
And he gave me a furlough.

So I got on the bus, and when it pulled into Atlanta,
I got off and went in the station. It was two Marine MPs.
They walked up to me. One said, "Hey, boy. C'mere."

I started out with my little bag.

"What you doing with that uniform on?"

I say, "I'm a Marine."

They say, "There ain't no damn nigger Marines. You
going to jail."

I give them my furlough papers. They tore 'em up right
in my damn face. Said I was impersonating a Marine.

They started to turn me loose. Say, "You go in there
and pull that damn uniform off. You ain't got no clothes
to wear, you go to the relief."

I say, "I'm not impersonating a Marine. I *am* a Marine."

"You going to get it."

They took me down to the city jail and had me locked up. That night a Marine captain came in to get some white Marines who've been locked up for bein' drunk. I knew a captain when I see a captain, so I ask him to get me out, too.

"Ain't no nigger Marines. We heard about you."

I was there the twenty-third, the twenty-fourth. And they took us out to pick up trash and garbage. And there I was in jail on my first Christmas in the Marine Corps.

When the Navy chaplain came in for Christmas prayers, he wouldn't even talk to me.

Finally, a Marine major came in. It must have been the twenty-eighth. And I convinced him to call Colonel Woods, even though he thought I was making up a bunch of lies. He didn't know about Montford Point, being as it was a brand new camp.

Colonel Woods told the major to get me out now, and he told me to go home and don't worry about any papers.

Colonel Woods is dead now. But I got his picture. Colonel Samuel S. Woods, Jr. The first commanding officer ever commanded black Marines.

General Larsen was somethin' else. He was the commanding general of Camp Lejeune. One day he came over to speak to us at this smoker. No Negro was allowed to be on Lejeune unless he was accompanied by a white Marine to go to a specific place with a chit stating what he was going to do there. I'll never forget when he walked in. It was the first general we had ever seen. Here I am, a hard charger, thinking I want to be a general. I want to be like him.

Well, he started talking about the war. He said, "I just came back from Guadalcanal. I've been fighting through the jungles. Fighting day and night. But I didn't realize there was a war going on until I came back to the United States. And especially tonight. When I come back and I find out that we have now got women Marines, we have got dog Marines, and when I see *you people* wearing *our* uniforms, then I know there's a war going on."

Goddamn. You never saw so many Coke bottles fly. Knocked him down. And there was a riot that night. The first black riot in Marine Corps history.

Well, I went from private to first sergeant in just 23 months and became the sergeant in charge of training all the black Marines. When we shipped out to the Pacific, we moved supplies to the fighting units that were all-white. After that, I took the first black unit into Tsien Tsin, the first to step on Chinese soil. In Korea I fought in a weapons company, which, of course, was integrated by then. But over the years, I was so unhappy sometimes in the Marine Corps, I didn't know what to do. If there's ever a man should be prejudiced as far as the white man is concerned, I should be. 'Cause some of these officers kicked me every way but loose.

Back in '57, when I was sergeant major right here in Camp Lejeune, the executive officer of headquarters battalion got half drunk and called me into his office.

He say, "C'mere, boy."

I've been called boy so many times you automatically move like a robot even knowing you wasn't a boy.

He said, "How 'bout a drink?"

"No, sir. I don't drink during working hours."

"You think you too good to drink with me?"

He shoved the bottle in my face. And when he did that, I turned right around and walked right out. If I had hit him, I would have been in the penitentiary for striking an officer.

Another time I was in a general's office, and he was talking on the phone. He says, "Now, Colonel. The problem is not how many watermelons you have. It's how many niggers you got to eat 'em."

After he hung up, he look at me, and he said, "I'm sorry."

I say, "What did the general say?" When a general is on the phone, I don't know what he says. "You don't owe me no apology."

He said, "Ed, I'm telling you, ain't but one of your kind. Thank you very much."

And the sergeants could get to you, too. But by me being sergeant major they had to watch their step with me.

Take this time at Camp Geiger. This gunny sergeant

was reporting in, and he telephoned my quarters. This was 1963.

"Did you know what the damn chief clerk of yours done this evening?"

"No. What did he do?"

"He assigned me to stay in a room with a damn nigger."

I says, "Is that right?"

He says, "Yes, sir, Sergeant Major. And I'd rather sleep on the parade ground under a flagpole than to sleep with a goddamn black nigger."

So I says, "Well, I can take care of you tonight. Tomorrow, I'll assign you to your permanent quarters. I make it a practice to do everything I can especially for my staff NCOs."

So I arranged for this gunny to have the VIP quarters that night in the staff NCO club.

The next morning I told my driver to go down to supply and draw out a half a tent, five tent pegs, and one pole. I said, "You know one Marine don't rate but half a tent."

So I'm sitting there in my office with about 25 yards of campaign ribbons, a bucket of battle stars, and each one of my sleeves look like a zebra. Ain't no way in hell a man could not know I was not the sergeant major.

When the gunny walked in, he stopped and looked at me as though he saw a ghost.

He said, "Are you the sergeant major?"

I said, "Well, Gunny, you are familiar with the rank structure, aren't you?"

He said, "You not the one I talked to last night, are you?"

"Why sure I am. Sit down."

I made him drink some coffee, and the cup was rattlin' like it was a rattlesnake. Then I drove him out to the parade grounds, up to the flagpole, and said, "Here is your quarters. Now you pitch your lean-to on the flagpole like you requested." And it was raining like hell.

When I came back, the tent was running full of water. I said, "Get this tent trenched out like it's supposed to be. You are ruining government property."

Then he said, "I'll stay with that fella."

I told him he would have to get this black sergeant to

agree and bring him to my office. Well, it was all right with the sergeant, and the gunny moved in.

In about three weeks, I went down to the club and this black sergeant had a white woman, and the gunny had a black woman. Having the best time you ever saw. And a few months later, the gunny and the black woman was married. They live up here near me now and got two children. Doing real fine.

But I never let any of these things make me prejudiced right back. Especially in combat. Especially in Vietnam. I am the sergeant major. I take care of all my men, black and white.

Now when the Tet Offensive broke out in January of 1968, I was sergeant major of the 1st Military Police Battalion in Danang. At the time, our headquarters was right across from the main airstrip. Well, the rebels was trying to get to the headquarters of this Vietnamese general. And they made a breakthrough down on River Road. So we had this blocking force right between the general's headquarters and the rebels.

The colonel and I was in a bunker at the time. The fighting was going on for about an hour, and we figured everything was going pretty smooth 'cause we had radio contact and everything. Then Kenny called in. He said, "Send help! Send help!"

I thought to myself, That's not the way Kenny calls.

And the colonel said, "What the hell's wrong out there?"

Kenny said, "The whole area's moving. The whole area's moving. Send help! Send help! They got us surrounded." Then he said, "Help! This is my last transmission."

And it was just like a breath was rolling out. And that was his last transmission.

And I told the colonel, "Let's go."

At that time I carried a shotgun, a pistol, and a grenade launcher. And two bandoliers also.

And when we got to the scene, you never saw a fire fight more horrifying in all your life. The boys were in a spot as hard as it could be, but they was holding it.

And I looked up, and the best radio operator you ever saw—name was Rick—was hit and pinned down out there maybe 50 yards. They saw him out there in this field, and they were trying to finish him off. They was shooting with automatic fire, you know. And every time Rick'd move a little, they would fire out after him. Just tryin' to finish him off.

Rick was hollering, "Mother. Mother."

I could stand it no more. I started out. And the colonel said, "No. No. Just wait. Just wait."

I said, "Sorry, Colonel."

This wasn't a black boy. He was a white boy. I knew I might get killed saving a white boy. But he was my man. That's what mattered.

And I took off. Ran through an open field. They was firing from a tree line. And I got maybe 20 yards, and I was hit on the head. It hit my helmet. And it spin me around, knocked me down. And I got up and started again. And another round hit on the side of the helmet and knocked me down again. And I started crawling. And it seemed like round after round was kicking at the dirt all around me.

And I jumped up then, and I started running. Then I got to him. Then they opened up everything they had right there into that position. And I fell on top of him to keep him from getting hit again, and this fragmentation grenade hit us and ripped my flak jacket all into pieces. And it got me in the shoulder and arm.

Then our people opened up all they had. And the Cong started moving back. And the colonel came out to help me with the stretcher to bring Rick back.

And then I went back and found Kenny. Kenny was killed. He was still holding the transmitter in his hand.

Then they tried to get me to go to the hospital, but, hell, I wasn't going to no damn hospital then, because my men was still scattered around and I had to get 'em together.

Well, I got pieces of steel still in me. And my wife still digs them out when they start coming up to the skin.

They gave me the Bronze Star for pullin' Rick out. And Rick wrote me this letter. It says, "Sergeant Major, I thank you for my life."

Hell, he was one of my men. Black or white, I would

have done the same even if I got shot to hell in the process. And I was forty-eight at the time. And that boy couldn't have been much over twenty-one.

When I had my retirement party, I kinda wished that boy could've been there. Wouldn't that have been nice?

Well, sir, about three weeks after that party, we were having some friends over for dinner, and we were out on the patio. Sergeant Major Washington and his wife. He's a black sergeant major. And another black lady. She was teaching at the Marine base. And my son and some more kids were playing in the yard. It was just about dusk hour.

At this time, a car drove up. And four white Marines started throwing hand grenades. They were white phosphorous. Threw one right through my station wagon. Threw another at this lady's Cadillac. Guess they thought this was my Cadillac. And they threw another one into the house. And another one hit the Marine emblem on my gate. And everything was lit up like Christmas around here.

A white friend of mine saw them, and he took off at a high speed, and he did get that tag number. And some of the state troopers came out here and helped me put some of the fire out.

The Marine Corps never did nothin' to them at all. Three of them got transferred or discharged, although they were supposed to be held pending an investigation. Being a sergeant major in the goddamn Marine Corps for 17 years, I know damn well that when a person is awaiting disciplinary action, he can't be transferred, discharged, or do a damn thing. I got pissed off. I've fought for 30 years for the Marine Corps. And I feel like I own part of this ground that I walk on every day, especially this that I own. So I went to the Naval investigator, and he said a report was turned over to the commanding officer. He said he talked to these guys who were trying to destroy my family and myself. He said they told him they didn't understand how a nigger could be living this way, sitting out there eating on a nice lawn, under that American flag I fly everyday.

I went to the deputy sheriff, an old buddy of mine, and he got hold of the boy who was still on the base. He told the boy I didn't want him to serve no jail, I just wanted him to pay the damage he did. The boy's daddy telephoned me from Tennessee about he didn't have no money. I ain't never heard a white man beg to any black man like that in all the days of my life. A Southern white man. Well, he paid it.

You know, when they threw those grenades at my family, my friends, and my home, I thought back to the time the Ku Kluxers came and took Mr. Sam Brewster away. I was nine or ten at the time.

We heard all these cars blowin' horns. My grandfather said, "The Ku Klux is comin'."

My grandfather had a pistol. If the Ku Klux had known he had a pistol, they would have pitched camp at our house till they found it. Grandma and Granddad kept it in the top drawer of the chifforobe. He went and got that .44, turned out the lights, and looked out the door to see what would happen. The rest of us jumped under the bed and waited to see whose house they gon' bust into and who they gon' take away and beat up.

Mr. Sam Brewster lived four doors away. There was a lot of hollering and screaming going on. We heard a shot. And he was dragged out. They took him up to Lookout Mountain. Tied him to a tree. Took a whip, and beat that man like you never seen the like before. They thought he was dead. But he got loose and came back and laid down on the front porch of my grandfather's house.

I don't know for sure why they did it. But I think it had something to do with the store owner across the street—this white man—and Mr. Sam Brewster's wife. She was a real high yellow type. In fact, her family looked white. You couldn't tell the difference to save your life. The store owner wanted Mr. Sam Brewster's wife, and in those times you weren't suppose to do nothin' about it. But Mr. Sam Brewster was a big strong type, and he wouldn't have it.

The next day the store owner's arm was bandaged. That's how we knew he was Ku Kluxer. And that evening, they burned his store down—the Negro people did.

Whenever the Ku Kluxers would come, I would be terrified. It was the damnedest thing. And I thought about that many times when I was overseas, and I had those beautiful machine guns. I would just wish to hell I had somethin' like that back in Alabama when those sonof-abitches came through there. I would have laid them out like I did those damn Congs. The same way.

I just don't see how black people survived down there in those days. I just don't see it.

Staff Sergeant
Don F. Browne
Washington, D.C.

Security Policeman
31st Security Police Squadron
Tuy Hoa
November 1967–January 1968
Air Force Special Elements Activity
U.S. Air Force
Saigon
January 1968–November 1968

We thought we were really shit-hot.

There were eleven of us. All Air Force security police. It was a unique organization. It was called the Air Force Special Elements Activity. Our primary duty there in Saigon was to escort VIPs who worked in the American Embassy after curfew hours. But there were several other jobs.

The Army took care of the exterior of the American Embassy compound. The Marines took care of the lobby of the main building, the Chancery. We took care of everything else. So when the American Embassy was hit during the Tet Offensive and six Viet Cong got inside the Chancery, we had to go in and clean 'em out.

It was a suicide mission at the Embassy anyway. I don't see any other reason for it. What was the purpose of them blowing a hole through the wall in the building and going inside? They had to realize that once they went in, they'd never come out, I would think. But then, Asian philosophy is strange.

I was career Air Force when I got to South Vietnam in 1967. And I was rather pro-military. Vietnam, as I was told and as I read at the time, was about us trying to prevent the Domino Theory, you know, the Communists taking South Vietnam and then the Philippines and marching across the Pacific to Hawaii and then on to the shores of California.

My folks are both ministers in Washington, D.C., and they had always wanted me to go into the ministry. I started singing in the church where my mother was the pastor when I was very young. And I still sing. I've won the Air Force worldwide competition for top male vocalist four times. But I never felt the call to be a preacher.

I went to Howard University on a football scholarship, and I was starting fullback right away. We were rolling along there with a three-game winning streak, and we ran up against Morgan State. And they taught us how to play football.

I didn't do anything academically that first year and flunked out. After knocking around at a job as a laborer for a period of time, I decided that maybe the service could do something for me. It was July 1959. I'd always wanted to be in the Air Force. I was just fascinated with planes. I'm in seventh heaven when I'm flying even as a passenger. I wanted to be a pilot. But I could not pass the physical because of my eyes, and, truthfully, I couldn't pass the written exam. I became a security policeman.

My first job in Vietnam was bunker security guard out on the perimeter of the air base at Tuy Hoa. We were there for three months protecting the F-100s. Through some disagreement with the host commander, the Korean troops decided that they would no longer provide security on the outer perimeter, so that burden fell on the security police, too. And we had to formalize search and destroy teams, and go out looking for Viet Cong encampments. Because at night they would attempt to penetrate the base.

I remember the first night we went out. I guess maybe 15 of us. We were at least 1½ miles from base. And without any warning, you just begin to hear whistles go by you. Then you hear the shots. So the sarge told us we were being attacked.

I learned how to love mother earth. Not knowing from which direction the projectiles were coming, you just hug the ground and lay tight. And you shoot at sounds. If something moved in front of you—something caused by the wind, maybe some rodent running through—you fired at it.

I'm sure the incoming didn't last longer than five or six minutes. But it seemed like an eternity. Then we pressed on.

When we arrived at an encampment, it was totally empty. These VC were pretty smart. They weren't going to sit there and wait for us.

A couple of weeks later, we more or less surrounded a camp. There was a very brief fire fight. We went from hut to hut. All we found was these two guys sitting in the corner, all huddled up, in this hut. They were not armed. I'm almost ashamed to say these were very old warriors. In excess of forty years old, although to tell the age of a Vietnamese is difficult. I guess they simply couldn't escape fast enough. We just turned them over to the ARVN for interrogation.

When we reported to the special contingency at the Embassy, we wore fatigues with no insignia, no ranking. They didn't want your rank to be known. Our names were on an access roster with just your name and social security card number.

We worked out of the Embassy basement, and the civilian who was in charge of us had an ammo cache in the back of his home in downtown Saigon that would sink half the city.

Besides escorting the VIPs to their different homes around the city, we had several side jobs. Like running escorts, training guards for the homes of the VIPs, doing background investigations on Vietnamese employees.

Every week money was brought into the country at Tan Son Nhut airport which had to be delivered to the Embassy. It was one of those things you didn't ask questions about. But it was supposed to be millions of dollars for the Embassy payroll. I imagine they did other things with the money, too. We had an armored car in front and one in back. And here's this Volkswagen bus in the middle with the money. We're flashing lights and telling everybody to get out of the way and all that, escorting it downtown to the bank to be counted and then from the bank to the Embassy.

I had one special job. To train Chinese Vietnamese or Chinese Nungs to guard these homes of the VIPs. Most of the people that we recruited came up from the Cholon district, which was south of Saigon. The Nungs were supposed to be known for their fighting capability, their aggressiveness, their tenacity and whatever. And in the evening hours, we would make regular post checks on these folks when they became guards.

One day one individual walked into our training camp that we had in Gia Dinh. He was much taller than the average Vietnamese. This guy is almost 6 feet. But he's a super guy. Dressed well. We gave him the baggy fatigue uniforms, and he immediately went out and had them tailored. We were teaching hand-to-hand defense and combat techniques and weapons firing. The whole spectrum. And this guy was number one in everything. He was kicking *our* behinds in the hand-to-hand combat.

About the time that this guy graduated, the guard quit who was guarding the house occupied by this real big wheel who handled money for USAID. He had a chauffeured driven car, and the chauffeur had a shotgun. So what better troop to put on that house than this new 6-foot Vietnamese? So we put him on there.

The policy was then that when you hire these folks, you get a Vietnamese detective to run a background check. We had a Vietnamese detective firm on contract to the Embassy. Most of the people we caught were really just draft dodgers, trying to stay out of the South Vietnamese Army.

About two weeks after the tall Vietnamese went to work, I get a call from the detective agency. Their office is downstairs from mine in downtown Saigon. The detective says, "We have a problem. Could you come down and see me?" I went right downstairs.

He says, "Would you believe that this man is a graduate

of the North Vietnamese NCO academy?"

Of course I was flabbergasted.

I called the Embassy and passed the information on right away. They said, "We need to latch on to this guy?" Then I went to the Embassy to brief them directly. And they said, "Good Lord, let's get over there and get this guy."

From the time I left my office, went to the Embassy, and got to the USAID guy's home, the tall Vietnamese is gone. In the meantime the detective had taken it upon himself to call this individual and question him over the phone.

When we got the full record on this guy, we found out he was the top graduate of the North Vietnamese NCO academy. Trained in Hanoi. A North Vietnamese. Really one of their really shit-hot guys.

As I reflect back on that now, I think of how stupid we were.

The guys in the contingent were really pampered. Because of not wanting a lot of visibility, we were given extra money to do this and that. It was something like $500, $600 a month. So I just banked my military check.

And food and lodging was taken care of. We lived together in a villa about 2 miles from the Embassy. We were eating steaks all the time. And the little mama san who cooked for us had her little vegetable garden there. This other brother in the contingent who is from North Carolina wrote home and had some seeds sent back. For mustard greens, turnip greens. And he showed her how to fix greens Southern-style. So living there was a welcome change from a base. We enjoyed it.

We had access to any kind of weapon we wanted to carry. There was no kind of rule that you had to carry any particular kind. I usually carried the Swedish K that you can fold up and put in a briefcase and a 9-millimeter Colt.

Well, we had this white guy we called Brute. He was big, weighed at least 230 pounds, over 6 feet 4. He was the typical example of all brawn and no brains. We had an armored vehicle made with so much armor on it that it would only go about 20 miles an hour. That was our contingent vehicle. We titled it the Beast, but in parentheses we painted the word "Brute."

Well, Brute carried a little bit of everything. He would have a M-1 carbine, a M-16. He'd have a .38 on one hip, a 9-millimeter on another. A pistol in a shoulder holster under each armpit. And he had a strap of grenades across his chest.

I said, "Brute, stop and think for a minute. You're carrying all these different kinds of weapons. How're you going to carry all the ammunition for them, too?"

One evening I had the VIP patrol with Brute. We were going to escort some secretaries home from the Embassy after the curfew. I got on the elevator in the Embassy with Brute, and the elevator would not move. That's how heavy he was. And this Marine guard said to Brute, "My God. If one round hits you, it would blow up half a block."

Down in the Cholon district, you had the American commissary. And outside the perimeter of the commissary there must have been hundreds of kids peddling whatever. You have to push them away to get in.

Brute kept saying how smart he is and how he's going down to Cholon to put one over on these little kids. What he had in mind, nobody knew. We kept telling Brute, "Leave those kids alone."

One day one little kid ran up to Brute and showed him what Brute thought was a couple of hundred dollars in Vietnamese money. He rammed it in Brute's pocket.

He says, "You number one GI. Don't look how much money I have. Police may arrest me. I tell you what. You can have all this money for twenty-dollar MPC."

All Brute saw was dollar signs.

So he reaches in his pocket and gives the kid the MPC note, and the kid turns his hand loose out of Brute's pocket and runs. Brute takes out the money to count. I think he had an equivalency of a dollar. Vietnamese money was highly worthless. There was one note worth less than a penny. No matter the quantity, you could get very little valuewise.

Now Brute wants to kill every Vietnamese kid.

When I first came to Saigon in January of '68, we kept receiving intel briefings that something was imminent.

There was some indication that a big Communist push was coming. They had said there would probably be a lot of terrorist activity. They expected a lot of VC to infiltrate the city. Those who were already planted in the city would begin to do their thing insofar as setting off of massive rocket barrages. The purpose of that, as we were told, was to discredit the presence of the United States military. They wanted to show that even after all these years our presence really has not assured a safe environment, not even in the cities. The cities were the ultimate target for what we ended up calling the Tet Offensive.

In the afternoon on January 30, the Embassy guy came by and told us tomorrow's the day. We had heard this before, so I really didn't give it a whole lot of thought. But we were placed on immediate standby, which meant that we couldn't leave the villa.

It was funny. You always have power fluctuations. This particular day, the power went out. And just like any American, when the power goes out, you bitch and complain about the air conditioning. So you open up the windows, and you suffer. And there's no TV.

About four o'clock in the morning, the squawk came over the radio. There were some fire fights in various parts of the city. We were told to go to our various positions. I went up to the roof. We sat around looking out into the city, and you could see the rockets come in, the afterbursts and all.

Then around six-fifteen the emergency net went off, which entailed a recall of all security officers and related personnel to report to the Embassy. They said bring the Beast. When they added that, we knew something was wrong.

So we go rumbling down there with this three-quarter-ton truck with half-inch armor plate, tires looking like donuts, and two M-60s, one facing the front and one facing the back.

And the guys who stayed out at the training site in Gia Dinh, they came in from that area.

When I get there, I see this gaping hole in the big 8-foot-high wall that surrounds the Embassy compound. The hole is on the side that runs along the main thoroughfare in front of the Embassy. A Viet Cong sapper team of about 15 had attacked the Embassy around two-forty-five.

I thought to myself, They have really done it. Now they've gone too far.

By the time we got there, the Marine guys had already secured the lobby area of the Chancery. The Army had landed a helicopter right on the roof. And the Army had strung a ring of men up around the Chancery. I learned later four Army MPs and a Marine had been killed in the fighting.

Then I heard the Army guys saying, "I believe they got inside. I believe they got inside."

Then I saw this big powwow taking place of the powers that be. They said there must be some Viet Cong in the building, but we didn't know how many.

Then our boss came over and said, "Well, Brownie, the decision is that you and your guys have to go in and flush them out." There was no direct order to take them alive if you can, just get them out of there.

Knowing these sappers are suicidal, I just couldn't understand why the Army guys couldn't have done this. They are the experts. We're the Air Force. We're lovers.

It was about seven by then.

The plan was to start from the top floor and work down. So here comes Brute with all his equipment to get on the elevator with me and this other brother to go to the top three floors. Another team of our contingent would work the next three floors at the same time.

If you heard something, you were to yell "Score event." The guy would call it back to you, and you'd know the noise you heard came from a friendly.

We got to the top floor, and it seemed like there were a zillion offices. You could hide anywhere. This was going to be shaky. Checking all of those offices one at a time. All the closets. Behind every desk.

You talk about doing some tall praying. You didn't know what to look for. All you knew was that in this building there are some people bent on eliminating the breath in your body. And they know they got nowhere to go.

We would open the doors very carefully. One guy would

go right, one would go left, and the last to come in would come up the middle. That would work fine as long as there were no desks right there at the door. Each room was different. And we didn't have time to get a floor plan to know how the rooms were set up.

The top floor was very hair-shaking. It took us about a half-hour to clear it. I kept hoping that the other guys would run into those dudes.

So we take the elevator down to the next floor. When we went into the second room, I moved left, the other brother was on the right, and poor Brute came down the middle. Then we heard some scuffling over in the back corner. Everybody got quiet. Real quiet.

I threw a grenade over in the corner. And then we just started shooting in that area.

When we got through shooting, there was no more noise. So now the question becomes, Who's going to go over there and see what we have shot? Brute decides to be the hero.

He went from behind one desk to another until he found this one guy. He was wasted. He had been hiding more or less. He had an AK-47 with one banana clip. If he gets off a burst for five seconds, he's out of ammo. He had on black pajamas and those rubber-tire sandals. He looked to be maybe in his middle twenties.

Now it's for real. Until you come face to face with the VC, it doesn't seem so real. This is real. And who knows when you open this next door, there may be five or six guys there waiting. Or somebody not dumb like this one guy fumbling around behind a desk.

As we cleared the rest of the floor and the next floor, we heard gunshots from the other team. By the time we got down to the lobby, the five they killed were all stretched out in a row, lined up like ducks. We didn't bring our guy down. Left him up there for the medic folks. We shoot 'em, you drag 'em.

So we got six VC out of the Chancery. They never saw any classified material. They were just lookin' for a place to hide.

They had told Ambassador Bunker to stay away until the fighting was over. The rankingest guy that I saw there was a three-button Army general, Frederick Weyand, commander of the United States forces in the area, and this guy, Barry Zorthian, who spoke for the Embassy.

It would have been impossible to totally prevent what happened to the Embassy. But we did a lot of dumb-shit things over there. The wall around the Embassy was a barrier to honest folks. Just like a lock on your front door. But if a burglar wants to break in, he will. So who was watching the wall where the VC blew the hole. We needed more Marines than two on guard. And better equipped. This was a war zone.

And the VC would watch you all the time. They knew your pattern. And we would, most of us, do the same thing at the same time every day.

In Tuy Hoa they would set the claymore mines out in the daytime. The VC would be watching in the bush. They know exactly where they are so they can sneak up at night and turn them around against you. We would broadcast over an open airway. The Vietnamese would learn some English. So we're telling them when we were coming and what time and how many of us are coming. They'd sit back and wait. We would even bomb the same area the same time day in and day out. So the enemy would sit in their caves till the bombing is over. Then they would come back out and have a picnic. We won't be back until tomorrow. Same time. Creatures of habit.

I got so I enjoyed the city of Saigon. The real difficulties came mostly after curfew, when the Vietnamese police, the MPs, and our group were the only ones allowed on the city streets.

The guys in our outfit went to a club on Tu Do Street—"the street of flowers." We called it our club. Being favorite customers, we were accustomed to getting more than normal favors from the proprietor, which meant girls.

Not too far from the main gate of Tan Son Nhut was Soul Alley, where you could find Cambodian girls in bars who could readily pass for black females. And in the Soul Kitchen, which was run by this brother in the Air Force, you could buy soul food that tasted like back home. Chitlins, ham hocks, cornbread—the works.

If you could drive around Saigon in the daytime, you could drive in any city in the world. Saigon prepared me for driving in West Germany. Saigon had no speed limit.

The big thing during rush hour was to burn rubber from traffic light to traffic light. Especially guys who were driving jeeps and cars that had some pickup. What really aggravated you was waiting at this red light when, invariably, a Vietnamese guy would pull in front of you on a pedal bicycle, loaded with bricks.

One day, coming from the Embassy, I was drag racing this Vietnamese up the strip to the Saigon River. I was in a jeep. He was on this Honda. From red light to red light, he would win one, I would win the other.

When we got to the last traffic light before the bridge, I knew the one who got there first wouldn't have to give up the lane closest to the center. The four lanes would become two after the light.

When the light turned green, he zoomed off in the lane that would merge with mine. There was no blockade. The road just quit. At the bridge. He had to turn into my lane or go into the river. And that river was so thick with pollution it looked like syrup.

I don't think he realized what was happening until too late. The last I saw of that young fellow and his Honda, they were both airborne. And he was screaming "Ahhhhhh."

A lot of Army MPs who would go around checking on their people would go through a narrow alley or street and never come out. There's no way to turn around. And it's very easy to drop a grenade in the back seat of an open jeep. And that's how the MPs usually drove. Which I thought was ludicrous.

One time I was out checking cars in my closed jeep, and I had a grenade thrown at me. It bounced off the side. It was a dud.

Another time I was following an MP jeep, and for some reason, I stopped to talk to another guy who was on the road. The MP jeep went on. About three or four minutes later, we heard this tremendous explosion. Naturally, we responded. When we were about to run into this alley, this guy said, "Don't go up there. Let's get out and go on foot." We found the jeep blown up by a grenade or several grenades. The two Army guys, obviously dead.

Snipers were the biggest danger in the city, however. Especially at night. And sometimes a guy would ride up on a Honda next to a GI on a cycle or in a pedicab and just shot him right there on the spot. You learned to duck at any sound, watch the movement of anyone.

It got to the point where we were told to always be armed, even in daytime. And if a Vietnamese, be it man, woman, or child, refused to *di di mau* or tried to get away, the authorization was to go 'head and shoot 'em. We were told not to hesitate.

One guy in our contingency was traveling in the Cholon district. A girl on a Honda bike stopped beside him. He told her three times, "*Di di mau.*" She didn't. Maybe it was difficult for her to get away through the traffic. Maybe she didn't understand the Vietnamese he was speaking. Well, he shot her. The white mice showed up, and just took the body away. She was not armed. There was no report. It was just one of those things.

During the spring and summer of '68, the Viet Cong were just shelling Saigon indiscriminately. I remember one night I was in bed and all of a sudden this tremendous explosion went off. My whole life passed before my eyes. I grabbed a helmet, flak vest, and my weapon. I went up to the roof, and this three-story building that stood next door was nothing but total rubble. There were several Vietnamese casualties, and one baby fatality.

One of our guys ran out the front of our villa and was shot in the leg by someone. Then the Army MPs showed up. This second lieutenant jumped out of his jeep and left it unattended with a M-60 machine gun and all the ammunition in the world on it. So he yells, "Go get my jeep. Go get my jeep." By that time, some Vietnamese or Viet Cong is standing by the jeep, just about ready to take off with it. They fired a couple of shots and he disappeared into the woodwork. Now everything is really tense.

Then this dumb-ass second lieutenant felt that the area wasn't lit up enough. He fires off a hand flare that sounds like an incoming round. Everybody just dives into the street or tries to grab something to pull over them. The second lieutenant is standing there looking dumb.

Needless to say, we wanted to kick the second lieutenant in the rear.

Then everything calmed down, and we took care of the wounded.

When I heard that Martin Luther King was assassinated, my first inclination was to run out and punch the first white guy I saw. I was very hurt. All I wanted to do was to go home. I even wrote Lyndon Johnson a letter. I said that I didn't understand how I could be trying to protect foreigners in their country with the possibility of losing my life wherein in my own country people who are my hero, like Martin Luther King, can't even walk the streets in a safe manner. I didn't get an answer from the President, but I got an answer from the White House. It was a wonderful letter, wonderful in terms of the way it looked. It wanted to assure me that the President was doing everything in his power to bring about racial equality, especially in the armed forces. A typical bureaucratic answer.

A few days after the assassination, some of the white guys got a little sick and tired of seeing Dr. King's picture on the TV screen. Like a memorial. It really got to one guy. He said, "I wish they'd take that nigger's picture off." He was a fool to begin with, because there were three black guys sitting in the living room when he said it. And we commenced to give him a lesson in when to use that word and when you should not use that word. A physical lesson.

With the world focused on the King assassination and the riots that followed in the United States, the North Vietnamese, being politically astute, schooled the Viet Cong to go on a campaign of psychological warfare against the American forces.

At the time, more blacks were dying in combat than whites, proportionately, mainly because more blacks were in combat-oriented units, proportionately, than whites. To play on the sympathy of the black soldier, the Viet Cong would shoot at a white guy, then let the black guy behind him go through, then shoot at the next white guy.

It didn't take long for that kind of word to get out. And the reaction in some companies was to arrange your personnel where you had an all-black or nearly all-black unit to send out.

Over the next months some of us in the contingency were sent on secret operations in the Delta similar to the Phoenix Program. We would get the word that certain people were no longer necessary or needed to be removed. Our group never got a high-ranking VC. It was always a local person in the village who was coerced by the VC into being a leader, to get the community to rise up in arms against the allied forces. ARVN troops engaged in everything we did, but when it came to the interrogation or the torture, we were specifically instructed not to do that. The ARVN troops did that.

I remember this one ARVN sergeant took one of these old guys into this hut and strung him up from his ankles. The guy wouldn't talk. So the sergeant built a fire underneath him. When his hair caught on fire, he started talking. Then they stopped the fire.

When we passed through those villages, we really had to watch out for the kids. They would pick up arms and shoot at you. And we had to fire right back.

When we were going out from an operation not very far from Vung Tau, we went through a hamlet we were told was friendly. Quite naturally, you see the women and the children. Never see the men. The men are out conducting the war.

We had hooked up with some Army guys, so it was about a company of us. As soon as we got about a half mile out down the road, we got hit from the rear. Automatic gunfire. It's the women and the children. They just opened up. And a couple of our guys got wasted.

The captain who was in charge of this so-called expeditionary group just took one squad back to the village. And they just melted the whole village. If women and children got in the way, then they got in the way.

In another village we sent an advance party to recon the place. It was fairly empty. But when we got there, this kid come running out of a hut. Looked to be about fourteen or fifteen years old. He was told to halt. And he didn't. He ran into another hut, and gunfire started coming from the hut. So two GIs took defensive measures. Dropped to the ground and fired into the hut. We went inside. And here's the kid with the gun. Dead. And then mama san comes out of the other hut boohooing and all.

I'm willing to bet that a lot of those grenades that were thrown in the back of Army jeeps were done by kids. The very kids the GIs befriended with candy or whatever.

When it was time for me to leave, my staff had a dinner in my honor at one of the restaurants. My secretary, my interpreter, and the clerk were there. And the Vietnamese who helped with the training. And they put me at the head of the table.

On the menu was pigeon soup. And each bowl had a pigeon head in it with the eye open and the beak. I ate the soup. I didn't eat the pigeon head.

And as custom goes, I had to toast each person at the table with what was like rice whiskey syrup. I made it to nine of the twenty sitting there. That was Saturday. I didn't gain full control of my senses until Tuesday.

And just before I left, one of our maids tried to sell me her baby boy for about the equivalent of $200. She wanted me to bring him back to the United States and raise him.

She had difficulty with English so I couldn't philosophize with her. I just told her that in American society we just don't buy children like that.

When the North Vietnamese started taking over South Vietnam in 1974 without too many shots being fired, I felt let down. But I never had any faith in the ARVN. As long as they knew that the American platoon was 2 feet behind them, they would fight like cats and dogs. But if they knew that they didn't have American support real close— like right behind them—they would not fight.

When I watched on TV the cowardly, shameful way we left Saigon and left the Embassy, I felt hurt. I felt betrayed. I didn't feel very proud to be an American.

We destroyed what we couldn't carry with us. We ducked our tails and ran.

Why wait ten years and thousands upon thousands of lives later to just turn it over to the Communists? We could have done that at the very beginning.

Late that year I got accepted to officers' candidate school, after failing six times. General David Jones, whom I worked for in race relations in West Germany when he commanded the Air Force in Europe, wrote a beautiful letter to make that appointment happen.

I've made captain and will retire at that rank. And I

still sing when I can. Swing stuff. I don't do much disco. You could call it a cross between Lou Rawls and Johnny Mathis. When I was stationed in Nevada, I worked as a replacement in the lounges at the Sahara, the Dunes, the Landmark. That was great. That's the top of the line.

When I think back, there were a lot of things we did in that special contingency unit in Vietnam that we didn't get credit for. We couldn't talk about it. Or put in for commendations. In fact, we were even under oath not to talk about what we did for five years.

But we really wanted some kind of commendation for what we did at the Embassy during Tet. Some of the Marines and Army guys got medals. But that was out of the question for us. You weren't supposed to report our activities. They were secret.

All we got was the Vietnam campaign medal. Everybody got that. If you flew into the country and stayed overnight during the war, you were eligible for that.

So at the famous battle of the American Embassy, officially, we were not there.

Specialist 4
Robert L. Mountain
Millen, Georgia

Mortarman
25th Infantry Division
U.S. Army
Cu Chi and Dau Tieng
June 1968–December 1968

"Burns! Burns!"

I'm calling out to tell him that I'm hit.

"Burns, I'm hit. Oh, God. I'm hit."

But Burns, he's getting into the bunker.

Burns and I built this bunker together. Burns and I were good friends. He was a brother from Texas. He'd been through Tet and in the field a lot. He was gonna go home in like two months, so they had taken him out of the field and put him in supply. Apparently he had been a good troop.

On this particular night, Sergeant O'Hanlon said to us, "Sleep inside of your bunkers, because of the incoming mortars."

Prior to that we hadn't had a hell of a lot of incoming. And it's hot as heck over there, so nobody likes to sleep in those bunkers. We slept just lying right outside the bunker. Burns was lying next to me. We were maybe 10 feet from the bunker.

I guess it was three in the morning, December 23. The round came in, messed me up, and Burns didn't get a scratch.

I looked. My right hand was stinging. This piece of white bone was sticking up where my little finger was. There is just a splinter where my ring finger is.

I heard some rounds going off again. I think they were outgoing. I could see Burns crawling to go into the bunker.

I tried to sit up, and all I could see was just blood, blood everywhere. I looked at my right leg, and it was just blood. I turned on my stomach to push to go into the bunker. When I pushed with my left foot, that's when all hell broke loose. Oh, it was just a tremendous amount of pain. But I managed somehow to crawl on over to the bunker.

The firing didn't last long, and immediately the guys came over.

People were hollering, "Medic. Medic. Medic."

They had to take the top off the bunker to get me out, because I went in head first.

Burns is standing there, and Burns turned to walk away. I'm calling, "Burns. Oh, Burns."

I'm just hollering as loud as I can, but it's like no sound is coming out of my mouth.

I don't know whether Burns didn't want to talk to me because he had seen too many people get hurt. Or he didn't hear me. But I could tell he was crying before he turned away, and I never had seen Burns cry before.

They took me over to the battalion aid station, and the medic asked me if I was in pain and did I want any morphine. I told him yeah. So he gave me a shot, and the pain began to subside.

Then I saw the captain, a brother. He'd only been there three weeks. He was kneeling by me and said, "You're doing everything you can to go home, aren't you?" I had gotten wounded a few weeks earlier, but just slightly.

The morphine is taking effect. I've seen my fingers, but still I don't know how bad I'm wounded. I wish I had looked at my foot.

They medevaced me to Dau Tieng. But when I got there, they said I would have to go to Cu Chi to have surgery. I said okay. When I got there, I wanted some water. But they said, "You can't have water. You're going to surgery."

Then I hear them say, "What's your mother's name?"

But I'm going deeper and deeper into this sleep.

And I hear the word "amputate." Amputate.

They might be explaining something to me, but I can only remember that word.

When I woke up the next morning, my foot was strapped in this big ball of Ace bandage. They had my hand all in a cast. I knew it was hurting.

So there was a sergeant walking through, medic, white guy. I said, "Why do they have my foot in there?"

I was thinking maybe they tilted it down like this and just had it bandaged up.

He said, "Didn't the doctor tell you?"

"No."

"You sure the doctor didn't tell you?"

"No."

He said, "Well, you don't have one there."

I said, "Damn."

I was thinking, What's my mother gonna say when she hears this? I got my foot cut off.

And immediately, a urologist comes in. He's saying, "How are you doing?" Blah, blah, blah.

He pulls back the sheet, and he commenced to looking down there. And I looked down and see all this shit. Oh, my goodness.

I didn't know what the hell was wrong with my right thigh. There is a gash down to my knee. There is a 4-inch gash in my penis. They've taken three fragments out of one testicle, and it is all mushy. There is a catheter in me. Never even seen or heard of a catheter before. And my left foot is gone.

The doctor could probably see through my face that I'm most concerned. He said, "Wait a minute. Wait a minute. Everything is all right. Everything is fine."

I said, "Thank you."

They had just cut the foot portion off, making me a Syme's amputee. My leg went just straight down. The ankle joint was still there, and the heel flap was folded over to make a big fist.

When they took me to Japan, I had to go to surgery

twice, because the bone marrow at the stump was rotting, and they wanted to drill some holes in the bone to get the calcium to come down to get it to grow.

I got back to the States on February 8. And when they were taking me from the plane at Fort Gordon in Augusta, Georgia, I saw my mother for the first time. They were carrying me on a litter. And she just got on the litter with me. And she was crying and hugging me.

I had never seen my mother cry before. She was very strong. Very strong.

My mother, she's a guidance counselor in the junior high school in Millen. She went to Savannah State College and had a master's degree from Fort Valley State.

I played the trombone in the marching band in high school. I was into sports, too, but I never really got to play. I tried out for basketball, but you didn't get to play unless you were extremely good or tall. And I was neither. My mother came and just yanked me out of practice. She said, "You know you can't play basketball. And your nose bleeds besides."

So I just kept playing the trombone, and when I went to Savannah State, I was in the marching band. Mama started buying me this expensive Conn bass trombone. It was beautiful.

After the first quarter, I told Mama, "I'm not going back to school."

She said, "Why not? I've got your money for the next quarter."

I said, "I'm in the Army. I volunteered."

She was stunned. She couldn't believe it. I had just turned eighteen. It was a very unpopular decision. Small town. Teacher's son. Parents want you to go to college, get married, buy a home, live happily ever after. The great American dream.

But I wanted to play in the Army band. I had seen them on television and in my hometown. I heard a lot of groups play. But it was just something about those dog-gone Army bands. I guess the pomp and circumstances.

Before I left for boot camp, Mama told me not to worry if I ended up in the war. She said you could be sitting here in the backyard and you could get killed by a stray bullet. She was very strong.

When I got to Fort Benning, these guys started yelling at you to get in line, do this, and do that, and we don't even have fatigues yet. I knew then, I ain't gonna like this man's army.

I called my mother and I said, "Mama, I don't think I want to be in the Army. I want to go back to school."

She said, "Well, I can't help you. You can't get out now."

I thought it would be just that easy. Call Mama, and I'll go home. But no. It wasn't that easy.

At the time, I did not know why we were being pushed so, drilled so hard, being brainwashed. Trained in guerrilla warfare. Told the Vietnamese were killers. Told to be prepared to defend yourself 24 hours a day. As you would approach the hills, you would see villages that were just replicas of what they had in Vietnam. As we advanced, even in the classroom setting everything became more and more like a war zone. We would sit in foxholes and eat C-rations. And even at noon, they would have aggressors attack us. It really became warlike.

When I went in, I had a lack of interest in the war. I didn't even have contact with the war through the media. It was like it wasn't there. But after a while, I began to see myself almost as a soldier in Vietnam without having been there.

I didn't get in the Army band. I auditioned at Fort Benning, but they said, "We don't need any more trombone players. Maybe you can join one when you get to Vietnam."

And it was strange, because I want to go to Vietnam now, because I want to shoot just one Communist to see how he looks when he falls. That's stupid as hell, but this is the way they had me programmed. I've been playing war games. The Communism wants to captivate our allies. And if we're going to have allies, then we're going to have to come to their rescue. I'm an American fighting man. I serve the forces which guard democracy, my country. Gung ho. All the way. Not from enthusiasm, but from training. This is my profession.

When we were approaching Tan Son Nhut airport, I saw some heavy terrain. My fears are coming to play. But we still have on our dress greens, and I'm thinking the

war must be some other place. Then they took us to the
9th Replacement unit nearby, and I hear this *whoosh*. I
was told they had a fire mission. Nothing is incoming,
but I'm afraid as hell. This is something they can't train
you for back home. You know about the weapons, how
to attack a hill. But they don't train the ears.

I had my first meal in this service club. This lady brought
me this half-baked, half-fried chicken. She must have
knocked the garlic over on it. I can do without garlic.
And there were brothers sitting around in their fatigues,
feet up in the chairs, smoking their cigarettes, drinking
beer. But I'm thinking with every lift of the fork, When
is the top coming off this place?

The first three months in country I was a forward observer. Carried a radio for a sergeant, small as I am,
carried a doggone radio, extra battery, grenades, smoke,
and an M-16. Suppose to be a mortarman. Helicopters
would pick us up for eagle flights in the morning, or we
would go on night ambush at night. We would make contact, depending on the strength of the enemy forces, or
we would call in artillery or an air strike. I had auditioned
for the band at Dau Tieng, and this warrant officer told
me if you can get yourself transferred to the band, we'll
take you.

I'm a PFC. How in hell am I going to get myself transferred out of the field in Vietnam?

Excuse me. I didn't curse until I went to Vietnam.
That's where I learned to curse. Learned to drink. Pabst
Blue Ribbon. Learned to smoke. Kools.

One time we were completing a sweep, and we got hit
in an ambush. It was maybe one o'clock in the afternoon.
After lunch. We were a little sluggish. Smoking cigarettes.
On our way to the purple out-zone, where we catch the
helicopter to go back in.

We were coming down this old trail. The weeds had
grown up. Walking along the hedgerow. And this man
opened up with everything he's got. Grenades. Machine
guns. AK-47s. It's just like *voooom*. It's on you. I mean
they are all over you. About 50 yards out. And I had read
it in the book. You approach an area when most of you
are going to be killed when they open up the ambush.

They allow you to get in there. The killing zone. We are in the killing zone.

Luckily, the sergeant yelled, "Pull back. Pull back."

I started running back. I ran by this Mexican-American. With the radio on, I didn't think of helping him. Somebody would grab him. His glasses was knocked off. His chest was torn open. His mouth was just going. But he wasn't saying anything. I just saw all this blood and everything.

We called in the Cobras. And after they worked over the area, they went out and got him, and put him in a bag and sent him in.

One night we set up an L-shaped ambush at this crossing outside this village. Charlie is suppose to come down this street. All of a sudden GIs—I guess about 15 of us— are taking off guns, hats, shirts, pants, everything. This place is just loaded with black ants, and they would sting. Man, those ants burnt our behinds up. It was like we were standing in hot water.

We were making so much noise when somebody said, "Here comes Charlie."

I'm thinking, Well, damn, you know they have to know where we are. They had to hear us.

But they just came walking right on up the trail. I still can't understand this. We sprung the doggone ambush in our undershorts, supposedly killed four of 'em. And we don't have no bodies. Haven't got a damn thing to show for it. You can go out there and see where there was some blood.

I don't know where these guys go when you kill 'em. It's just that they just vanish. Somewhere. I don't know. Maybe the Twilight Zone.

When they moved us from Cu Chi to Dau Tieng, that's when the shit got bad. The Iron Triangle. Oh, man. That place is not fit for God, let alone man. That was a tough assignment. And after we got pinned down, that's when I began to rebel.

I mean you have to know my mother. How quiet I was when I grew up. I would do boyish things and get punished. But if Mama said do A and B, I would do A and B and that's all. I would not tarry over to C's territory.

Now I'm really afraid. I'm walking around constantly in fear. And I'm thinking about survival first.

Then one night this brother, a medic, has to go out to show his replacement how to get set up on ambush. The brother has been through Tet, all this shit, never been wounded. He rotates out of the field next week to go home. I don't remember his name, but he was a good guy. The new medic comes in. Big thick mustache, gung ho White guy. Wants to do his job. Brother has got to show him. Luckily I didn't have to go out that night. They're gone 20, 30 minutes. We hear boom. That's all. All of a sudden, rat race. We've got to go and get these guys.

They hit a trip wire, artillery round attached to it. The brother is gone and two other guys. The new medic didn't get a scratch on him. Not one scratch. It was really disheartening on everyone, black and white.

Then one day the entire company is working in that Iron Triangle. In very tall weeds. The darn man must have hit us from behind. We had to figure now how the hell we going to get out. If Charlie had been up high, he could have just picked us off. Apparently he was down on ground level, and they would fire every once in a while to let you know they're still there.

There is no direct visibility, the weeds are so tall. But from the weeds moving, Charlie knows where we are. And I got on the radio with the damn antenna. And you move, and the darn thing makes a lot of noise. I can't be quiet.

The rest of the company is standing out of the way, just laughing and saying, "Y'all better get your butts over here. We gettin' ready to get out of here."

We decided we would throw grenades, put our guns at our sides, and run like hell. Charlie would shoot at you in a minute. But if you'd run, he'd leave you alone. Charlie didn't follow you too much over there.

Then this black sergeant pushed me on the shoulder and told me to go first. I told him I was carrying a radio, so I'm not walking point. He turned to some other brother and told him to do it. He said, "I ain't doin' it."

He pushed me again. "Get your ass on up there."

I said, "I'm not suppose to walk point."

We stood and argued for a few minutes.

And he said, "Goddammit. Get your ass in the back."

And he took off. He led the way. Nobody else would do it. I kept my eyes open behind me. And we got out okay.

When I came in country, there were two forward observers like me. So I'm waiting for another guy to come in country, so I can rotate out and don't have to do this ground pounding. I can sit around reading Mickey Spillane.

When the third guy comes in, Sergeant O'Hanlon, this big Irishman, decides we need three forward observers. That means I don't get out of the field. I'm highly pissed about it. And he tells me about the heavy shit he's been through and calls me a coward. I was not. I wanted some equality, to be treated just like he had done my predecessors. And they were all white.

I guess there was this racial tension between us. O'Hanlon is monitoring my daily operation, scrutinizing everything that I do. I was like a thorn in his side. I was just a dangling participle that you don't know what to do with.

So one night he asked me to go out on ambush with this black sergeant. The one who told me to walk point. I went slugging over there with my radio. The black sergeant said, "You going out with us tonight?"

I said, "Yep."

"Goddammit. You don't have to go. You keep your ass here."

I waited until they got out of sight and walked back to my platoon. O'Hanlon saw me coming. Oh, my goodness. Sergeant O'Hanlon had a fit. He gave me hell for not going. Told me I was a goddamn coward.

I said, "Hell, Sergeant. You can call me anything you want." I just never was aggressive, and this war is no place to be aggressive in.

All of a sudden, he decided to take me out of the field. He will give me an assignment that's going to keep me in the back all day. Company barber. That would be my job. I'd never have to go in the field again. But first I would have to cut his hair.

I told him I didn't know how to cut hair. So I didn't

want to cut his hair. I had never even seen a white guy
get his hair cut.

The sergeant said, "Nope. You gonna be the company
barber. You got to cut everybody's hair. You gonna cut
mine first."

I darn near cried. Here is my chance to have a permanent job out of the field, and I can't cut this man's
hair.

Johnson put this thing around the sergeant's neck and
gave me these damn clippers and some scissors. Johnson
was trying to tell me about comb it up and clip it. Comb
and clip. It just didn't make any sense.

When I finished, it was indescribable. It was terrible.
O'Hanlon cursed me. "You goddamn ass. Look at my
head."

When he cooled down, he said, "You just stay there
and work that damn gun." That's where I was suppose
to rotate to in the first place. That's what they trained me
to be. Mortarman.

After I got to Vietnam, I see the Vietnamese people
are some hundred years behind us. People got oxes pulling
carts. You know, I'm thinking, something is wrong here.
These people have been left behind, and I don't know
why. I just stayed away from them.

One day I did walk through the village that was just
outside the wire. Every other evening, it seemed, we'd
get sniper fire from the village. Sniper fire, sniper fire,
sniper fire. Walk through there, nothing but women and
kids. Well, somebody's shooting at us.

So we got a fire mission to stop the sniper fire. I was
the gunner, the one that looks through the sites, sets the
elevation and the deflection. We might have fired six rounds
from my gun and more from the other two. That was a
pretty heavy dropping for this little area. And afterwards,
nobody would shoot at us from that village anymore.

Apparently the South Vietnamese complained to our
ARVN counterparts, because people calling themselves
the CID came up to investigate. They said we were firing
on children. They found the fins from one round from my
gun.

I think one woman and some kids got killed.

I don't feel anything about it.

It was war. And there is no proof that any one gun per se killed them.

When you have a fire mission, your forward observer is telling you what to do, where the target is. When you fire, no matter what the elevation, you don't actually know where your round is going to hit.

When I got back to the real world, it seemed nobody cared that you'd been to Vietnam. As a matter of fact, everybody would be wondering where have you been for so long. They would say, how did you lose your leg? In a fight? A car wreck? Anything, but Vietnam.

I stayed in the hospital for almost a year for five more operations. They were still trying to get the stump to heal. And as soon as I got out of the service, it was right back to Savannah State. Back to school was all that was on my mind the whole time I was in the war. I felt like I had slept for those two years and came out with a disability.

I wanted to play again in the marching band, and my former director was still there. He said come play in the concert band. It was thought at the time that I could not march. I didn't go to the concert band. Those dreams about a marching band dissipated forever.

I was not using my mind a great deal in classes, because I felt I've been to the war and I'm disabled. I would drink all the time. I would smoke all the time. Nobody cares. No matter what you do, nobody's going to recognize it.

I met Dottie in college, and we started dating. I mentioned to her about my disability. I was always a little shy because of it. Never made love to a woman that I didn't tell first. I just put it right out there. I knew probably the fellas had told her. And she asked me if it made me feel any less of a man.

As little as it sounds, what she said made a significant impact on my life.

I said, "It does not. I don't have any limitations."

We got married, and now we have three children.

When I was in Japan, I thought I was going to have to walk on a peg leg until I saw a brother walking with an artificial prosthesis. I said, Wow, that thing really looks neat. When they give me one, I'm gonna walk on it with no cane or anything.

But the one I got had to be big at the ankle. Cosmetically it was undesirable, and when I would hang around the gym and play basketball, it would break, and my foot would just be dangling until I went back to the hospital.

And the darn thing ain't healing. Even with three more operations. I just didn't want to go back to surgery anymore, so I let them make a BK amputee, cutting the leg off 6 inches below the knee.

The new prosthesis doesn't break. Because of where the torque is applied, there's no pressure in that ankle joint area. Nobody can step on your toe and snatch the darn thing off. I can jump higher. I'm thinking I can run down the basketball court. It has just opened up a whole new, new world. And now I want to run. It is as if you say to yourself, I don't like to jog, and you don't think about wanting to jog until you find out you can't jog. But I don't open up yet. I'm afraid the prosthesis will break. And I don't know how to suspend it to get maximum performance.

I graduated with a degree in sociology and worked at counseling in the prosthetic treatment centers in Veterans Administration hospitals, first in Mobile, then in Indianapolis. I guess the counseling is a spin-off from my mother. But I needed to focus on the needs of others, 'cause I didn't need to have so much time to think about myself.

In a few years I'm very comfortable with the prosthesis. Everybody tells me you don't have an artificial leg. You don't limp. I'm touching the rim when I play basketball. I'm playing softball with able bodies. And they are telling me how fast I can run, how fast I can run. And though I've never seen anyone with a prosthesis run before, I'm thinking that there are guys out there with one leg who do run. And I'm thinking that if that is true, then I am one of the best.

If I was going to run, I needed someone to work with me. At the VA Medical Center in Indianapolis, I met Douglas Moorman, a management analyst who was in the Army Reserves, had run track in college, and played for the Minnesota Vikings until he was hurt. From a standing start, I ran 100 meters in 16 seconds. I was dead tired, because I was out of shape. So Doug put me on an endurance program. I needed to work myself to the point where I could run a mile. But when I ran a lap, the prosthesis didn't run out just right. I developed new pressure points. I needed a little piston action. That meant a little snugger fit. And the bony prominent may need a relief area. We got the bugs worked out, and I got to the point I could run three, four laps. Then I could work on speed.

Another friend, Mark Gregg, began to pace me. One day I was actually outrunning him. I thought he had slowed down. But I was really faster. Mark wasn't pulling my leg. And it was just amazing to me.

Then I learned that in 1981 the newly formed U.S. Amputee Athletic Association will hold the first national track meet at Tennessee State University. I think I was the only one of 900 athletes who came who was training to run and run only. So I set the first U.S. records for the 100 meters and the 400 meters. And I won the high jump and long jump, too. But the time for the 100 meters was under the world record for an amputee of 13.7 seconds. I was at 13.07, but the U.S. organization was not sanctioned by the world amputee association yet. Magella Balanger, the Canadian, a BK amputee like me, still had his record.

Now I want a real track coach, and I found him in Gordon Mendenhall, a high school coach in Indianapolis. Gordon said, "Biomechanically, I don't know anything about what's going on with you." But when he saw me run the first time, he couldn't believe it.

Like many amputees, I was starting the race from a standing start. Gordon put me in the starting blocks. We would do nothing but starts. He would ask me, "Where's your eyes? Where's your hands?" Then we would work on the middle of the race. Then the end of the race. I always thought these guys just ran down the track and just leaned at the end. If you just lean, you will end up all over your face. There is a way to lean, a way to recover from the lean. Gordon was polishing me off, and I was beginning to feel like a professional athlete.

Meanwhile, some Canadian runners put the word out on me to Balanger. They had seen me in a meet at Georgia Southern College. In the 100 meters I had to race against a guy with a leg off above the knee, and guys with whole legs, but missing arms. I thought it was unfair, but the officials said, "We've only got one heat. Y'all have to run together." So I ran. I just left the whole doggone field. But 10 feet before the finish line I fell. My prosthesis was not on tight enough. It was the only race I didn't finish. The only time I wasn't first.

In February 1982 I go to Windsor, Ontario, for the indoor games sponsored by the Canadian National Amputee Association. I'm thinking Balanger. I win the 60 meters, the 200, the long jump, and the high jump. My time in the 60 is 8.3 seconds. A world record for amputees. But Balanger did not show. And I'm running just about two seconds slower than Herschel Walker.

When I came home, Indianapolis gave me a beautiful press conference. About a 100 people were there. They were calling me the Mountain Man. And I got named to the national team that would compete in September at the world meet in Edmonton, Alberta. But I didn't have $800 I needed for the trip.

Two days before I needed to leave, Tom Keating, a sports writer, put this story in the Indianapolis *Star* about how a disabled Vietnam veteran needed help to go to the track meet. And that night Emroes, a sporting goods store, gave me the $800, and another caller offered an anonymous gift of $800 more. Then people came by my home and just dropped $1, $2, $5 in this bucket. It was like a telethon. It was a tremendous feeling. After a while, we had $2,000. We couldn't take any more.

When I'm leaving, it's butterflies. How can I lose after what these people have done for me back home?

When I get to Edmonton, I'm introduced to Balanger. And he sort of shakes me up. This cat is telling me he is running 12.8 in 100. I knew if he was running 12.8, I was in big trouble. Butterflies again.

The first event was the 100 meters, and we took off. When the gun snaps, I don't see anybody on the line but me. I go down the track. I don't look left. I don't look right. When I crossed the line, I looked back and I saw him. I know I ran under 13. But the Canadians say 13.1. As it turned out, Balanger's psych game didn't work. And he didn't have the speed either. And I now have the world record.

The second event is the 400 meters. I don't want to run it, because it takes the energy out of you. Everybody had a fit. Our teammates said, "Run, Mountain. Run, Mountain." I just jogged around the track and finished last out of seven. Balanger not only won, he broke his own world's record.

But Gordon had been training me for the 100 and 200. I wanted the 200 record, too.

When the 200 came, I was really shaking, because everybody told me you'd better win after the way you embarrassed us in the 400.

They put me in the far lane, lane 8. Coming out of the staggered start, Balanger was in lane 2. I never saw anybody, I just took off. Psychologically, he was beaten. I was starting in front, and if ever I'm in front, there ain't no comeback because I never let up.

My time was 26.01, 2 seconds lower than his world record.

Now I hold two world records, four national records, and four indoor Canadian records.

I sent Mama the medal I won in setting the world record for amputees in the 100 meters. She put it beside my Purple Heart.

Lieutenant Commander William S. Norman Norfolk, Virginia

Airborne Controller
U.S.S. Ranger
November 1963–May 1964
Airborne Controller
U.S.S. Coral Sea
January 1965–July 1965
Combat Warfare Officer
Commander, Carrier Division 3
September 1969–June 1970
U.S. Navy
Yankee Station
South China Sea

It was one of those long nights on watch. In the combat operations room. Carrier Division 3. The command ship. On Yankee Station. In the South China Sea. In 1970. In the middle of the war.

I was directing aircraft. Giving orders. Whatever you are supposed to do militarily, I was doing it and doing it well. But at that point I decided to get out of the Navy.

I was not frustrated by the war as much as I was frustrated by the role of blacks in the Navy in that war. I wasn't really certain by then that our best vital interests were being served by the war effort. Yet the Navy was asking black people to take part in a war while subjecting them to institutional racism—institutional racism intentionally.

You could go aboard a carrier with 5,000 people, and you would find the overwhelming majority of the blacks in the lowest level in jobs, in the dirtiest jobs, down in the laundry room, down in the bowels of the ship. You walk into the areas where I work with all the sophisticated computers, and it would look as if there were no blacks on the entire ship.

The commander of the carrier division felt that I was very good, that I had been promoted to lieutenant commander early, that I had a good career, and that I, therefore, ought not to be getting out. He felt that I was being affected by a lot of the other things that were going on in Vietnam. But Vietnam was secondary to my feelings of what was happening to blacks who were a part of the war. And I didn't have the kind of disaffection with the war that would cause me to refuse to do certain things. When I gave directions, I made certain that they were effectively executed in a timely way.

Everybody knew how I felt about equal opportunity. I pushed actions on board ships. I used to write to people back here and make suggestions on doing things in equal opportunity. I felt that the system was set up in such a way as to perpetuate racism, and we were not doing anything about it. Other than symbolic things like trying to recruit blacks or work with a civil rights group. But the substance was not being done.

I didn't just write an ordinary letter of resignation. Most of it had to do with improving conditions for minorities in the Navy. I felt I had an obligation. My letter went through channels, and when it reached Washington, they wanted to know who it was who had written it. Of course it was embarrassing that it was done by someone who was getting out of the Navy.

It was perhaps just fate that when I was writing the letter, we got a new Chief of Naval Operations, Admiral Elmo Zumwalt. Because of my letter, we would meet and I would go to work for him. Most of the admirals opposed the changes we would make. They would call Zumwalt a nigger lover. And they would call me Zumwalt's Rasputin.

Probably the worst racial thing that happened to me in the Navy was on the second of my three tours in the war. We were in Japan. I had a date, and we stopped in this military place for a hamburger. I was in civilian clothes, and there was this chief petty officer in line in front of me. He had had too much to drink. He was talking to one of the Japanese clerks. He was being machismo and verbally abusive. He made some comment about the guy owing him some more money.

I said, "Look. You are wrong. Why don't you just pay the man his money and move on?"

The chief turned around, and he says, "What did you say?"

"You're wrong."

And he said, "You're a lying, fuckin' nigger."

And he punched me.

I immediately grabbed him and let him know my rank so that there was no misunderstanding. I was a lieutenant JG at the time. And he still was mouthing off. So I pulled out my ID card—I did know the rules—and he kept on. So I called the shore patrol, and I decided to put him on report. I couldn't punch him back, which was on my mind.

The next day we got back on the carrier, and you would never believe the parade of people that came to see me, up to and including the executive officer of the ship. They were saying he was an outstanding chief. He never had gotten into trouble. He was drinking. And that it ought to be excused.

I said, "Look. This can't be tolerated. This chief knew that I was an officer. I can't believe that you are telling me that this ought to be called 'extenuating circumstances.'"

The chief was brought around to apologize. And the executive officer urged me to drop the charges of disrespect, which I refused to do. To me there was a much higher principle that I was concerned about. But I left before anything ever was done about the chief. And I am certain that nothing ever was.

I admire people who didn't always push every race issue, because they were doing everything proper, correct, by the book. They were the soldier's soldier, the sailor's sailor, the Marine's Marine. I don't put them down. It was tough. But I would raise holy hell every time. I would be ready to go to any authority. I was always very proud, probably still am now. There were just certain things that I was never willing to tolerate from anybody. I felt the same way about segregation.

I grew up in Norfolk, Virginia, and the separate but equal doctrine. Everything was separate, from the theaters to the hotels to everything. I lived in a neighborhood that was all black except for some Filipinos and Puerto Ricans. We didn't think about them as such. It was white people and the rest of us.

You could not find two people who were more gracious and more ordinary than my parents. My father worked for the Naval shipyard as a carpenter. Worked very hard all of his life. My mother did what mothers did at that time—worked at home. Was a mother of five children, housewife, manager of the house. And occasionally she did day work for extra money.

During those days I was not a crusader. Not consciously. I was not conscious of going out trying to break the segregation laws. There were just things that I was not going to tolerate. It was incomprehensible to me to stand by willingly and allow myself to be limited for artificial reasons. I just have a strong belief in myself. It was the way I was raised.

I can recall getting on buses and being asked to move to the back. I wouldn't sit in the direct front, but I would clearly sit farther than where the unofficial line was. If whites got on, you had to move back if there were more seats in the back. The bus driver inevitably would say, "Hey, you. Get to the back." I would sit there and wait for someone to throw me out. But they wouldn't. They didn't want to make enough of an issue out of it to throw a kid out.

Perhaps some of the things we did in the segregated environment was not too dissimilar from what Solidarity is doing to Poland today. You may not have gone out and stood before a bayonet, but you did as many of the little things that you could to erode the system and show you did not accept it.

I remember when I was a senior in high school. In 1955. I was always president of my class and president of the student government. I recall going to a citywide meeting of student government presidents. There was one particular white guy who said he was going to be going to the Naval Academy. That sounded exciting. So I went to the recruiting station and told the recruiter I wanted to understand something about the Naval Academy. And he simply wouldn't give me any information. And he said

he didn't want to waste his time going through the tests.
I was irate. To his mind, blacks didn't go to the Naval
Academy. Interestingly, there was a few at the time. A
very, very few. But I didn't know it.

I took an undergraduate degree in mathematics and
chemistry at West Virginia Wesleyan College, was an exchange student in the Soviet Union for six months, and
then started teaching mathematics at my high school. In
1961 I got drafted. And I just made the decision to go into
the Navy because I didn't think I wanted to go into the
Army and because of what that recruiter had done to me.

I qualified for the Aviation Officers' Training Program
and was the only black in my class at Pensacola, Florida.
At that time there were very few black officers. In fact,
on a ship as large as a carrier, you might be the only one.

We had what they called smokers at flight school. And
they would set up boxing matches. One day the sergeant
was standing around and said, "We have to have some
boxers. Who volunteers as the battalion boxers? Who
boxed before?" A few hands went up. "Who else would
like to volunteer?" I never fought before. And back home,
in the streets, I was not known as the one that was raising
all the hell. But the sergeant quote volunteered me unquote. After all, I was black.

The first boxing match I was a hero. They give you
some training, not much. But I was just too proud to be
beaten by anyone. I boxed someone else who had never
boxed, and I just kind of beat the hell out of him and won.

When it came to the second smoker, I fought a guy
who knew what he was doing. He was not one of those
quote volunteers unquote. He had done Golden Gloves
stuff. He won the fight. I got him some good ones, but
he really punched me. Of course, all my people thought
I was robbed. And although the scoring was close, he did
a job on me. That's when I retired.

I did not experience the terrible, overt racism that older
black officers did who went through before me. At least
at the officer level, the Navy was priding itself on being
ahead of what was happening in society. But the discrimination was still there, just not so open.

No one, for instance, would tell me that I couldn't go
to the swimming pool in the officers' club area. If I went

with my group, no one ever paid that any attention. But if I went by myself, the people would start getting out. And I use to have fun making them do it.

I remember I was in the band, and the band was going to New Orleans to play in the Mardi Gras. The bandmaster called me in and said, "I had an experience one time before where there was a black in the band we took to the Mardi Gras, and people threw things at us. I would suggest that you not go." When I complained to the sergeant, he said, "Look, you are an outstanding cadet. But you are down in the South, and those sort of things happen. We are doing this for you. We are trying to protect you from incidents. We are not giving you an order, but I think you ought not to push this anymore." And before I could do anything about it, they had gone.

I was equally outspoken when I went to Advanced Technical Training School in Glen Cove, Georgia. Jerry Allen and I were the only black officers. Coming back from our dates one night, we were driving along and the police stopped us. We demanded to know why we were being stopped since we weren't doing anything. The police threatened to break Jerry's jaw. So when I got to the base, I went to the base attorney and asked him to file charges against the police for racial harassment. He said, "We don't have jurisdiction over there." Of course, the big problem was the base didn't want to have any trouble.

And when I was stationed in Meridian, Mississippi, the executive officer once asked me if I wouldn't mind not coming to the officers' club because they were going to have a lot of guests from town. Just like Pensacola, the request was made under the guise that they didn't want me to be uncomfortable. Though I hadn't planned on going, I made a point to go there that particular time.

In 1963 I was on routine deployment into the Pacific. While we were in Japan, we received orders to go down to the South China Sea. I was on a carrier, the *Ranger*. None of us thought that much about it other than we were going south. We ended up in the waters off Southeast Asia. Because of the confidentiality of the mission, we were not to even mention what action we took even to other people on the ship. We were not to tell anyone back home, including relatives, that we were even in the area.

I might add that although it was the initial stages of the
Vietnam War, particularly for the involvement of our
forces, at the time, most of us weren't able to deal with
it as a war as such. Most of us didn't recognize the impact
of what was happening or how it was developing. Only
afterwards did we make the connection of what was taking
place.

I was in an airborne early-warning squadron. As the
airborne controller, I was directly over a pilot, a copilot,
the radar operator, and a technician. We would direct
bombers to particular targets. The bombers we had were
old, single-propeller aircraft and light attack jets. They
were carrying light weaponry, 500-pound bombs or less,
not the kinds of things that would cause tremendous damage. There was no napalm. Their mission was to destroy
routes and roads, and stop the supplies coming in from
the North to the South. Most of the missions were over
into the Laotian area. At that time it was not identified
as the Ho Chi Minh Trail.

Some of our people had had Korean experience, but
most had never dropped anything or anything other than
on practice targets. So there was a certain measure of
excitement. And most of us didn't envisage a great deal
of danger. There was no air contact with the enemy. Occasionally, there would be some small-arms fire that you
wouldn't notice until after the plane was inspected. No
one was being hurt. And no one was getting any battle
fatigue, because these were not daily bombing missions.
We would sometimes go three, four, five days without
doing anything.

When the intelligence people briefed us, we were told
that we were trying to stop quote Communist insurgency
unquote. That was the battle cry, and there was no real
questioning of that. And the assumption was that the action would be over soon. By cutting off the main supplies
to the guerrillas, they would be hurt severely. And we
believed that they didn't have any enclaves of friendly
support in the South. It was a very simple operation. And
in all candor, most of us looked at it rather simplistically.
You are trying to support a friendly country. It was a
limited engagement. We were not thinking about a war.
War in Vietnam was associated with the French period.

When I went back in January of 1965, we had a comparatively major situation. We were regularly assigning carriers to Southeast Asia. It was taking on the atmosphere of a combat zone. And we spent a great deal of time understanding the secret rules of engagement. There were specific conditions under which you could fire. We were told how far you could go in pursuit if anyone came after you. The MiGs would come out to test us and turn back in. But you could not go into hot pursuit of them into the North. We were in Cambodia and Laos, but you simply did not cross the DMZ. It was going to be a war fought under certain parameters. And it clearly was going to be limited. And that was somewhat of a comforting factor, because we thought that we had a clearly defined engagement, fighting for honorable causes, supporting a country that was being overrun by the neighbors from the North.

In the intelligence briefings we were hearing more about the geopolitical aspects of what was happening out there. There was no question as to who the good guys were. The North Vietnamese were aiding and abetting a guerrilla group against the legitimate, elected government of South Vietnam. I saw this as typical efforts of Soviet aggrandizement. A war of national liberation was being extended south to take over the people against their wishes. It seemed to make sense that the national interests of the U.S. was to stop these kinds of efforts. That's what I'd been trained to think, and it made sense.

At first there were mild operations. Like checking fishing boats for guerrillas. And it was kind of fun, flying down low to take a visual look. If they looked suspicious, we'd call in a nearby boat to investigate. We would fly in support of some of the land forces, and occasionally the ships would go in for some shore bombardment as they were asked for it.

The things started to intensify. The war became real.

It started becoming real when they started putting heavier bombs on the planes. When they started loading napalm.

It started becoming real when we started getting fewer and fewer "bingo" fields. Those were fields in South Vietnam where you could land if something happened to you and you couldn't get back to the carrier.

It started becoming real when we started putting more emphasis on escape and evasion.

It started becoming real when the missions stepped up. When the targets of opportunity were getting closer and closer in the North, across the DMZ. And the more you started doing that, the more you faced the SAM emplacements.

It became real when the first pilot didn't come back.

A guy we called Bush Bill as the first person I knew who didn't come back. He was flying an A-6 off a carrier during night operations. We were in flight school together.

In that early stage, the tendency was to treat those kinds of deaths like you would the accidents that always happen on a carrier. Every time you take off from a carrier and every time you land, there is danger. And there is just a macho feeling among pilots that these accidents will happen on a carrier. And we tended to list the people as MIA as opposed to KIA until we were absolutely certain. We held out hope that they would be recovered, captured, anything but dead.

There was no feeling that we were in a war of attrition.

When I returned in 1969, I had the role as electronics warfare officer and combat information officer in the combat center for Carrier Division 3. In essence, I was representing the flag commander, giving the order to fire, the order to pursue or to change the rules of engagement. From just bombing roads on my first tour, we had advanced to a major war. There were bombing raids now into the North. We were bombing Hanoi. Yet there were certain kinds of power dams you couldn't touch.

By now, I had gotten married, taught at the Naval Academy, and finished a degree in international relations and national security policy. So I began looking at Vietnam from an academic view. I began questioning the rationale for what we were doing and the effectiveness of our efforts. It was no longer a war in which a few people were being killed. Large, large numbers of people were being killed. And everybody knew about it. It was in the papers, on television. And there were demonstrations against the war back home. I was seeing the war from a perspective that I had not seen it before.

And now I was getting all the intelligence information. Our resources were so fantastic that we could listen to the North Vietnamese pilots talking to each other as they prepared to take off on their runways. You would really know what was happening everywhere.

And in the command room, where four of us maintained a twenty-four-hour watch, you would have a tremendous quantity of time to think. And I would think and think and think.

It was still clear to me that there was Communist aggression from the North. But it was less clear that it was an aspect of Chinese or Soviet orchestration than it was a matter of the North and South going at it in a struggle for unification. And I wondered if the war was worth the American effort. Worth the number of people I saw getting killed. Worth the attrition that was taking place in the country. Worth the protection of a government that was appearing to be increasingly corrupt. Was it a typical example of Communist aggression? Was it a war of national liberation in which the North was not aligned with any other country? Were the Vietnamese simply trying to get everybody out? Was the war part civil, part aggression?

And I would get the feeling that we were going at what we were doing in a halfhearted way, not with any degree of confidence that we were fighting a winnable war using all the power that we had. The Communists were winning it guerrilla-style, but not because we couldn't stop them if we wanted to.

In all three tours I never once set foot in South Vietnam. I had made arrangements that last time to fly over to see my brother, Kenneth, to join him in Danang. He was working with a special intelligence group. A soldier's soldier. But before we could get together, he got hurt. Hurt so badly he still has trouble walking to this day.

I thought about him. Thought about all the people being maimed and killed. And you kept saying, Why?

When my letter of resignation reached Admiral Zumwalt, he asked me to hold off and work with him in the whole area of improving conditions for people in the Navy.

Zumwalt was really quite strategically oriented and an extraordinarily professional Naval officer. To the surprise of many people, he started asking questions about everything when he took over. He had commanded the naval forces in Vietnam and had lived with his family in the Philippines. So he had a great feeling for nonwhite people in general. I agreed to be his special assistant for minority affairs, but I didn't have any high expectations that he was willing to go as far as I was wanting to go.

Shortly after I arrived, we decided to have a group of black officers and their spouses come to Washington to talk about various problems that they had been experiencing in the Navy. We did the same thing with enlisted personnel. This was an opportunity for me to have them legitimize the recommendations I would be making.

One of the admirals listening in began to talk about how much he loved his stewards as if they were his own children. At the time, the steward's rates were closed to all but blacks and Filipinos.

"This boy that I have working for me is just like a son and a close friend."

One particular wife said, "Admiral, how old is this *boy* that you're talking about?"

And he says, "Oh, he's almost forty."

Zumwalt heard that.

And he heard the senior officers snicker when the enlisted men talked about the black hair products they wanted placed in the Navy exchange. Or the need to wear their hair a certain length.

Zumwalt was outraged.

Afterwards, he said to me, "I was looking at those flag officers, and they did not understand any of what was taking place here. I think I made a serious mistake. I have put so much emphasis on trying to ensure that everyone would be treated equitably that I was losing track of the fact that there are some differences, such as cultural, which have to receive some special attention."

At that point he started getting an emotional involvement in what he had to do. And that made it easier to get changes made. But I wanted him to understand everything from a logical approach, to see the intellectual basis.

Eliminating discrimination and ensuring equal opportunity seemed so right to him that he could not understand why others didn't deal with it from a logical basis. Even if the whole world was full of bigots, he just could not understand how a senior military commander still wouldn't be committed to equal opportunity and treatment because it made good sense from the point of view of mission effectiveness. Otherwise, you were not allowing your resources to develop. It was very simple.

In less than three years, we instituted some 200 programs. We had a new Navy. The first ships were named after black heroes. The first black was promoted to admiral. Ten percent of our NROTC units were set aside for predominantly black colleges. We guaranteed that blacks would be on promotion boards, assignment boards, and would make their way to the command colleges. The steward's rate was opened up to anyone, not just blacks and Filipinos. We opened all rates to women and welcomed them into the Naval Academy. And we relaxed the rules on haircuts and allowed beards.

A lot of people didn't like what was happening, and Zumwalt and I got called every name imaginable.

The flag officers were especially resentful that I was so outspoken, just a lieutenant commander, and Zumwalt always supported me.

One admiral did everything he could think of to block me or get me to quit. He would question the legal aspects of each new effort, unaware, of course, that I already had done so. He would offer me orders to this fabulous assignment, or he would try to find something he considered more important for me to do. Always, I said no. Finally he called me in to tell me that the Navy had been making some progress and now I was setting it all back by creating enemies.

You know, I was always able to find out any information I needed about the effective implementation of our equal opportunity programs, about race relations or any race crisis. It was not because I had Zumwalt's signature in my hip pocket. Not because I didn't have the power to get a Naval investigation going. But because the admirals and senior people almost always talked in front of their stewards and drivers as if they didn't exist. And the drivers and stewards would pass information on to me in a matter of hours.

In spite of everything that Admiral Zumwalt was willing to do for me in terms of promotions and assignments, I decided to resign from active duty in 1973. I really did believe we needed a period of consolidating the gains. I was so much associated with change and a kind of bellicose manner. We had had to use a meat cleaver instead of a rapier at first to get everyone's attention. And there were too many very, very senior officers who would love to have gotten me in a situation in which I was no longer with the CNO. And they never had any reservations about saying it.

And so I went to work for Cummins Engine Company in the area of corporate action and responsibility.

When I heard that Saigon had fallen, I felt angry. I'm sort of competitive. I don't like to lose at anything. We had put all this effort and lives into this, and we lost. Then when I saw the people climbing over our Embassy trying to get out, I felt a certain degree of disgrace and sadness.

Then I began to feel deceived, deceived by our foreign policy-makers. There was no question in my mind that if we were not prepared to go to the limit to keep South Vietnam from falling to the Communists, then we should not have done anything. We should have been willing to commit more resources. We could have bombed the dikes in North Vietnam, used stronger tactical weapons—not nuclear weapons. Gone to the heart of North Vietnam and bombed them. Maybe up until the Tet Offensive, we could have done a large quantity of things. And we didn't have all the daily media to inform us on how much was going on. After Tet, that kind of escalation I think would have caused rioting everywhere back home.

Even when we pulled our forces out, I wondered, Why give up now? Even if we had had to maintain a permanent presence like we have in South Korea, that would have been a far preferable solution than the Communist takeover.

I realize Vietnam was an evolutionary process, from our clandestine role, to a covert one, to the wide-open participation. But I think we muddled through because our policy-makers had the sense that there wasn't the national resolve to fight the kind of war that would win. When it came time to take strong actions, it was too late.

I think the people who were there, like me, were doing

their duty as they understood it. We were fighting for the honor, the integrity, and the national interests of this country. What upsets me now and will always is that there were policy-makers with a perception based on a set of conditions that was not reality.

I finally did get to South Vietnam. One of the first things I did when I became Zumwalt's assistant was to tour all the Naval facilities throughout the world. When I went to Saigon, Danang, and other places in the war, I met with black soldiers, sailors, and Marines, and talked with them. I discovered a militancy of a nature that I've never seen before in anyone.

These men belonged to a generation that was far, far more outspoken than any generation of black men before them. So they get over there, get introduced to the drugs, the killings, the uncertainty, and they still had to put up with racism within the service. They were there to kill and be killed. About ready to die. To do first-class dying. Yet in terms of their assignments and promotions and awards, they were getting second-class treatment. It created a special brand of bitterness.

And many of them came back home with less than honorable discharges, caused by their anger and outspokenness. So they lost their veterans' benefits, which weren't so great anyway.

I don't think you can call Vietnam a success story for the young blacks who served there. A few stayed in service and did very well. But those who experienced the racism in a war we lost wear a scar.

Vietnam left a scar on them that won't go away. The black soldier paid a special price.

Today I am a group vice-president of Amtrak, the National Railroad Passenger Corporation, responsible for five corporate departments handling marketing and business development, including the computer services, information systems, and strategic planning. I'm also a captain in the Naval Reserve.

And you know, until now, I hadn't thought about Vietnam for five years.

Specialist 4
Robert E. Holcomb
New York City

Armorer
4th Infantry Division
Pleiku and An Khe
February 1970–October 1970
101st Airborne Division
U.S. Army
Camp Eagle
October 1970–December 1970

The FBI was on a rampage looking for me. Around the Fourth of July 1969. So I called the FBI, and I told them I was out on the Long Island Expressway. And they came and picked me up and put me in manacles again. Then they took me to Whitehall Street, where everybody in New York City gets inducted.

One of the agents said, "Holcomb, this time we're gonna make sure you take the oath so in case this time you leave, you'll be a problem for the Army and not us. We don't wanna be bothered with you anymore."

They took me inside to say the oath, and I refused. So they took me outside.

The other agent said, "Listen, Bob, if you don't say the oath, we're gonna lock you up forever. You just won't be seen around anymore."

So I said, "All right." And we went back inside.

I raised my hands and said the oath.

I was sworn into the Army in manacles.

Then the agents took the manacles off, and they left.

It was really a strange scene. Because there were a lot of very young Spanish guys who were very proud to be getting inducted into the Marine Corps while this was going on with me. They were excited about becoming Marines and getting to wear that uniform. They couldn't understand me. They thought I was a degenerate or something. But they didn't say anything. They just stayed as far away from me as they could.

I had evaded the draft for more than a year, but my antiwar views were shaped long before, while I was a student at Tennessee State University.

After two semesters at Indiana University, I transferred to Tennessee State in Nashville to get farther away from home. I was rebelling from the middle-class values and way of life my parents, both schoolteachers, were grooming me in. I think my first protest came in a march for civil rights that Martin Luther King had organized back home in Gary when I was a junior in high school. I had printed a huge sign to carry in the march. From the time I could hold a pencil, I was always drawing something. The sign said, "*Nunc Es Tempes*." "Now is the time."

Tennessee State was a hotbed of social and political unrest in the mid-sixties. Black awareness was on the rise. People like Nikki Giovanni, Kathleen Cleaver, and Rap Brown would be on campus and join our marches. We staged sit-ins at the governor's office and mansion, protesting poor living conditions for black people in the state, some of whom lacked food, decent shelter, and even real toilet facilities. We got into Che Guevara's theories on guerilla warfare, read Mao's little red book, and the revolutionary writings of Camus and Jean-Paul Sartre.

We thought the government was gonna begin to be more and more oppressive, especially to black and other minority people. So some of us even took our philosophy to the point that we felt we should arm ourselves and develop skills so that we could survive in the hillsides. We were essentially carrying the student movement into a revolutionary mold.

We wanted the war in Vietnam to cease and desist. We felt that it was an attack on minority people, minority people were being used to fight each other. Some of us would give safe haven to soldiers who went AWOL from Fort Campbell, Kentucky, because they did not want to go to Vietnam. They would hope to stay around the college campus scene until things just blew away. But they wouldn't blow away. You had to do something about it; otherwise, they'd be following you for the rest of your life.

I was arrested for violations of curfew after a riot. And for that and other infractions of school policies aimed at stopping protests, I was expelled. As tensions between the police and the black community continued to rise, I decided to leave Nashville. I just had the feeling that I was under surveillance and one day I'd be walking down the street and someone would roll down his window and I would be shot. The revolution I left behind petered out like it did everywhere else. Free love came into the picture. Drugs came into the picture. There was always police repression. And there was Vietnam.

I decided to move to New York to continue my art study. Soon afterwards, I got a draft letter. At that point, I decided that I was gonna resist, because I didn't believe in the war. I had read tons of books about the war, including literature from Cuba and from China and from Hanoi itself, material that had filtered here through Canada and other sources. Wars are only fought over property, really. And the war in Vietnam was basically about economics. As I saw it, we were after a foothold in a small country in the Orient with rubber plantations, rice, timber, and possibly oil. And the people. A cheap source of labor, like you have in Hong Kong and Taiwan, making designer jeans and the insides of TV sets. That's what I understood the war to be about—a war that was not really for the many but for the few. I didn't have any problems fighting for capitalism, but I was not interested in fighting for a war in which I would not enjoy the rewards.

I considered the conscientious objector status, but I couldn't do that because I was not a religious fanatic. I decided that the best thing for me to do would be to leave the country. I was not interested in being locked into Canada. I was not interested in Cuba, because it had a very pure form of socialism and didn't permit the kinds of freedoms that I was accustomed to here. I did not consider myself an African. I was concerned with the better distribution of wealth and authority at home. I never really left the idea of capitalism and the idea of democratic government. I would have gone to a European or African country.

I went to the passport office in New York, and they told me that my application would be delayed because I didn't have a draft status that would permit them to issue me a passport. I filled the application out anyway, and I left. A few weeks later, an uncle who lives elsewhere in New York called to tell me that agents had come to his apartment looking for me because they knew that I applied for a passport.

I couldn't work because I couldn't file a social security number. I was basically hanging out, living with friends, and getting a little bit of money from my artwork or from house painting. My family did not support my ideas, so I really didn't have any support from them. They wanted me to straighten up, perform as I was trained to, forget my ideas about changing the government, and go into the Army. After a while, I was at the point I was no longer in a viable position to do anything constructive with my life, so I decided to turn myself in.

I was charged with draft evasion. The FBI offered me an option. I could work for them as a plant, an informant, or I could go to the service. For two weeks they kept me locked up in the Federal House of Detention hoping to sweat me into working for them. They wanted to plant me within various black or radical groups, like the Black Panthers, the Student Non-violent Coordinating Committee, and the Symbionese Liberation Army. They said we could start off in New York, but there might be other cities involved. They would provide me with an apartment and with a subsistence allowance. For each person that I helped them capture on an outstanding warrant, they would pay me from $1,000 to $3,000. My questions to them were, Would I get concessions against the charge against me, how long would I have to do it, and would I be permitted to carry an arm to protect myself? They offered no promises of leniency or a time when I could get out. And no, I wouldn't be permitted to carry any kind of weapon. I said no deal. I did not want to fulfill that kind of role, especially unarmed.

Then I went before a federal district court judge and told him I'd prefer to go to war than go to jail or be an informant. He stamped my papers approved to go into the Army.

When they took me to the induction center on White-hall the first time, the agent said, "You're not gonna go anywhere, are you?"

I said, "No."

He took the manacles off me and left me in the hands of the Army. The Army treated me just as they did any other recruit. They didn't know what my history was. I was free to roam around, so what I did was to roam around and roamed right out of the building.

I got in contact with the lady I was living with, Felice Mosley. I told her I was going into the war, and she got cold feet about waiting for me. We resolved some issues. We broke up. And, after two weeks to rest and recuperate with a friend, I told the FBI to pick me up.

After I finished basic training, they made me a security holdover for two months because they weren't sure whether I'd be subversive to the government in a war situation. I had to go over to the G2 every week to prove to them that I'd be a loyal trooper and fight for the red, white, and blue. Finally, they said, "Fine. We're gonna take you through a little more training in AIT school, and from there you'll more than likely go to Vietnam."

But an odd thing happened before I left Fort Gordon, Georgia. I was training some troops on how to fight with a bayonet. One of them came running down a path to stick the dummy with his bayonet. It was a guy I was in college with who had his ear severely damaged when he was beaten by the Nashville police. I thought to myself they must be taking all of us who were involved in any sort of black political struggle and putting us into the Army as soon as they could so we wouldn't be a problem anymore.

I landed in Cam Ranh Bay in January 1970. It was just a big sand bowl. There was nothing there. It could have been a Long Island beach with some nondescript buildings. It could have been the beach in Mexico with some nondescript buildings. It could have been anywhere. The headquarters of the 4th Division in Pleiku seemed the same way. Little Army buildings. A desolate-looking area. Nothing that reflected the difference in the culture of Vietnam. After two days, I told my commanding officer to send me to the field immediately. I was bored. And I wanted to be somewhere where I could get involved more with the Vietnamese people, but not necessarily fighting against them.

I started off repairing small arms. The 2nd of the 8th Mechanized was like a reaction unit for the division. We were mobile by track or helicopter. And we patrolled Highway 19 from Cambodia to Qui Nhon.

During the Cambodian incursion, we went in about 2 miles deep to secure the roads for the 101st Airborne. In the sense that we uncovered an awful lot of munitions, I think that operation was a victory. But it also was a defeat because we pushed the VC more into Cambodia, involving them more with the Cambodian people. And that helped lead to the overthrow of the Cambodian government by the Khmer Rouge, who then destroyed 2 million of their own people.

It was during those operations around the Cambodian border that I really thought I would get killed. It happened twice.

We were on a regular search and destroy mission, breaking through this jungle trail with one tank and about ten tracks. Most of the people were on foot except the track chief and the driver. I'm the last person in the whole line of tracks. I was carrying an M-60 machine gun. I was walking.

Then we made some contact. It wasn't the sporadic pop, pop, pop you would hear when there are maybe just a small group of people fighting. Just an absolute wall of noise.

I immediately turned backwards and began to spray the back to make sure that nothing is coming up from the back.

When I turned around forward, everybody was gone. I presumed they had pulled off the trail. But I really didn't know where they had gone to. Your adrenaline is pumping so hard it seems like your chest is gonna burst. I just had a terrible sinking feeling that—that I was just gonna be left there.

I was the only one there.

I got down as low as I could. Then I began to crawl across the tree stumps to the side of the trail. I crawled into some bushes, but I still didn't see anyone. Five minutes. Ten minutes. I began to try to crawl towards where I thought there were some troops. Always there was the fear of getting killed by your own troops as you get closer and closer, because they don't know who you are.

Finally, I saw one of the tracks off the trail, and some people hiding beside it. I was scared to wave at 'em. I was scared to do anything.

Then I heard somebody yell, "All clear."

So I yelled to a track driver, "Hey, Tex!"

And everybody turned around with their weapons aimed in my direction.

I said, "It's Bob."

So they said, "Oh, hurry up."

I got up and started running. And everything was okay.

This other time I had to guard this sergeant, a white guy, on our way to Cambodia. I don't even know how they picked him up. He was busted for raping a Vietnamese woman. His thing was that he just felt that they were animals and didn't deserve to be treated like people.

I was told to give him a weapon in case we get into a fight. I only had one spare weapon, a defective M-79 grenade launcher. It didn't have a safety catch on it, so you couldn't load it unless you were ready to fire. I told him not to load it unless we made contact and he's ready to fire. He loaded it anyway. He was sitting slightly behind me with the weapon lying across his lap, facing towards me.

We went across a bump, and it went off, just an inch behind my back, and exploded in the woods somewhere.

I turned the .50 around on him. It didn't turn around as far as I wanted it. So I got up out of the track, pulled my M-16 and told him to get off the track. Just leave. He wouldn't move, so I kicked him off.

He went and asked this other track to let him on. They radioed me, "Papa Charlie, what's happenin'? Why are you leaving this guy here?" I clicked my radio off and told my driver to drive on. I guess he got picked up.

This sergeant wasn't the first American I knew about messin' with the people. In my third week in country, I was assigned a detail to take cases of milk that had spoiled out to the helicopter port at Fire Base Oasis. The port was beside this road where people on motorbikes go by. And these two GIs began throwing quarts of milk at the people on the bikes. Some of them would get hit and fall off the bikes and get injured.

My first reaction was, Jesus Christ, like why are they doing that?

My friend and I, supposedly in charge of the detail, went over and told them, "What the fuck's a matter with you? You're doing this today. Do you realize what's gonna happen tonight? Fuck with the people in the daytime, and you can expect mortars at night."

That night, we got mortars.

One time our commander decided to give this village a lesson. The villagers had lied and said that there weren't any VC there, but the VC were there. They shot this one guy hiding in one of the bunkers. After he was killed or almost dead, the captain ordered him tied to a tank and dragged around the village. It was a psychological thing. Let the people know what can happen to them if they don't inform on other VC.

It was something I didn't want to see. But there were a lot of soldiers in Vietnam who would run out with cameras to take pictures of dead enemy. Like here in the States, when people hear the siren, they run out to see who got hurt, who got shot, who's arrested. That's something I never did in Vietnam. I could never really relate to taking pictures and sending them back home. Saying this is a picture of a dead gook, or a dead dink. I couldn't understand the psychology of that at all.

I use to give away supplies, food, equipment to the people. And not to just anybody. We'd have to have some sort of relationship. Either they are giving me some intelligence information or they have befriended me. I'd give them those big cans of beans, peaches, carrots, poncho liners, blankets, boots, socks, T-shirts. But no weapons.

Or I might just buy something I didn't need or want to be friendly, to gain trust.

I remember a woman asking the people on the track in front of me if they wanted to buy a little bottle of eucalyptus oil. They didn't want to buy any. She came by my track, and I told her I would buy some. Then I asked her what was happening around this area.

She was looking kind of nervous. "Well, they been some VC come by here."

I said, "Really?"

"Yesterday. I no know if they still here."

I did loan a Vietnamese a weapon once. He was my scout. He had been an ARVN once. And while assigned to me, he was not supposed to have a gun. But we had gone down into VC Valley in an area by the Song Ba River. And we got in some sniper fire the first day. He was just kind of hiding. I was looking out for him, so he didn't get shot. But I said to myself, "Gee, this is real bad, man. In the middle of a goddamn war, he's the only one without a piece." I had a .45 that I never used really. I always had my M-16.

I told him, "Listen, I'm gonna give you a .45, but you can't strap it on. You gotta put it down in your pants somewhere, 'cause you're not s'posed to have it."

He's the only one I gave a weapon to, only because he was a scout. I wasn't afraid of him turning on us. He was loyal to us. And from then on he was like an ally that you wouldn't believe.

He pointed out to me about not firing right away when there is contact. Don't fire. Don't do anything. If you fire, they see where your fire is coming from and they can always fire back. Even though I've seen that kind of thing in movies, you don't think about it in the war.

Another thing he would do. Whenever we approached an area he was concerned about, he would always pull my coat, say, "Wait a minute, Bob." Then he would go up first to check it out. Which was unusual for ARVN troops.

A couple of weeks later, he gave the pistol back to me because he didn't want me to get into any trouble.

When we were out in the jungle, we lived on the ground, slept under a tank or track. But the real scene was going to the latrine. Especially at night. It was a scene. Every time.

You could piss anywhere. But if you had to go to the latrine, you'd always try to plan it so you didn't have to go at night. You could always go in the daytime. But you always seemed to need to go in the middle of the night.

And then, there had to be this big preparation. You start off by asking, "Is there any toilet paper around?" Then you try to find something that's suitable and not too scratchy. Then you have to remember where the goddamn thing is. Usually away from everybody else and with no security. When you find it, it's usually sitting out there like a throne.

The moon made things so bright that you were so obvious out there. You're scared, first of all, of being shot. When you think everything is cool and don't see anything moving in the bushes, you actually had to sneak up on it.

Then, when you pull your pants down, you are not only dealing with the mosquitoes, you're concerned about whether or not there's a scorpion underneath the seat and you'll get your nuts bitten off. Or get your ass bitten off. Or you'd get up there and bang, something blows up under the seat. And there you are, wounded with your pants down, and you're crapping all over yourself.

Once you get there, you try to make things happen as fast as possible. You try to relax yourself real fast. You sit with your piece loaded. And you're looking around, saying, Gee, I wish everything'd hurry and come on off, so I can get outta here. Finally, everything happens. You immediately jump up. You don't button your pants up. You just kind of hold them on and scurry off to some safe place.

Guys would get real horny out in the field, especially when there are no women. Then when you would get near a village, a little boy would approach you about his sister or someone.

"Hey, GI. How you doin'?"

You'd rap a little.

He would say, "Hey, you wanna boom boom?"

And if you said yeah, he would say, "Oh, man, I got beautiful, beautiful, my sister. She right down street." Or wherever.

"How much is it gonna be?"

"Five dollar." Three dollars, or whatever.

"Aw, she really beautiful."

And you go wherever the person may be. Down in a ditch off the side of the road, behind a house, behind a tree, or next to a water buffalo.

"Okay. Five dollar."

And you go ahead and take care of business.

But when you get there, there's this little, scared Vietnamese woman sitting on her ankles, nervous. She takes down her black pajamas. She doesn't have much pubic hairs, because she's so young or they don't grow much. You're s'posed to have sex with her, and you kind of have this sinking feeling like this is just the worst ever. Nothing really attractive that I wanna sleep with. And then I'm scared of some kind of venereal disease. Then you try to figure out how you're gonna do this. Or can you even get it up to do it, because you're not even excited. The girl doesn't speak English, and she's just trying to do it as fast as she can and get the hell outta there.

One day I was first in line. The girl was laying on the side of a ditch. She takes her pajamas off, and I'm about to screw her. But she has this pained look on her face. Her eyes are closed in a grimace, because she isn't into it at all. She wants to make the money. And I started laughing, because of her reaction. I couldn't do it.

Of course, she felt embarrassed because she thought I didn't think she was attractive. I had to tell her, "Listen, I'm really sorry. I just can't do it."

When I went back, I told her brother or whatever, "It was okay."

And he said, "Yep. She beautiful."

Our guys wanted to know how it was. This is a communal thing between all guys who were in the war. I said, "It was all right." I didn't say that I couldn't do it. Partly because of pride. Partly because I didn't want to blow their heads about it and turn them off so they didn't get any. A lot of troops came to Vietnam, eighteen- and nineteen-year-olds, and had never slept with a woman before. And they could die before they ever did. Or that girl would be the last one any of us would ever screw.

When all of them came back, some of them said, "Yeah, she was nice."

There was a girl in Qui Nhon I liked. I really had a good time with her.

She wasn't terribly attractive, but she had a really beautiful body.

She worked in a PX, and I met her through a buddy. She wasn't aggressive. She wasn't into profiteering from American GIs. The people in Vietnam liked the GIs. They were not into the government, but they were into us as people. Like she asked me what I did back home, what my hometown was like, what I felt about her people. I felt she sincerely liked me.

She lived in one of the old French houses. It has a flush toilet. I was in heaven. And the first night seemed so exotic, because there was a mosquito net over the bed. I was in paradise.

We ate some river lobster. I played my tapes. John Coltrane, Eric Dolphy, Pharoah Sanders, Miles Davis, the Beatles. And she gave me pastel-blue pajamas to wear.

The next morning, I told her, "Wow, this is really nice. I really like being here with you."

She said, "This has been great for me, too. I've been with other GIs, but I really like being with you."

I gave her money. I gave her gifts, poncho liners, some blankets. And I saw her again.

Towards the end of my tour, people started getting very hostile towards each other, because it was getting late in the war. And there were a lot of drugs around. And a lot of people were taking them. The Communists were making sure the American soldiers got them. And others were making sure drugs were available, because they could make a lot of money. Drugs took a great toll on all soldiers.

Some guys were choked to death in their sleep, because they drank too much alcohol or were taking drugs. Some ODed. They were mainly not really smoking grass so much anymore, but taking "number tens," which are

something like Quaaludes, and speed. And that was devastating, taken together. Of course, there was the scag.
And whether you smoked it or snorted it, you got really
fucked up.

One night, two white guys were playing this game in
a bunker along the perimeter checkpoint as you leave the
base camp at An Khe on the way to Qui Nhon. They had
been taking speed and number tens. So they began to play
with this grenade. Taking the pin out and putting it back
in. They did it for a time, until one of 'em made a mistake
and dropped the pin. When he found it, he was so nervous
he couldn't quite get it in, and the grenade exploded. It
killed him. And his partner was critically injured.

Another night, we had come in for a stand-down. I was
laying in bed, just about to go to sleep. We hear this burst,
and the bullets went through the tent. Everybody jumped
off on the floor. We didn't have any weapons, 'cause
they'd always disarm us when we'd come in. What happened was this black soldier had taken some drugs, and
he just sort of went crazy. A lot of his anxieties and hos-
tilities came out. He got an M-16, and he sprayed a sergeant, killed him and two others.

After another stand-down, we lost a second lieutenant.
A white guy. He had been in country about six months.
And he had made a lot of enemies because he was really
tough on some of his people in the field even though the
pullout had started. Someone wired a claymore mine to
the door of his hootch.

When I went over to the 101st Airborne, I heard stories
that the white guys would stay close to the black guys in
the field because they thought the VC and NVA didn't
shoot at the blacks as much as the whites. And there were
signs the Communists put up in the Ashau Valley which
told the black soldier this was not his war. Finally, in the
3rd of the 506th, about 20 black guys refused to go to the
field for a good week. They thought more blacks were
going to the field, because blacks were less likely to get
shot at. They were confined to quarters and threatened
with Articles 15 until they ended their protest.

A few of us black soldiers were able to get into positions where we could have some freedom, make our lives
a little better, even though we were in a war that we didn't

really believe in. But most blacks couldn't, because they didn't have the skills. So they were put in the jobs that were the most dangerous, the hardest, or just the most undesirable. A white soldier would probably get a better position. And Hispanic soldiers and Jewish soldiers and Polish soldiers would catch some flak, too. But not as much as a Blood.

I couldn't escape it completely with my skills. I wanted to do combat art. But they wouldn't let me do it. I ended up redoing maps out on reconnaissance patrol, or painting emblems on tanks. I painted a lot of panthers. Our unit was called the Black Panthers.

I came home the day after Christmas. When I changed planes in Seattle, I put on some civilian clothes. But I felt so uncomfortable that I put the Army clothes back on. Before I returned to New York, I went to see my parents in Gary. It really made Christmas for 'em. They told me that I was right in protesting the war and that they felt bad telling me to go. Then they made a bed for me upstairs in my old room. But I didn't really feel comfortable sleeping aboveground in a bed. So I moved down into a corner of the basement and put everything around my bed. Gun here. Stereo here. All your pot right here. Just like in the war. Then I could go to sleep.

At first I would wake up with my arms and hands all scarred from hitting the walls. I was having dreams in which I would run out of ammunition and we were getting overrun. And this VC is coming at me with a machine gun. I jump him, and I'm killing him.

Then one night, I was sleeping with my lady, Fern. I'm having the same dream. I sit up in the bed, and I am getting ready to kill Fern in my dream. But she felt me go through this stuff and screamed. I woke up in time to pull my punch, and I yelled out, "What in the fuck am I doing?"

And the dream was gone.

When South Vietnam started to fall, it was a drag. Watching the ARVN run to the sea on television. That was a drag. I couldn't see it. I kept saying, these cats want what we want. To be able to express yourself. They know the Communist thing doesn't work. But they were fleeing. And when I saw them driving all those tanks and shit into the ocean, I felt bad, real bad. Especially 'cause I had to dig those motherfuckers out so many times back in 'Nam.

I don't think we failed to win the war, because we didn't fight a war.

When Ho Chi Minh asked us for help against the French, we should have told him we can't help him militarily against the French but we can use pressure to get the French out. Once the French were gone, we should have dealt with Ho Chi Minh, instead of letting the country get divided and backing puppet government after puppet government which did not work. We would have saved a lot of money, a lot of lives.

But if we were really gonna fight a war against Ho Chi Minh, we should have gone to Hanoi. We should've gone into Laos and Cambodia immediately. The American fighting forces are superior. The war would've been won in that sense of winning and losing.

One night in 1981 I got a call.

"Hello, is this Bob Holcomb?"

"Yes."

"This is Felice Mosley."

"Holy smoke."

She had run into a mutual friend of ours.

"This is great. Do you wanna go out for a drink?"

She said no. She was not in New York. She was living in Washington.

I began to think, Why is she calling me after eleven years?

She said, "My son is eleven years old now, and he's really a good boy. His name is Christian."

"Are you trying to tell me something?"

She was telling me that this was my kid. When I went into the Army, I was under the understanding that our relationship was over. She assumed that I had died in the war because I didn't come to look for her after the war.

I agreed to come to Washington to see him.

So I take a room at the Hyatt, and a knock comes on the door. There she stands. This is the same woman.

"This is your son, Bob."

There he is. He walks in and says, "Hi."

I am pretty speechless.

She gives me a kiss and says, "Hi."

And her fiancé comes in and says, "How're you doin'?"

"Fine."

We have a drink. Her fiancé leaves. And the three of us sit and stare.

"I got a couple of gifts for you."

I give her some flowers and one of my paintings. And I give him two paintings. And we go downstairs to eat dinner.

I'm just sitting there. I don't know if I'm interested in her anymore. I'm in love with my lady in New York. What's going on? My head is just kind of blown. What the hell am I doing down here in Washington with her and meeting my son for the first time?

So we finish eating. And Christian asks if he can spend the night with me. I say sure. And I get her a taxi to take her home.

Christian and I decided to stay up late. We walk for about four or five hours all over Washington, talkin' and tryin' to get to know each other.

I asked him, "What did you think happened to me?"

"Mom wasn't sure. I thought you got killed in the war, 'cause you didn't come to visit me. But all my friends are really gonna be jealous, because you're alive and my father was a soldier in Vietnam."

Then he told me that at school he was taught that we won the war. I told him that's not what happened.

Then he said, "Did you win any medals in the war?"

I was not into that, but I did not want to squash his pride. I'm glad I did eventually go and serve my country, even if the war was not in my best interest. But I was not proud of those medals. They had no meaning. I couldn't remember the actions they were for. I was gonna burn 'em up. But I was glad when Christian asked about them that I had given them to my mother to keep. Now I could give them to him.

As time went on, we got warmer and closer to each other. We now got a pretty good relationship. We tell each other we love each other.

The next year Bobby Muller, president of the Vietnam

Veterans of America, asked me to join the second group of veterans going back to Vietnam. They wanted a black person in this delegation, and they knew I agreed with their efforts to open channels of communication with the Hanoi government to get its help in returning the remains of missing Americans and to assist in reuniting American fathers with children they left behind.

I felt excited about going. Other Americans had been there since the war, but we were the first veterans.

We flew into Hanoi from Thailand in an old Russian propeller-driven plane. It was so small you'd bump your head going in the doorway. Some of us were a bit nervous when we landed, because the guards on the airfields carried AK-47s.

The officials in Hanoi read statements that we were all—Vietnamese and Americans—victims of the war. And that the war wasn't the fault of soldiers like us.

One of the interpreters, named Quang, asked me how many people I had killed over there. He had worked with the VC. I told him that was a terrible question to ask. "I don't really know. I never shot anybody face to face. And I didn't go around making body counts after a fight." He thought I was offended, and he apologized.

Later, I met another interpreter, Duc Lu. I asked him, "What were you doing during the war?"

He said, "I had been in grade school, but I couldn't finish because of all of your bombing. It blew up the school, and I had to go to school in underground bunker in countryside."

Now, I felt embarrassed.

You could see in Hanoi a few black Russian limousines, a few Russian planes, and the military hardware. But there was no evidence the Vietnamese were getting the technology from the Russians for factories, schools, and hospitals. They are not industrialized yet. They are still pretty much out there in the field.

Saigon, now called Ho Chi Minh City, was bustling. The bars on Tu Do Street are closed, but the Majestic is open. They were selling Jordache jeans on the streets. You had to be careful of your watch riding around on a cyclo. But you didn't see computer games and television sets. The economy is down 80 percent. And people are still making it with old pieces of cars and other materials from the war days.

One day I was sitting at an outside café, when two people acting like lovers came by and shoved a big wallet down my shirt. They gave a real fast rap and walked away real fast..They were brother and sister. Their father was an American. And they wanted me to get some letters and their picture to him. The mail had been cut off by Hanoi since '75.

In Saigon, we got some smiles, some expressions of surprise, and some hostile looks. Hardly anyone in Hanoi though gave us a look of contempt. Mostly stares. I think it's because the North Vietnamese never really saw us that much, experienced us that much.

On May 30, our Memorial Day, our delegation shared a moment of silent prayer for our fallen comrades. I prayed that the effort had not been wasted and that it wouldn't be if we could have some economic and cultural exchanges with the Vietnamese despite the Communist takeover. I thought those in the North are starved for contact with the rest of the world and those in the South have still got that big taste for the West.

When I left, Duc Lu asked me for some film. He was gettin' married, and he wants to take some pictures. All he is guaranteed is his kilos of rice and his job in the government. With the economy being what it is, he can't get any film.

He noticed that I had been drawing along the trip, and he said how much he liked them.

He said, "You know, Bob. If you come back to Vietnam and stay a while, I can make you a rich man with your art."

I said, "Duc Lu, you're really not suppose to think like that."

"What you mean?"

"That's free enterprise."

He was real embarrassed.

He said, "I'm sorry. Please not to tell anyone."

I smiled.

And he kissed me good-bye.

Just before I left, I bought a miniature fishing boat for Christian in the airport terminal. It was made from a water

buffalo horn. It represented a better time, a better tradition in Vietnam. Before there were helicopters, B-52
craters, Agent Orange, and AK-47s.

When I got home, I gave him the boat and asked him
would he like to go with me the next time I visit Vietnam.

Christian said, "Yes. But, Dad, what would I do there?"

**Captain
Joseph B. Anderson, Jr.
Topeka, Kansas**

Platoon Leader
An Khe
June 1966–June 1967
Company Commander
Cambodia, Phouc Vinh
May 1970–April 1971
1st Cavalry Division
U.S. Army

Shortly after I got to Vietnam, we got into a real big fight. We were outnumbered at least ten to one. But I didn't know it.

I had taken over 1st Platoon of B Company of the 1st of the 12th Cav. We were up against a Viet Cong battalion. There may have been 300 to 400 of them.

And they had just wiped out one of our platoons. At that time in the war, summer of 1966, it was a terrible loss. A bloody massacre.

This platoon had been dropped in a landing zone called LZ Pink in the Central Highlands to do a search and destroy operation. It was probably eight o'clock in the morning. They didn't realize that they were surrounded. After the helicopters left, the VC opened up and just wiped 'em out. They knocked out the radios, too, so nobody knew what happened to them.

My platoon happened to be out on patrol some miles away. We were the closest to the area of their intended operation. So when there was no word from them, I was given instructions to move in the direction of where they had been dropped and try to find where they had gone.

This is my first operation. I'm new in country. People don't know me. I don't know them. They have to be thinking, Can this platoon leader handle it? I was only a second lieutenant.

We went into a forced march all day. When it got dark, we pulled into a clear area like a landing zone and put our perimeter out and set up for the night. Headquarters wanted me to keep moving and keep searching through the night. I knew it wasn't a smart thing to do, because you could get ambushed. You can't see what you're doing in the dark.

Around ten or eleven o'clock, they opened up on us. They were still there. We fought all night long, until six in the morning.

I learned very quickly how to call in artillery, how to put aircraft over me to drop flares and keep the area lighted up so they couldn't sneak up on me.

I was calling the artillery in within 35, 40 yards of my own people, as tight as I could without hitting us.

I can't remember wondering if I was ever gonna get out of this. I just did not have time to think about it. I was just too busy directing fire to be scared.

After we drove them off, we began to fan out and search the area. We found the ambushed platoon just 50 yards away. About 25 of them were dead. There were four still alive, but badly wounded. They must have played dead, because all the bodies had been searched and stripped of weapons and equipment. Then four more members of that platoon who had gotten away came out of the jungle to join us. Only one of my men had been hurt. He was shot in the hip.

For rescuing the survivors and driving off the VC battalion I received a Silver Star. But most importantly, the action served as a bond between my platoon and me. It was my first chance to react under fire, and it had gone well. My men knew I could handle the responsibility.

I was an absolute rarity in Vietnam. A black West Pointer commanding troops. One year after graduation.

I was very aggressive about my role and responsibilities as an Army officer serving in Vietnam. I was there to defend the freedom of the South Vietnamese government, stabilize the countryside, and help contain Communism. The Domino Theory was dominant then, predominant as a matter of fact. I was gung ho. And I thought the war would last three years at the most.

There weren't many opportunities for blacks in private industry then. And as a graduate of West Point, I was an officer and a gentleman by act of Congress. Where else could a black go and get that label just like that?

Throughout the Cav, the black representation in the enlisted ranks was heavier than the population as a whole in the United States. One third of my platoon and two of my four squad leaders were black. For many black men, the service, even during a war, was the best of a number of alternatives to staying home and working in the fields or bumming around the streets of Chicago or New York.

Earlier that year, French National Television hired Pierre Schoendoerffer to produce a film about America's participation in the war. He had been with the French forces at the fall of Dien Bien Phu to the Communist forces in North Vietnam. After visiting different operations around the country, both Army and Marine, he settled on the 1st Cav because of the new approach of our air mobility, our helicopter orientation. And he wound up with my platoon because of its racial mix—we had American Indians and Mexican-Americans, too—our success in finding the lost platoon, my West Point background and ability to speak French. He and the film crew stayed with us day and night for six weeks, filming everything we did. They spoke very good English, and I didn't speak good enough French. And Schoendoerffer had as much knowledge and experience about the war as any of us.

The film would be called *The Anderson Platoon*. And it would make us famous.

During the filming in late September, we encountered another Viet Cong battalion in a village right on the edge of the coast. A couple of scout helicopters had been patrolling, looking for enemy signs. The Viet Cong fired on them and shot them down. We were already lifted off that

morning, going to another location, when we were di-
verted to the scene. In air mobility. The basic concept of
the 1st Cavalry Division. And it worked.

My platoon was the first one on the ground. We blocked
a northern route of egress, and then we started to sweep
south through the village. It's amazing. We walked through
the village, through their entire battalion, to link up with
our company on the other side. And they never fired a
shot. To this day I don't know why.

Meanwhile, the division piled on. We put about a brigade in, three battalions, and surrounded the village about
a mile across. We did it so quick, they were fixed. They
couldn't escape. And with artillery, aircraft, and naval
gunfire off the coast, we really waged a high-powered
conflict. But not without casualties.

Around noon, my platoon sergeant, a white guy named
Watson from Missouri, and some of his people were
searching holes in the ground, and they threw a grenade
in to see if any enemy were in it. The enemy was in there
and threw the grenade back out, wounding Watson and
three others. We had to pull back to get them out on a
medevac.

I made Owens the platoon sergeant. He was a black
guy from California who was as professional as they come.

Around four o'clock, another platoon got in trouble,
and we started moving to help them. Owens's squad
moved on the attack first, then he got hit in the head, a
bullet crease. And we had to consolidate our position and
medevac him out.

I remember very distinctly chastising my organization
for firing during that night. I felt they were spooked and
just shooting at shadows. The next morning, there were
all kinds of bodies out there, where the Viet Cong were
trying to slip out to escape the encirclement.

That was one lopsided operation. We lost only four or
five men, maybe thirty wounded. But the Viet Cong lost
more than 200 killed.

After a couple of weeks, we got Watson and Owens
back.

There were only a very few incidents of sustained fighting during my tours. Mostly you walked and walked,
searched and searched. If you made contact, it would be

over in 30 or 40 minutes. One burst and then they're gone, because they didn't want to fight or could not stand up against the firepower we could bring with artillery and helicopter gunships.

In the jungle you couldn't count on tanks and APCs for support. You couldn't count on gunships supporting you in contact unless they were already overhead. You had difficulty getting supplied at all. You just didn't get it unless you carried it or it could be kicked out the door of the chopper.

Sometimes we could move easily. There were other times you moved maybe 25 yards in an hour, cuttin' and choppin' your way through bamboo every step.

Snakes weren't the big problem. Mosquitoes and malaria were.

And every once in a while, we'd run into a iguana. And it would scare somebody 'cause it would be so unique and ugly-looking. And the meeting would be so sudden.

I made it a policy not to follow trails and paths. That way you avoid ambushes and punji sticks. And none of my men got hurt from that. I just didn't allow them to take the easy way. And it's very difficult to keep 30 men who're tired or bored or frustrated or scared from making mistakes. But the bigger mistake would be to let them get away with something most of the time and then have it come back to hurt or kill them one time when they did not expect it. The lesser price was to take the more difficult route, the one that is least likely to be ambushed or booby-trapped.

Whenever we would go into villages, as the film documents, we would set up our medics to treat the children and the people. We would tend to scars, wounds, whatever. Give them aspirin and soap. We'd give the kids gum, cookies, C-rations. If we wanted to eat off the land, we would buy a chicken or buy a pig. And the film noted that this was probably the first army in the history of the world that did not take what it wanted.

I lost only one man during the first tour. Just one man in my platoon.

Oddly enough, it was not from enemy fire. It was friendly fire.

I guess it was in October. We were in a fairly heavily

populated area in the An Lo Valley. On the coast in III
Corps. We were conducting night operations to keep the
Viet Cong from moving around among the population. It
was around four-thirty in the morning. One patrol came
back in earlier than they were supposed to to my platoon
headquarters. They should've come in after daylight. So
one of my men on the perimeter threw a grenade out at
the noise, thinking it was enemy movement. I don't know
whether they were trying to come in or whether they were
lost. The grenade landed among them, wounded three not
too seriously, but was close enough to Shannon that it
killed him.

Shannon had been in country about eight months, longer
than me. He was a rather quiet white guy from California.
A rifleman. Did his job all the time. A good soldier.

I did write a letter to his folks, telling them he did an
exceptionally good job. I did not describe the circumstances under which he was killed, because we were directed not to put those kinds of details in letters whatever
the case may be.

When the film was about to be released for viewing on
American television, there was some concern among CBS
officials about his family's reaction to his body being shown
after the incident. My wife wound up calling his family.
She explained what would be seen in the documentary
and asked if they had any objections. They didn't.

The film describes the grenade as an enemy grenade.
Which is not the real circumstances.

Speaking of phone calls, I had to make a different kind
when I got home. Reese, my radio operator, had gotten
his girl friend pregnant in North Carolina before coming
to Vietnam. She had the baby while he was there. In the
film he is shown with a couple of young Vietnamese ladies
in a club during R & R in Saigon. He wanted me to call
his girl friend and convince her that this was done purely
for the film. Being from North Carolina, how would that
look for him to be seen with those women on national
television?

I made the call. And she thanked me. She said she was
a little embarrassed, but it was not that big a thing.

I returned to Vietnam in June 1970. I'm a company
commander now. A captain. And I went directly into

Cambodia, about 15 miles over the border, trying to locate enemy food and weapon caches. We're dealing with the NVA now.

We set up the first night, and the first thing I did in the morning was send out a patrol just to make sure that nobody set up the ambushes. The patrol, five of them, got hit instantly within 50 yards of the perimeter. Only two of them made it back. I didn't know what the status was of the other three.

I put a platoon together to go out and try to find them. And they really drew heavy fire, B-40s and AKs. Then I sent another platoon. This went on for two days. That was very unusual for them to stand and fight. What we didn't know was that we were on the edge of a major supply cache. And they were fighting to defend it.

Meanwhile, I was calling in artillery. We couldn't get much air support because we're too far away from our bases in Vietnam. We couldn't get more troops in because the jungle was so thick. Supplies had to be kicked out of helicopters from treetop height. That's how tight it was. We as a company were operating independently.

On the third day we finally ran them off. It must have been a company of NVAs. And we found our three individuals. All three were dead. I'd rather that not have happened. But I would have rather it have been the patrol that got hit than moving the whole company and get 15 or 20 people ambushed.

My medics went out to put the bodies in body bags. But they couldn't do it. The bodies had begun to decay, and the maggots got to them. It was just too emotional and stomach-wrenching for the medics. They broke down. They were throwin' up. So I had to go out and personally put the decomposed bodies in the bags myself. It was a responsibility that I could not pass on to anybody else. I was the commander.

We found 10 tons of food supply—corn, rice, and so forth. And about 50 tons of Soviet weapons and ammunition. It was the largest cache ever captured by the Cav.

Michael Davidson, the Second Field Force commander, flew out to congratulate us. He had known me at West Point. He had been the commandant at the time I was a cadet.

There was a great amount of criticism about us going into Cambodia. But from that time in June until I gave up the company in November, we didn't receive another single shot. We'd wiped out all their supplies and demoralized them so greatly that they were not ready to fight. As we ran our patrols, we would find they were trailing us so they could eat our garbage, the stuff we'd throw away.

As a company commander, I did not have any feel for the political and international ramifications of going into Laos, going into Cambodia. But as a guy who had to live or die by how well the enemy was equipped or fought, there was no doubt in my mind that the correlation was very great between us going into Cambodia and then not taking any more heat from the enemy.

I had a great deal of respect for the Viet Cong. They were trained and familiar with the jungle. They relied on stealth, on ambush, on their personal skills and wile, as opposed to firepower. They knew it did not pay for them to stand and fight us, so they wouldn't. They'd come back and fight another day. We knew that we could not afford to get careless with them, because you pay the price. But they were not superhumans. And they did not scare us.

The NVA were more like us in being oriented to organization, numbers, and to some degree firepower, although they didn't have as much as we did. But they were as motivated as we were. They didn't pay the same attention to detail, to preparing for battle, to digging in. They were there doing the basics, doing a job.

During that second tour, I could see that drugs were making an impact on American forces, but in the field the men would tend to police themselves and not let drugs endanger the unit. What was very clear to me was an awareness among our men that the support for the war was declining in the United States. The gung ho attitude that made our soldiers so effective in 1966, '67, was replaced by the will to survive. They became more security conscious. They would take more defensive measures so they wouldn't get hurt. They were more scared. They wanted to get back home.

I spent my last months in the base camp at An Khe,

an aide to the commanding general. Being featured in *The Anderson Platoon* had obviously helped my career.

Being in the rear meant clean showers, shaving every day, and air conditioning. It meant eating in the executive dining room. And since the general called his wife every Sunday night, I could call mine, too.

One night, Lola Falana came through for a show. She was invited to a special reception, and I got to dance with her. When I called my wife on Sunday night, I said, "Guess who I danced with? Lola Falana." And my wife said, "I thought you were in combat."

Career officers and enlisted men like me did not go back to a hostile environment in America. We went back to bases where we were assimilated and congratulated and decorated for our performance in the conduct of the war.

The others were rejected, because the nation experienced a defeat. The nation heard stories of atrocities, of drugs. Everyone who was in Vietnam was suspect. And that generalization is unfair to apply to all the people who were there. In two tours I just did not experience any atrocities. Sure, you shot to kill. But personally I did not experience cutting off ears from dead bodies or torturing captured prisoners.

Long before Saigon fell, it was clear to me the United States was not willing to win the war. So the only alternative is to lose the war.

When Saigon did fall, the only feeling I had was, you might expect that considering how things deteriorated. There was no remorse, no feeling of life wasted.

I was at peace with myself about my behavior and my contribution to the process. I went over there and I did what I had to do. I didn't volunteer for it, but I bought into it when I signed up for the Army.

Personally it was career-enhancing. A career Army officer who has not been to war during the war is dead, careerwise. I had done that. I received decorations. Two Silver Stars, five Bronze Stars, eleven Air Medals. And *The Anderson Platoon* brought me a level of notoriety and recognition. I was in a very good position for promotion and future responsibilities. But in 1978 I decided

I did not want to cool my heels for the next eight to ten years to become a general. I was not prepared to wait. I resigned my commission, worked a year as a special assistant to the U.S. Secretary of Commerce, and joined General Motors as a plant manager.

The Anderson Platoon won both an Oscar and an Emmy.

As time passes, my memory of Vietnam revolves around the film. I have a print, and I look at it from time to time. And the broadness and scope of my two-year experience narrows down to 60 minutes.

Sergeant
Robert L. Daniels
Chicago, Illinois

Radio Wireman, Howitzer Gunner
4th Infantry Division
September 1967–November 1967
52nd Artillery Group
U.S. Army
November 1967–November 1968
Pleiku

I never been away from home when I joined the Army. I never been on a train before I went to Fort Campbell, Kentucky, for basic training. I never was in a plane before they took me to Fort Sill in Oklahoma. That was AIT. Seems like we would have gone somewhere for a few months or so. But we went straight from there to Vietnam. Three months after I got in.

Flying over all that water, I was scared to death. I thought we would never get there, and I didn't know whether I was coming back.

When we landed in Cam Ranh Bay, it was like I had never seen anything like it before. Just open land. A lot of sand. Grass. Water. I was in a strange land.

I was scared to death.

We came up poor on the South Side of Chicago.

I don't even remember my childhood. I don't even remember a birthday cake. I don't remember a birthday party. I don't remember my father takin' me to places like parks and to the movies.

The only thing I remember is my grandmother always put up a tree every Christmas, and she always gave us something.

My mother left my father when I was three. I remember that they used to argue all the time. They got married too young, I think. They was seventeen. They didn't finish high school, and there wasn't no money. I didn't know where my father was. I knew my mother was working, and she lived somewhere else. My grandmother raised me.

My grandmother took care of her kids and her kids' kids. They were livin' on and off with her and my grandfather, about 15 of us brothers, sisters, and cousins altogether. There was always five of us in my bedroom.

My grandmother always told us to try to go to school, and we all graduated from high school. But I wasn't too interested in school, because I never had anything to wear. I only had one pair of shoes at a time. Tennis shoes. We always had a coat. But no nice clothes, like a suit or a tie. They couldn't afford to buy me them. So I didn't go to the dances and benefits at school. I was too ashamed. I was a timid person.

I sometimes think the way I came up and didn't be no dope addict is a surprise, because I had to learn so much from the streets. But one thing my grandparents instilled into me was staying away from the wrong crowd. When I found out they was the wrong crowd, smokin' dope or messin' with people, I would just go off to myself. I was a loner.

Before I went into the service I worked at the post office in Skokie as a sub for about a year. I decided to enlist 'cause it didn't seem like I was gettin' anywhere. And I felt it was gon' make me sort of like grown up. I didn't have anybody to sort of rear me into becomin' a man. And I thought the GI benefits would help me go to college since I didn't have no money for college.

When my mother realized I was gettin' ready to go away into the service, she gave me a birthday party. It was my first birthday. I was nineteen years old.

All we did the first days in Pleiku was fill sandbags.

Then they taught me about the switchboard. But I spent most of my time on the 105 howitzers. There were six guys around it. Each guy has a different job. One guy tilts the artillery. One guy might be on the telephone runnin' from one gun to another. My job was either cleanin' it or help loadin' it.

It seems like at first they was always shellin' us, and we would run to the bunkers. I use to wonder sometimes why we would run to them. The way they were built, if a shell would hit it direct, it wouldn't do no good anyway. It was only made with a whole lot of sandbags on top. It ain't nothin' like a house. Maybe it was just to keep you from gettin' some scrap metal if the round hit near it.

One night we was goin' to sleep. I was just wearin' them green things they give you, like shorts. I thought I heard things comin' in. I jumped up, got my rifle, and put my belt on. I was runnin' out the back way, tryin' to get to the bunker. The sergeant told me to go back to sleep, because it wasn't what I thought it was. Everybody laughed 'cause I had all these guns and just my shorts.

When I went on guard duty, you hear noises. You shoot, because it be so dark out there. But I didn't never see anybody. All I know, I was scared.

Before I went to Vietnam I was told they were helpin' the people from Communism, so they could try to be a free country. The Communism didn't let the people control their own rights. But it looked like we were fightin' 'em altogether. You didn't know who was who. One Vietnamese look like he be on your side, and then at night he might be VC.

When I see the Vietnamese comin' in to clean the barracks, they didn't say nothin' to me. I didn't say nothin' to them. I didn't know who was who. I didn't trust 'em.

Sometimes we had to drive trucks from one place to another. Guys'll stop on the road, and the Vietnamese be sellin' beer or something. I never did stop. I was too scared.

One time I was goin' to pick some sandbags up to bring 'em back to my base. I was drivin' a five-ton, and I had two flats on one side. The other three trucks that was with me, they had just left me 2 miles down the road all by myself. I didn't stop, but I was goin' so slow. And I didn't have a shotgun at the time. Charlie could've just picked me off. Now that scared me.

When there was nothin' to do, I stayed in the barracks and read the *Jet*, or just wrote letters.

It took me six or seven months to walk down to Pleiku village. I was too scared at first. You might just get shot just walkin' around.

My friend and I went to this little place that made trick pictures, like you holdin' yourself in your hand. They had warned us before we left not to be active over there with the women sexually in case you catch something. I was too scared anyway, because I didn't know who the women was.

In November '68 I had about a month left. When I think about it now, I should've been gone since I was out there 14 months already. They were tellin' me to go to the field. I told 'em I didn't wanna go.

They told me they didn't have any sergeants out there, and they needed one to drive out this amtrac. They said you gotta go 'cause you the only one.

It was dangerous out there, and I didn't know what might happen. I didn't know where I was goin'. I never been out there. And it was almost time for me to go home.

I had a shotgunner, but it wasn't like no company or battalion goin' together.

We spent the first night in the field in some tents. Got up that next morning. We had a long way to go. Up to Kontum.

We was way out in the boonies like, and they kept saying we was almost there. They said they was hookin' me up with somebody else. Somebody I don't even know. I didn't even get a chance to see 'em.

It wasn't no main road. It was like a old dirt trail.

There was a minesweeper in front of us. Then a couple of tanks. We was fourth in line, the last vehicle.

We hit this mine. Got blew up. Blew the track straight up in the air.

I thought it was all over.

When that thing blew up, I never heard nothin' like that before in my life. That was the loudest sound I ever heard in my life.

It blew us right out of the track.

When I came down, the track fell on my leg.

We didn't have the cover on it you put over the top if it rains. If that would've been on, we would've got trapped in there.

I don't know whether the shotgunner got killed or not. He was on the other side with his machine gun.

I was just burnin' up. I was burnin' everywhere.

It ain't no gas stations in the field. You run out of gas, you just run out of gas. It no tellin' when somebody might come by and bring you some. So we had these gas cans with us. They must've exploded, too.

Fire was runnin' all up my fatigues.

Somethin' just kept tellin' me, Pull your leg out. Pull your leg out. My left leg. I was steady diggin' and steady tryin' to get it out, and I finally got it out. I just nearly tore my right hand off.

I was never taught to roll over when you on fire, and I start runnin'. And that's what I did wrong.

It felt like I was in hell.

I just was screamin' and screamin'.

So the guy that was in the tank in front of me told me to lie down, and he put it out with the stuff they carry.

So they had me sittin' on the side of the road waitin' for the helicopter. It must have took 20 minutes. They gave me something. Maybe morphine, and I sort of passed out.

I had third-degree burns everywhere. The skin was just hangin' off my left arm. My right arm was burned completely to the bone. My face was all burnt up. It was white.

I remember in the hospital in Japan I kept tellin' 'em I was cold. I couldn't get covered up, because I was burnt all up. They kept puttin' some white stuff all over my body. And they kept puttin' me in a tub and takin' the dead skin off.

In the hospitals back here they took skin grafts off my leg and put 'em on top on my head, on my forehead, and on my arm.

I caught gangrene in my right hand, and they took the thumb off. The hand just kept getting bigger and bigger.

Finally my doctor told me that he had to take it off, because gangrene was gettin' ready to go all through my body. Well, I didn't want to die. So they cut it off.

They had to take veins out of my legs, too. I have a little limp now. I figure it's just poor circulation.

They wanted to do some plastic surgery on my ear to make it look like the other one. I didn't go back. I was just tired of hospitals. I don't know how many operations they did on me. They said I had somethin' they call severe trauma.

Two Christmases had gone by me in the hospital.

That doctor say if I wasn't a young man, I wouldn't have made it.

I got my discharge papers May 6, 1969.

I came home and stayed with my mother.

I didn't come home the way I went. I went a tall, slim, healthy fella. You could look at me now and tell something had happened. I was either born like that, or I was in the war. I'm scarred all over. It ain't no way you can hide it.

After six months, I started goin' to school at Northwestern Business College. Using the GI benefits. I got a associate arts degree in accounting, and they sent me all over lookin' for a job.

I tried maybe 40 places in two years. But I never did get hired.

They would say I didn't have experience. Or they would make excuses like, "You think not having that hand would interfere with your doing this kind of work?" I thought, How would that interfere sittin' there at a desk? Or they would tell me they would let me know, but nobody never did call me back.

I got discouraged. I guess I just gave up, because I kept gettin' turned down. Nobody never really wanted to give me a break. I was black. A amputee. And it was an unpopular war. Maybe they didn't like the idea nobody from Vietnam workin' in they profession.

That was in 1975. I stopped lookin' for a job. I've been livin' on disability and Social Security.

I stay home most of the time. Just readin'. I'll walk my daughter sometimes. But as far as goin' out to plays or out to dinner, I don't do that. I wouldn't know how you s'posed to carry yourself. Like in a nice restaurant,

I couldn't cut my own meat. And I'm gonna be stared at anyway.

In 1981 Social Security stopped sending me checks. So I have been havin' trouble with this house note. And somebody stole my car. The Social Security wrote me this, "We realize that your condition prevents you from doing any of your past jobs as a foot soldier, but does not prevent you from doing . . . various unskilled, light one-armed jobs." But it was Social Security that told me I was disabled and could have the money when I was discharged.

This lady, she said, "What do you expect, Mr. Daniels? To receive Social Security for the rest of your life?"

I started to tell her, "Yeah. My hand is gonna be missin' for the rest of my life." But I didn't say anything. Maybe Social Security thinks I've lived too long.

It's funny. When I see the Vietnamese who came over here, I just wonder how they start so fast. Get businesses and stuff. Somebody helpin' 'em. But the ones that fought for they country, been livin' here all along, we get treated like dirt.

I know you gotta help yourself, but you can't do everything. I can't hire me.

Sometimes I feel I'm worth more to my wife and daughter if I wasn't around because I got the insurance. Like you don't get your insurance until you die, right? Sometimes that what I think. Sometimes.

When I was nineteen, I know I didn't know too much about what's goin' on. Except you s'posed to fight for your country. And you come home. But where is my country when I come home?

And now I read where the people in Vietnam still havin' the same problems they had before the United States went over there. I read they say they wasn't no war. Well, what the hell they sent us over there for? I read the Americans lost. It was nothin'. Nothin'.

But I wish I—I would've—I would've came back the way, you know, I went.

I might have realized which way my life would've went.

All I did was lost part of my body. And that's the end of me.

Specialist 4
Arthur E. "Gene"
Woodley, Jr.
(aka Cyclops and
Montagnard)
Baltimore, Maryland

Combat Paratrooper
5th Special Forces Group
75th Ranger Group
173rd Airborne Brigade
U.S. Army
An Khe
November 1968–December 1969

I went to Vietnam as a basic naïve young man of eighteen. Before I reached my nineteenth birthday, I was a animal. When I went home three months later, even my mother was scared of me.

It began on my fourteenth day in country. The first time I was ever in a combat situation at all. We was in VC Valley, south of Pleiku.

I was a cherry boy. Most cherry boys went on point in the LURP team. I adapted so well to bein' a point man that that became my permanent position after this first mission.

We was in very thick elephant grass. We had sat down for a ten-minute break. And we heard the Vietn'ese talking, coming through the elephant grass. So we all sat ready for bein' attacked.

I heard this individual walking. He came through the elephant grass, and I let loose on my M-16 and hit him directly in his face. Sixteen rounds. The whole clip. And

his face disappeared. From the chin up. Nothing left. And
his body stood there for 'proximately somewhere around
ten, fifteen seconds. And it shivers. And it scared me
beyond anyone's imagination.

Then it was chaos from then on. Shooting all over. We
had a approximate body count of five VC. Then we broke
camp and head for safer ground.

After thinkin' about that guy with no face, I broke into
a cold sweat. I knew it could've been me that was in his
place instead of me in my place. But it changed me. Back
home I had to defend myself in the streets, with my fist,
with bottles, or whatever. But you don't go around shooting people. As physical as I had been as a teenager, there
were never life-threatening situations. I had never experienced anything quite as horrible as seeing a human being
with his face blown apart. I cried. I cried because I killed
somebody.

You had to fight to survive where I grew up. Lower
east Baltimore. What they call the Bottom. I lived basically three blocks from the waterfront. It was very difficult for us to go from one neighborhood to another without
trying to prove your manhood.

It was a mixed-up neighborhood of Puerto Ricans, Indians, Italians, and blacks. Being that I'm light-skinned,
curly hair, I wasn't readily accepted in the black community. I was more accepted by Puerto Ricans and some
rednecks. They didn't ask what my race classification
was. I went with them to white movies, white restaurants,
and so forth. But after I got older, I came to the realization
that I was what I am and came to deal with my black
peers.

I played defensive end, made all-city at Dunbar High
School when we won the city championship and was one
of the best football teams in the region. I was ranked
fourth or fifth in the state as a heavyweight wrestler. So
I was lookin' for this scholarship to college. It didn't come
through, and I didn't have the academics to go otherwise.
So I went into the Army primary as a lifer, because I felt
I could escape from my environment and get ahead in
life.

Being from a hard-core neighborhood, I decided I was
gonna volunteer for the toughest combat training they

had. I went to jump school, Ranger school, and Special Forces training. I figured I was just what my country needed. A black patriot who could do any physical job they could come up with. Six feet, one hundred and ninety pounds, and healthy.

They prepared us for Vietnam as a group of individuals who worked together as a unit to annihilate whatever enemy we came upon. They taught us karate, jumping out of airplanes, of course, and, not with any exaggeration, a thousand and one ways to destroy a human being, even decapitation with a piece of wire and two pieces of wood. But the basic thing is that we are the world's greatest fighting unit, and nothing will stand in the way.

In basic I noticed something funny. We Bloods slept on separate sides of the barracks. And it seemed like the dark-skinned brothers got most of the dirty details, like sweepin' up underneath the barracks or KP, while the light-skinned brothers and Europeans got the easy chores. But I didn't think too much about it.

We got to Cam Ranh in November 1968. And I got the biggest surprise of my life. There was water surfing. There was big cars being driven. There was women with fashionable clothes and men with suits on. It was not like being in a war zone. I said, Hey, what's this? Better than being home.

When I got there, my basic job was combat infantryman, paratrooper, 5th Special Forces Group. There was about 200 some men in my company. Thirty of us were blacks. Forty of us was Latin descent. We had some Italian guys. We even had some German fellows who came into the Army to get American citizenship. We had some fellas who had came over from other Special Forces units to get extra field duty. We were like a unit of misfits who were sort of throwed together and made into a strike combat unit. We would go out and capture prisoners, destroy a certain village, or kill a certain party because it was necessary for the war effort.

I didn't ask no questions about the war. I thought Communism was spreading, and as an American citizen, it was my part to do as much as I could to defeat the Communist from coming here. Whatever America states is correct was the tradition that I was brought up in. And

I, through the only way I could possibly make it out of the ghetto, was to be the best soldier I possibly could.

One day they stood us in a line at orientation, and this colonel asked if anyone interested in being LURP. I didn't really know what a LURP was, but I raised my hand. Then we went to another formation, and we was auditioned for being a LURP. They said a LURP was a individual who would go out in a five- or six-man group beyond support units of any type, and survey, capture, and destroy the enemy. Bein' a macho, strong young brother, I joined. I'm bad. It was exciting.

We were assigned to First Field Force, which hired our unit out as a recon unit to anyone who needed our services. Sort of modern-day gunfighters. Or low-priced mercenaries. We was stationed near An Khe. We lived rough. We only got hot meals maybe once or twice a week. We ate mostly little dry-good foods that were in plastic bags. You add hot water and spices, let it sit for five minutes, and you got a perfect meal. A lotta things we had to steal from other units—refrigerators, jeeps, or whatever. We were the type of unit that had no basic supplies. An' no rear area either. The only rear we had was a ass.

I was still a cherry boy—and that's what you stay until you get 90 days in country—when we had been dropped in a area s'pose to've been classified as a friendly area. We was goin' 'cross some water. I'm the point man. I'm on the other side of the stream, and now the team's comin' 'cross. All of a sudden, the whole world start to explode. People start to screamin' and hollerin' and runnin' around.

I had a white guy in the team. He was a Klan member. He was from Arkansas. Ark-in-saw in the mountains. And never seen a black man before in his entire life. He never knew why he hated black people. I was the first black man he had really ever sat down and had a decent conversation. Since I grew up in a mixed-race neighborhood, I was able to deal with him on his terms, and I guess he learned to deal with me on mine. And once you started to go in the field with an individual, no matter what his ethnic background is or what his ideals, you start to depend on that person to cover your ass. Arkansas and me wind up being best friends.

They was throwin' mortar rounds in on us. Man, you talk about mass confusion. Six of us runnin'. I was on the other side covering. A couple fellas on the rear end covering. Arkansas got hit in the chest. Another white dude got hit. They was in the middle of the water.

I started to cry and holler at Arkansas. He was layin' there with blood comin' out of his chest, comin' out of his mouth.

We called in for support. Support comes out. Helicopter full of soldiers lands in a clearing, but the troops would not even come out because contact was bein' made.

I went out in the water. Arkansas had ceased breathing. And I start to pounding in his chest and hollerin', "Dear God, please don't let 'im die."

Everybody say, "He's dead. He's dead. He's dead."

I said, "No! He cannot die like this."

I got to kickin' him in his chest. I'm stompin' on him. And he started breathin' again. And I pulled him from out of the water and dragged him to the helicopter.

There was so many in the helicopter, three of us had to hang on the skids on the underbody of the helicopter when we got out of there. And we were still under fire at the same time.

Arkansas and the other dude survived. But I found out it was friendly fire that we was under. It really made me angry. It made me angry for a long period afterwards. And I began to act a little strange. I was becoming a animal.

Then came the second week of February of '69.

This was like three days after we had a helicopter go down in some very heavy foliage where they couldn't find no survivors from the air. We were at LZ Oasis. We were directed to find the wreckage, report back. They see if we can find any enemy movement and find any prisoners.

We're headin' north. It took us ten hours to get to the location. The helicopter, it was stripped. All the weaponry was gone. There was no bodies. It looked like the helicopter had been shot out of the air. It had numerous bullet holes in it. But it hadn't exploded. The major frame was still intact.

The next thing we do is to stake out the observers to make sure that we were not being observed, that the area is safe.

We recon this area, and we came across this fella, a white guy, who was staked to the ground. His arms and legs tied down to stakes. And he had a leather band around his neck that's staked in the ground so he couldn't move his head to the left or right.

He had numerous scars on his face where he might have been beaten and mutilated. And he had been peeled from his upper part of chest to down to his waist. Skinned. Like they slit your skin with a knife. And they take a pair of pliers or a instrument similar, and they just peel the skin off your body and expose it to the elements.

I came to the conclusion that he had maybe no significant value to them. So they tortured him and just left him out to die.

The man was within a couple of hours of dying on his own.

And we didn't know what to do, because we couldn't move him. There was no means. We had no stretcher. There was only six of us. And we went out with the basic idea that it was no survivors. We was even afraid to unstake him from the stakes, because the maggots and flies were eating at the exposed flesh so much.

The man had maggots in his armpits and maggots in his throat and maggots in his stomach. You can actually see in the open wounds parts of his intestines and parts of his inner workings bein' exposed to the weather. You can see the flesh holes that the animals—wild dogs, rats, field mice, anything—and insects had eaten through his body. With the blood loss that he had, it was a miracle that the man was still alive. The man was just a shell of a person.

The things that he went through for those three days. In all that humidity, too. I wouldn't want another human being to have to go through that.

It was a heavy shock on all of us to find that guy staked out still alive.

With an open belly wound, we could not give him water. And we didn't have morphine.

And he start to cryin', beggin' to die.

He said, "I can't go back like this. I can't live like this. I'm dying. You can't leave me here like this dying."

It was a situation where it had to be remove him from

his bondage or remove him from his suffering. Movin' him from this bondage was unfeasible. It would have put him in more pain than he had ever endured. There wasn't even no use talkin' 'bout tryin' and takin' him back, because there was nothing left of him. It was that or kill the brother, and I use the term "brother" because in a war circumstance, we all brothers.

The man pleaded not only to myself but to other members of my team to end his suffering. He made the plea for about half an hour, because we couldn't decide what to do.

He kept saying, "The motherfuckers did this to me. Please kill me. I'm in pain. I'm in agony. Kill me. You got to find 'em. You got to find 'em. Kill them sorry bastards. Kill them motherfuckers."

I called headquarters and told them basically the condition of the man, the pleas that the man was giving me, and our situation at that time. We had no way of bringin' him back. They couldn't get to us fast enough. We had another mission to go on.

Headquarters stated it was up to me what had to be done because I was in charge. They just said, "It's your responsibility."

I asked the team to leave.

It took me somewhere close to 20 minutes to get my mind together. Not because I was squeamish about killing someone, because I had at that time numerous body counts. Killing someone wasn't the issue. It was killing another American citizen, another GI.

I tried my best not to.

I tried to find a thousand and one reasons why I shouldn't do this.

I watched the bugs and the stench that was coming from his body. I heard his crying and his pleading.

I put myself in his situation. In his place. I had to be as strong as he was, because he was askin' me to kill him, to wipe out his life. He had to be a hell of a man to do that. I don't think I would be a hell of a man enough to be able to do that. I said to myself, I couldn't show him my weakness, because he was showin' me his strength.

The only thing that I could see that had to be done is that the man's sufferin' had to be ended.

I put my M-16 next to his head. Next to his temple.
I said, "You sure you want me to do this?"
He said, "Man, kill me. Thank you."
I stopped thinking. I just pulled the trigger. I cancelled his suffering.

When the team came back, we talked nothing about it.

We buried him. We buried him. Very deep.

Then I cried.

I thought all hell was gon' break loose soon as I got back. It just about did, too.

They questioned me: "Was there any other alternative to killing him?" I stated the circumstances. His body had been eaten out. There was no feasible way to bring that man back and expect him to live.

They stated that there would be a court-martial procedure to find out if I had killed this man out of just plain anxiety or was it a necessity. They threatened me with a court-martial.

It never went to court. Nothing ever happened.

Now it begins to seem like on every mission we come across dead American bodies, black and white. I'm seeing atrocities that's been done on them. Markings have been cut on them. Some has been castrated, with their penises sewed up in their mouth with bamboo.

I couldn't isolate myself from all this. I had gotten to the conclusion today or tomorrow I'll be dead. So it wasn't anything I couldn't do or wouldn't do.

There was this saying: "Yeah though I walk through the valley of death, I shall fear no evil, 'cause I'm the baddest motherfucker in the valley."

I figured if I'm gonna be a bad motherfucker, I might as well be the baddest motherfucker in the valley.

I became the company initiator. It was my job to initiate any cherry boys that comes into the company. Even sergeants and officers asked to go in the field their first time with me.

I used to have a bad eye. It was a childhood thing that I grew up with. And I had a operation when I was fourteen years old that corrected the malformity, but the habit of keepin' my eye closed stayed with me. So around camp they took to callin' me Cyclops.

But the Vietn'ese, they called me Montagnard, because I would dress like a Montagnard. I wouldn't wear conventional camouflage fatigues in the field. I wore a dark-green loincloth, a dark-green bandana to blend in with the foliage, and a little camouflage paint on my face. And Ho Chi Minh sandals. And my grenades and ammunition. That's the way I went to the field.

I dressed like that specifically as the point man, because if the enemy saw anyone first, they saw myself. They would just figure I was just another jungle guy that was walking around in the woods. And I would catch 'em off guard.

When we first started going into the fields, I would not wear a finger, ear, or mutilate another person's body. Until I had the misfortune to come upon those American soldiers who were castrated. Then it got to be a game between the Communists and ourselves to see how many fingers and ears that we could capture from each other. After a kill we would cut his finger or ear off as a trophy, stuff our unit patch in his mouth, and let him die.

I collected about 14 ears and fingers. With them strung on a piece of leather around my neck, I would go downtown, and you would get free drugs, free booze, free pussy because they wouldn't wanna bother with you 'cause this man's a killer. It symbolized that I'm a killer. And it was, so to speak, a symbol of combat-type manhood.

The officers wouldn't want to be seen downtown. They had a facade to keep up. I would go downtown and cop women and dope for them. I would bring them back in this truck or sneak them through this tunnel that went from the back of this woman's house for about a hundred yards to our unit. I would get paid or I would get certain privileges.

One day in June my team went on a POW snatch. It was hot as hell. It felt like 120 degrees. I was wearing combat boots this time 'cause we would jump out a helicopter from about 10 feet into the elephant grass. I landed on a punji stick. It was about 2 feet long, sticking up in the ground. I don't know if my weight or whatever pulled the stake loose. But I just kept running because there was no use stopping.

It went right through my boot, my foot, everything. It just protruded through the top of the boot. I couldn't get the boot off. And I was told not to pull it through the leather. The base said if it doesn't give you that much problem, don't mess with it. They would get me out as soon as possible, but not immediately, 'cause they couldn't jeopardize the mission by comin' back out and get us.

They didn't get me out for three days. My foot swell up inside my boot. They had to cut my boot off. It just happened that I was lucky that it wasn't human urine on the stake, or my foot would've been amputated from infection.

After I got better, we was dropped off on the side of a mountain in the Central Highlands. It was so thick in there you could seldom see the enemy. We was to stay in the area five to six days and find out what type of enemy movement was goin' on in the area. There was suppose to be a VC village in the valley, but the village was empty. That first night, though, we observed somewhat like 500 NVA regulars coming through with heavy supplies from North Vietnam.

On the third night, we were setting up the night perimeter, and we heard this noise coming through the woods. The first thing came to mind was the enemy. We got ready. It sounded like so many of them we thought we would get overrun. And the enemy didn't come through. It was just about 200 monkeys. Something had scared them. Which is funny now, but it wasn't funny then.

On the seventh day, we were supposed to snatch a POW to bring back. So we went down on this trail, and they—they ambushed us. Myself, Reginald Solinas, a Mexican brother from California who is my assistant team leader, and one other guy got pinned down in elephant grass. The gunfire was so close that the grass was falling upon us. We laid in the grass for a while too afraid to move. Then us three crawled from under the fire and attacked two enemy positions. I think we got about 16 of 'em, but it wasn't feasible to sit around and count. We had to get out of there.

In movin' around so much we lost contact with the base, and they didn't know where we was. We were out of food and fresh water, so we started eating off the land—berries, weeds, anything. And we drank whatever water we came upon.

Around the tenth day, I started feeling feverish and cold at the same time. I was aching through my body. I was having nightmares and would wake up in cold sweats. My teammates would get on top of me, holding me down saying, "Hey, man, they out there. They on our ass. You got to be quiet, be cool." Solinas took up the slack. I was just out of it with malaria.

On the fourteenth day, we got pinned down on the side of this steep hill. We was in a trench. They was out there callin' to us, sayin' what they gonna do when they capture us. Kill you. Castrate you. Send your private parts home to your wife. But they didn't try to overrun us, because I think they didn't know how many there was of us.

Meanwhile, my mother got a letter stating I was missing in action. The base didn't know where we was.

On the seventeenth day, they found us. We had a instrument called a emergency beeper. It was sending out a sound that you could hear up to 5-mile radius. We were picked up on that beeper. At two in the morning the medevac helicopter came in and grabbed the other four members of the team and disappeared. Solinas and me, we're providing cover while they got on. Then the helicopter disappeared. We inadvertently got left.

Solinas looked at me, and I looked at him. We said, "Brother, this is it."

We was in an open field. We turned 'gainst each other's back and sat down. Placed our ammunition and our grenades in our lap. We locked and loaded. We shook hands, and we said good-bye to each other.

Then the helicopter came back and picked us up. We broke out laughing.

They think we got about 30 KIAs on that mission. And we sustained no casualties ourselves.

Some days when we came back on a POW snatch we played this game called Vietn'ese Roulette on the helicopter. We wouldn't be told how many to capture. Maybe they only wanted one. But we would get two or three to find out which one is gonna talk. You would pull the trigger on one. Throw the body out. Or you throw one without shooting 'im. You place fear into the other Vietn'ese mind. This is you. This is next if you don't talk.

It was never a regular means of deciding this one or that one. You never know their rank or anything until you start to eliminate them one by one. You would sit them down with the ARVN or *chieu hoi* who has come over to your side. So he's translating the conversation back and forth. If one talk too much, you might get rid of him. He has no basic information to give you. He just gonna talk to try to save his life. Or you just might say from the start, "Throw this motherfucker out." The other one will get to talkin'. And then you get that one word of intelligence, one piece of pertinent information.

One particular day we went out of LZ Oasis and captured three prisoners. We on the helicopter coming back, and we radio headquarters we got three bodies. They said, "We only want one." You had to determine which one of these guys you gonna keep and which ones you don't. We tied one by the foot to this rappeling rope, and he's danglin' on the rope. We even dragged him through the trees. He wasn't gonna say anything. The other two wasn't either. So we tied one more the same way, then the other one got to talkin'. We just cut the rope and let the others go. You have to eliminate the others. This was a war-type situation. These two soliders might go kill two of your soldiers if you turn them loose.

I guess my team got rid of about eight guys out of the chopper one way or another, but I only remember pushing two out myself.

One night we were out in the field on maneuvers, and we seen some lights. We were investigating the lights, and we found out it was a Vietn'ese girl going from one location to another. We caught her and did what they call gang-rape her. She submitted freely because she felt if she had submitted freely that she wouldn't have got killed. We couldn't do anything else but kill her because we couldn't jeopardize the mission. It was either kill her or be killed yourself the next day. If you let her go, then she's gonna warn someone that you in the area, and then your cover is blown, your mission is blown. Nothin' comes before this mission. Nothin'. You could kill thousand folks, but you still had to complete your mission. The mission is your ultimate goal, and if you failed in that mission, then you failed as a soldier. And we were told there would be no prisoners. So we eliminated her. Cut her throat so you wouldn't be heard. So the enemy wouldn't know that you was in the area.

This other time we were in a ambush site. This young lady came past. She spotted us. It was too late. We had to keep her quiet. We ran after her. We captured her. We gagged her.

We thought, Why kill a woman and you had no play in a couple weeks? We didn't tie her up, because you can't seduce a woman too well when she tied up. So we held her down. They didn't wear what we call underclothes. So there wasn't nothing when you tear off her pajama pants. She was totally nude 'cept for the top part of her body. But you wasn't after the top part of the body anyway. We found out she was pregnant. Then we raped her.

We still had five days to be out there without any radio contact. So we wouldn't let her go. We didn't want the enemy to know that we were there. She had to die. But I don't think we murdered her out of malice. I think we murdered her because we didn't want to be captured.

After a while, it really bothered me. I started saying to myself, What would I do if someone would do something like this to my child? To my mother? I would kill 'im. Or I would say, Why in the hell did I take this? Why in the hell did I do that? Because I basically became a animal. Not to say that I was involved in both incidents, but I had turned my back, which made me just as guilty as everybody else. 'Cause I was in charge. I was in charge of a group of animals, and I had to be the biggest animal there. I allowed things to happen. I had learned not to care. And I didn't care.

When I seen women put to torture as having Coca-Cola bottles run up into their womb, I did nothing. When I heard this other team raped a woman and then rammed a M-16 in her vagina and pulled the trigger, I said nothing. And when I seen this GI stomp on this fetus after this pregnant woman got killed in a ambush, I did nothin'. What could I do? I was some gross animal.

One time we went to a village to watch for VC, and

this young lady spotted us out in the field. We signaled her not to run, but I guess she didn't understand. We ran behind her to try to snatch her and keep her from notifying other people we were in the area. By the time she got into the center of the village, everybody start to runnin' out. Automatically in a combat-like situation you feel that your life is threatened, so you open fire on anything and everything that moves. It was like instantaneous. You couldn't stop it. That's how you're trained. We killed everything that moved. Dogs. Chickens. Approximately 20 some people, mostly women and children. No young men at all. Couple old men. We checked the huts, the bodies. Two was wounded, and we killed them. We was told not to leave anybody alive that would be able to tell.

I remember how we was told to set an ambush up for anything that walked down this trail, because it was being used as a supply route. And the people was givin' the NVA regulars food and fresh water. We saw Montagnards. They was all dead except these two kids that run away. I found them hidin' in the woods, 'cause this little girl, about three years old, started cryin'. Her brother was about five, and he was wounded in the stomach.

This little fella reminded me of myself when I was small. 'Bout the same complexion. Big head full of curly hair. I just could not kill him. So I brought him and his sister back.

I grabbed the little boy, and I put him against my body. He bled all over me. From the time I left from the helicopter pad to the first-aid station, everybody was talkin' 'bout, "Kill the little motherfucker."

I said, "Naw, you ain't gon' kill this one. He gon' live."

They took me directly to this officer, and he told me I will not bring another Vietn'ese living body into that unit unless I am specifically told to bring prisoners. If it happened again, I would be court-martialed.

With 89 days left in country, I came out of the field.

At the time you are in the field you don't feel anything about what you are doin'. It's the time you have to yourself that you sit back and you sort and ponder.

What I now felt was emptiness.

Here I am. I'm still eighteen years old, a young man with basically everything in his life to look forward to over here in a foreign country with people who have everything that I think I should have. They have the right to fight. I've learned in this country that you don't have the right to gather forces and fight back the so-called oppressor. You have the right to complain. They had the right. They fought for what they thought was right.

I started to recapture some of my old values. I was a passionate young man before I came into the Army. I believed that you respect other peoples' lives just as much as I respect my own. I got to thinkin' that I done killed around 40 people personally and maybe some others I haven't seen in the fire fights. I was really thinkin' that there are people who won't ever see their children, their grandchildren.

I started seeing the atrocities that we caused each other as human beings. I came to the realization that I was committing crimes against humanity and myself. That I really didn't believe in these things I was doin'. I changed.

I stopped wearing the ears and fingers.

I fell in love with a Vietn'ese girl, and I wanted to bring her back with me.

I met her in a geisha house. Most of the girls in there were orphans or prostitutes. Her mother was the mama san. She owned the place. I think her father was French. She was a very lovely and attractive young lady. She was cleaning up the place.

I had no physical relationship with her at all. The relationship we had was strictly intellectual. We just talked, had dinner. She would teach me some of the language and teach me about the customs and the food. I fell in love with her. And I tried to buy her for $1,000.

But her mother said, "No go."

Mai Ling, that was her name, was only sixteen and she had to go to school.

Now I was looking beyond the physical appearance of the Vietn'ese and lookin' at the people themselves. They were very pleasant, very outgoing, very beautiful people. I started disliking myself for what America, the war, and bein' in the Army had caused me to become.

But I was still a animal.

One day my best friend, Frank Koharry, a white guy

from Detroit, brought this axe over to me.

He said, "Hey, man. I want you to have this axe."

"Okay. What the hell you want me to do with it?"

He say, "I want you to hit somebody with it."

And I hit 'im. Hit 'im right there in his arm.

He just looked and said, "Nigger, you crazy."

He went to the aid station, and they bandaged his ass up. 'Bout 32 stitches in his arm.

But we stayed best friends. He would cover for me if I had got in any type of trouble. We was very close.

I took the axe out on one more ambush. And when I heard the VC come down the trail, I jumped out the woods and chopped a fellow's head off with it.

I was still a spec four, and I wanted a battlefield promotion to E-6, a high-ranking NCO. But the captain was telling me I had to take a test.

I said, "How the hell I'm a take a test if I'm out here fightin' and killin' people everyday?"

I was runnin' a LURP team. A Ranger unit. I'm takin' first lieutenants and captains to the field. I got shrapnel wounds. Me and my team was dropped in North Vietnam where American ground troops ain't s'posed to be. We hiding all the time. We become the Viet Cong. Because they got the tanks, the trucks, the airplanes now. We observing their troops, supply movements. Making drawings of their emblems if we don't know who they are. We never get discovered in North Vietnam. The whole time I was in the field, North and South, I never had anyone lose their life on my team. Never. I was good. That is the only test I need to take. I wanted the rank.

But this captain said no.

So we had what they call penlight flare. You had them big bullfrogs over there with the big warts. I took one of those penlight flares and stuck it up the frog's anus, went in the captain's office, and fired it at him.

I had a little farm, with some chickens and a cow. And a Puerto Rican buddy of mine, lived in New Jersey, was going home.

I told him, "Man, when you get ready to leave, I'm gon' kill these chickens, gon' kill this cow. We gon' have the biggest barbecue these people ever seen."

It comes to the day when it's time for him to go home.
I goes out, gatherin' up the chickens. We gon' cut the
chickens' heads off and have barbecue chicken.

So this same captain came up to me. He stared at me.
I had this chicken in my hand.

He said, "Don't cut that chicken up."

He wants it saved for the eggs, I guess.

"You cut that chicken's head off, I'm a have you court-
martialed."

I bent over, and I bit the chicken head off and spit it
in his face. And he throwed up.

My discipline was something to talk about. But a lot
of people felt in the unit that I was the best Ranger in the
company. When we went to the field, we were soldiers.
When we got out of the field, we was crazy. And we was
crazy together.

So they sent me back before the promotion board, and
this black sergeant happened to be a part of it. I had more
respect from the people in the unit than he did. He wouldn't
go near the field. Shit. Anything with the word F he
wouldn't fuck with. He was a certified ass. He did his
best to keep me from gettin' promoted, but they gave me
E-5 anyway.

Well, I happened to be downtown in the whorehouse,
when they called formation. I went back all drunk. They
had just dismissed the formation, when me and a buddy
drove up in a jeep. They called the formation again. The
sergeant called me, gave me my orders for E-5, and I
went back in the ranks. He called us back to attention,
called me back out, and took it from me. We had this
personal thing.

So on his birthday, which was three days later, he was
havin' all the officers in his barracks. They was partyin'.
Music was playin'. Me and some friends of mine got a
M-79 grenade launcher, got behind some sandbags, and
we M-79ed his birthday party.

A couple of people got hurt. The sergeant didn't get
touched. They thought it was incomin'. They had the
whole goddamn place on alert. Everybody runnin' around
tryin' to get their weapons. And we just went and got
drunk.

I think the captain and the sergeant was afraid of me.

I left Vietnam the end of '69. I flew from An Khe to Cam Ranh Bay, still in my jungle fatigues. I hadn't bathed in six months. I had a full-grown beard. My hair was so matted against my head I couldn't pull my fingers through it. I smelled like a cockroach on Christmas. Like Mount Rushmore in the springtime. I was funky. I was really funky.

Then they put me in this big fabulous airplane. I'm sittin' there with filth all over me. From my head to my toe. I felt like I was in the Twilight Zone.

We landed in California when it was dark. We were taken to some barracks. We took a shower, and they gave us some new clothes and a steak dinner. Then I got on another plane.

The same day I left Vietnam, I was standin' back on the corner in Baltimore. Back in the States. A animal. And nobody could deal with me.

I went home. I banged on the door. About four o'clock in the morning. I'm hollerin', screamin' in the middle of the street.

"Wake up, you motherfuckers. Get out of there. I'm home. Shit."

There wasn't nobody there.

I went and found my grandparents, and they told me my parents had moved a month before and where to find them.

When I got there, my mother wouldn't even open the door. She didn't even recognize me.

I started rappin' to her, tellin' her I was her son. And she finally let me in.

It took her a long time to adjust to who I had changed to be. She had heard so much negative rumors about Vietnam vets bein' crazy. She was afraid of me.

Before I got out the service, the My Lai stuff came out in the papers. Some of who had been in similar incidents in combat units felt that we were next. We were afraid that we were gonna be the next ones that was gonna be court-martialed or called upon to testify against someone or against themselves. A lot of us wiped out whole villages. We didn't put 'em in a ditch per se, but when you dead, you dead. If you kill 30 people and somebody else kills 29, and they happen to be in a ditch and the other

30 happen to be on top, whose guilty of the biggest atroc-ity? So all of us were scared. I was scared for a long time.

I got out January '71. Honorable discharge. Five Bronze Stars for valor.

I couldn't deal with goin' to school, because I wasn't motivated. The only friends I made were militant types, because they were the only ones could relate to what I was tryin' to say. I took all the money I saved up and bought weapons. Fifteen-hundred dollars' worth. Rifles, guns. I joined the Black Panthers group basically because it was a warlike group. With the Panthers we started givin' out free milk and other community help things. But I was thinkin' we needed a revolution. A physical revolution. And I was thinkin' about Vietnam. All the time.

I could never have a permanent-type relationship with a lady. It was always sporadic-type relationships. They couldn't understand what I was goin' through when the flashbacks started. Tryin' to talk to them, they wouldn't wanna hear it. Didn't want to hear no gross war stories. Hear about dead people. I just couldn't translate my feel-ings to a lady.

I couldn't discuss the war with my father even though he had two tours in Vietnam and was stationed in the Mekong Delta when I was there. He was a staff sergeant. A lifer. Truck driver. Jeep driver or somethin'. In a sup-port unit with the 9th Division. I couldn't come to terms with him being in a noncombat unit. He died three years ago. He was forty-five. He had a disease he caught from the service called alcoholism. He died of alcoholism. And we never talked about Vietnam.

But my moms, she brought me back 'cause she loved me. And I think because I loved her. She kept reminding me what type of person I was before I left. Of the dreams I had promised her before I left. To help her buy a home and make sure that we was secure in life.

And she made me see the faces again. See Vietnam. See the incidents. She made me really get ashamed of myself for doin' the things I had done. You think no crime is a crime durin' war, 'specially when you get away with it. And when she made me look back at it, it just didn't seem it was possible for me to be able to do those things to other people, because I value life. That's what moms and grandmoms taught me as a child.

I've had a lotta different, short-lived jobs since I been back. I've been into drug counseling in Baltimore City Hospital. Worked in the children's clinic at Johns Hopkins Hospital. In welfare rights as a community organizer. Always human service work.

I don't have a job now. But I would take any human service job, especially where I could show the black kids and the black people that we ought to stop looking toward the stars and start looking toward each other. That our greatest horizons is in our children. And if we don't bring our children up to believe in themselves, then we'll never have anything to believe in.

But they turn their backs on a lot of us Vietnam vet'rans. They say the only way to success is through education. I wanna go back to school and get my B.A., but I can't afford to. I gotta get out there and get a job. Ain't no jobs out there. So what I'm gon' do now? Only thing else I know how to do is pick up a gun. Then I'm stupid. I'm being stupid again. I'm not going forward. I'm going backwards. And can't go any further backwards. I done been so damn far back, I'm listenin' to the echoes in the tunnel.

One day I'm down on Oliver and Milton Avenue. Go in this grocery store. In my neighborhood.

This Vietn'ese owns the store.

He say, "I know you?"

I say, "You know me from where?"

"You Vietnam?"

"Yeah, I was in Vietnam."

"When you Vietnam."

"'68, '69."

"Yeah, me know you. An Khe. You be An Khe?"

"Yeah, I was in An Khe."

"Yeah, me know you. You Montagnard Man."

Ain't that some shit?

I'm buyin' groceries from him.

I ain't been in the store since. I'm still pissed off.

He's got a business, good home, drivin' cars. And I'm still strugglin'.

I'm not angry 'cause he Vietn'ese. I don't have any-

thing against the Vietn'ese. Nothin'. Not a damn thing.
I'm angry with America. When the Vietn'ese first came
here, they were talkin' 'bout the new niggers. But they
don't treat them like niggers. They treat them like people.
If they had gave me some money to start my life over
again, I'd been in a hell of a better situation than I am
right now. We went to war to serve the country in what
we thought was its best interest. Then America puts them
above us. It's a crime. It's a crime against us.

Me and some vet'rans started what we call Base Camp
One. We met at this church. It's to bring the comradeship
that we had in the service into civilian life. To get a pos-
itive foundation to grow on. Because we feel that we are
still in a combat situation.

We talk about the old enemy. The war. Our lives. The
ghosts. The nightmares.

We didn't gain no respect for the Viet Cong until after
we got into combat and found out that we had millions
of dollars worth of equipment which s'posed to be advanced and so technical, and they were fighting us with
whatever was available or whatever they could steal. I
don't think we were well trained enough for that type of
guerrilla warfare. But we were better soldiers, better
equipped. And we had the technology.

In fact, we had the war beat until they started this
pacification program. Don't shoot, unless shot upon. The
government kept handicapping us one way or 'nother. I
don't think America lost. I think they gave up. They sur-
rendered.

And this country befell upon us one big atrocity. It
lied. They had us naïve, young, dumb-ass niggers believin' that this war was for democracy and independence.
It was fought for money. All those big corporations made
billions on the war, and then America left.

I can't speak for other minorities, but living in America
in the eighties is a war for survival among black folks.
And black vet'rans are being overlooked more than everybody. We can't find jobs, because nobody trusts us. Because we killers. We crazy. We went away intelligent young
men to do the job of American citizens. And once we did,
we came back victims.

Sometimes I'm walkin' on the street. I see Kenneth

McKnight. I see Cook, James Cook. Brothers I knew in west Baltimore, in D.C.

One time I saw Kenneth on this corner. When I got there, he had turned down the street and was not there.

Another time I saw James on the other side of the street.

I called 'im, "James. Wait for me, man."

When I got over there, he was gone.

I ask this guy, "Did you see a brother standing right here?"

"No, man."

I still cry.

I still cry for the white brother that was staked out.

I still cry because I'm destined to suffer the knowledge that I have taken someone else's life not in a combat situation.

I think I suffered just as much as he did. And still do. I think at times that he's the winner, not the loser.

I still have the nightmare twelve years later. And I will have the nightmare twelve years from now. Because I don't wanna forget. I don't think I should. I think that I made it back here and am able to sit here and talk because he died for me. And I'm livin' for him.

I still have the nightmare. I still cry.

I see me in the nightmare. I see me staked out. I see me in the circumstances where I have to be man enough to ask someone to end my suffering as he did.

I can't see the face of the person pointing the gun.

I ask him to pull the trigger. I ask him over and over. He won't pull the trigger.

I wake up.

Every time.

**Radarman Second Class
Dwyte A. Brown
Washington, D.C.**

Radarman
Operation Marketime
U.S. Navy
Cam Ranh Bay
March 1968–September 1969

I didn't see the ugly part of the war. I enjoyed the war 'cause I was at Cam Ranh Bay. Cam Ranh Bay was paradise, man. I would say, Boy, if I got some money together, I'd stay right here and live. I wasn't even gon' come back to the United States. I was treated like a king over there. It was no war.

Cam Ranh Bay was the inland R & R spot. That's where the battle-weary people was supposed to come to have R & R in country. They could get everything.

And it was so beautiful, pretty country. Beautiful coral reef. And the sand. Miles of perfect white sand. And the white boys could surf all they wanted. Boy, they had their fun.

We had movies about twice a week. The EM club was open from like eleven o'clock to about ten every day. It had live shows two, three times in a week. USO would come through all the time, too.

The Army had it good; the Air Force, better. We had

it the greatest, the Navy. We had hot and cold running
water. Air conditioning. The Navy always had great food,
but this base was somethin' else. The Vietnamese did all
the cooking, and the blacks supervised the cooking. And
we ate like kings. Lobster, steak, everything. I must have
gained 40 pounds.

I had every luxury in my room. Complete stereo with
reel-to-reel tape. TV. Three-foot refrigerator full of beer
and booze. Cabinets. I had a closet full of clothes. When
you were on duty, you had to dress. But other times,
there was no dress code. If I wanted to put a suit on one
day, I wore a suit. Officers, enlisted men, be lounging
around all day, like the dress code was bathing suits and
sunglasses. And all the officers had a dog. I had three
myself. And Tiffany was my favorite. I called her that
'cause she was pure white.

And there was plenty of pretty Vietnamese women
over there.

And marijuana. Fact is I didn't even smoke marijuana
'til I went over to Vietnam. Didn't even know what marijuana was 'til I went over to Vietnam. And it was given
to us. We didn't spend money in the village for it. It was
a barter system. We'd bring them some steaks from the
base, or a mattress. They would just give us the stuff.

I tell you I ain't even know it was a war if somebody
didn't tell me. I mean I did have to be reminded sometimes
there was a war going on.

Nobody shot at the base but one time. In fact, we didn't
even carry weapons. That one time we thought we was
under attack. All of a sudden, the siren went off. General
quarters. So we brought the boats around, trained the
guns on this hill. We was getting ready to light them suck-
ers up. When we put the spotlight on, we saw two simple-
ass white dudes up there drunk, spraying the base with
two M-16 rifles. So they got a court-martial.

The only serious fighting at Marketime was between
black guys and white guys. There would be this power
struggle over the field. All the white guys wanted to play
softball. We wanted to play basketball. And we could go
into a barracks, and there would be nothing but Confederate flags all over the place. And one time they burned
a cross. And like some of the brothers was getting beat

up. And we were more or less head hunting, too. Payback. We knew that we couldn't get justice going by the book, because out of 500 people, it was only 38 blacks. That's why we started this club, Negro Veterans from Vietnam. We had to protect ourselves. So we lived together, this club. And the whites knew they better not cross our perimeter. This is my territory, this is yours. It was like a city within a city. I wasn't fighting the enemy. I was fighting the white man.

I joined up in '65, a year after I got out of high school. I was working as a stock clerk in Woodies department store in D.C. I come from a family of nine children. My father always worked two jobs, for Sealtest Dairy Co. and drove a taxi. I had three brothers who had been in the Navy, and I was just following them. And I wanted to learn a trade. They told me I could either become a radioman or a radarman. I chose radarman.

The first time I went to Vietnam, we spent the time sitting out there guarding a carrier. I said, Hey, I want to see some of the action. I thought I should be there to fight. Stop the Communism. I wanted to be *in* Vietnam. So I volunteer. I put in for a river patrol boat. So I got sent to Cam Ranh Bay. But when I got there, they said the boat I was s'posed to get on had just got blown out of the water by a mine. So they sent me into the operation center. Operation Marketime was for coastal surveillance, right? And I was in the front office, plotting the courses of the ships. I was radarman. I was telephone talker. The other brothers on the base was in the mess, doing the security on the boats, or seabees. We didn't have no black officers. So I was the elite one, because I was the number one plotter. I was like the spook sitting by the Navy door.

One time I be in the plotting room, and *Time* magazine have a whole bunch of big-shot business people from *Fortune* 500 seein' our operation. I know, 'cause I had the pointer. They told us, show 'em the good part, none of the ugly parts. We doin' this, doin' that, which was not true. Just make it look great, but in actuality it wasn't. Like a operation went foul, fucked up. Lost a whole bunch of lives. But we tell 'em it was a great operation. I can remember we had a contingent of the SEAL team come down. About ten of them. They had the run of the base.

They snapped their fingers—everybody jumped. Nobody messed with them. Shit they did was hushed up. But they had a operation, people lost their lives. Then the report that came out was a complete reversal of what happened. Said everything was great.

I went out on the patrol boats a few times. It was illegally, more or less. But I was bored. We were searching down the lines to keep the sappers away from the generator ship that was giving power to the base. They would be like a kamikaze person. He would strap a charge on his back, just float down the river with a reed out of his mouth, and he would just ram his body right to the ship. Boom. Gone. Blow a hole in the ship. Cause chaos. Or if we saw a little junk, or anything strange, we would go investigate.

One time we'd see bubbles on the surface of the water. It would be at night, okay? We had spotlights. He was trying to get through our lines. So we just dropped concussion grenades into the water. Let 'em explode. Bust his eardrums. That would do the job. And then wait a few seconds after the explosion. Then the body come up to the surface. Then we would just rake his body in, and we would just put him in a sack. We would get one like that once a week. And if that tactic didn't work, they would try maybe around land. Well, then, they would meet the Army people.

Sometimes in the plotting room the white guys would be all drunked up, and when they come down to tense situations, they couldn't perform their duty. Even ones ranked higher than me. But the captain knew that my stuff was good. And Captain Hoffman, he liked the Miracles, the Temptations. So I used to sit in his trailer and make tapes for him. He would let me do anything. I had his jeep at my convenience. The other officers come up when he was away and say, "Can I borrow the jeep, Dwyte?" "No. This is *my* jeep." I got to be a snotty mother over there. And if you wasn't a lieutenant commander or above, you don't even talk to Dwyte. This lieutenant got mad because I didn't salute. I told him, "You ain't got no rank, turkey. You ain't nobody. I work for Captain Hoffman. He got four bars." When he told Captain Hoffman, Captain Hoffman said, "Get out of here." Then Captain

Hoffman say, "Dwyte, you didn't have to do that." I
say, "I know it."

The captain was buckin' for admiral, so sometimes he
went down South to fight the war so he could get his
ribbons. When the captain was there, I worked. If the
captain was not there, I didn't have to work. So I'm
roamin' around free. I could go and get lost in the village.

One time I disappeared for three weeks, and nobody
knew where I was. Captain went down South. I ain't got
nothing to do. I'm gone. "See y'all."

I got my gun. I got my walkie-talkie. I got voice communication to the boat. So the brothers dropped me off
in my girl's village. I stayed in her house. I didn't need
no supplies. I ate what they ate. I slept on what they slept
on. And when the boat came back to get me, I just shine
my flashlight. And George, this brother, say, "Dwyte, that
you?" "Yep. Comin' in."

This other time six of us—all brothers—got caught
though. We had took the boat down the river, maybe about
10 miles. We pulled right up to this village, and we was
in there shacking up with the little village people. Early
in the morning of the second night, that village was attacked by Vietnam terrorists. The Vietnamese killing the
Vietnamese. You could raise the flap on the window and
watch them fightin'. I was kind of scared at first. But the
girls said not to worry. They ain't comin' in here. We're
gonna protect y'all. When the daylight come out, I walked
around the village. And the ARVNs be right there with
guns and everything. Then we got caught sneaking back
to the boat. The Army had sentry dogs and caught us off
limits in the village. They took us back in handcuffs, and
our people said, "All right. We'll take care of 'em." I
opened the door at operations, and Captain Hoffman said,
"All right, Dwyte. Go back to work."

After a while, we'd go to the villages and bring the
women back on the boat. See, the Air Force had built a
village. And the men could go there and buy some pussy.
But the VD rate got so great, they closed it down. So
every Monday, Wednesday, and Friday, the brothers would
sneak five dames on the boats and bring them into this
barracks. The white guys would stand in line outside, and
we would charge them. That's how we made money. Five

minutes cost about a dollar. All night, $20. But all night be only a couple of hours, you know. We'd have a man downstairs collecting the money. And then we'd have another guy up by the cubicles saying, "You go in that one. You go in this one. Times up."

It made the white boys mad that we had this business sewed up. But we did, because we controlled security and nobody could get on base except through us. And this was the paradox about it. The officers knew what was going on, but they didn't mess with us, because we were providing a service. One time the brother on the gate stopped this captain's car. He said, "Captain, what do you have under the blanket, sir?" He wouldn't let him on the base until he had a look. "All right. You got a little girl under there, don't you, Captain? All right, sir. We'll let you in this time, sir." That was a trip, because there was a contingent of Red Cross nurses 'bout a couple of miles down the road. And the American women, white or black, went with the American officers only. If you was enlisted, you couldn't get within striking range. I'm talkin' 'bout don't even look like you want to look at 'em. Even the black sisters. I went up to this black nurse. "No, brother," she told me. "Officer's pleasure only."

I wish I could show you a picture of the cave we had, the brothers. You could only get to it by boat. About a mile down the river. We would go there on weekends. It was like a oasis. We had our own generator power set up. So we got our music boxes hooked up. Brothers ran the commissary, okay? So everything was there. Steaks, beer, liquor. All the women. All the marijuana. Picnic tables. You go swimming right down there from this little grotto. It was like Paradise Island.

One day we had an open house. We invited everybody. The commander of the base came down and said, "You all, this is a good thing you got here." But after that, the white guys tried to crash it. And the executive officer said, "This is all black. That's wrong. We want the whites to be able to share in this also." We said no, and they made it off limits to us and everybody else.

Even so, I really had a ball over there. I didn't take nobody's life, and I'm glad I didn't lose mine. It was really paradise.

When I got out of the service, I started looking for a job. Then I became bitter. I always considered myself to be a good guy. I stayed within the limits of the law, okay? I don't bust nobody's bubbles. I remember pounding the pavement for about a year looking for work. I could not get a job because I was not an ex-drug addict. I was not an ex-convict. I was not an ex-Vietnamese. I had to be an ex-something before I could get work. Being ex-serviceman Vietnam meant nothin'. I said, Damn, I done sacrificed for my country in Vietnam and what do I get. I just became a street urchin. Different odd jobs around the city. I didn't want a regimentated type of atmosphere. In the service it was a hundred people telling one person to do something. I drove a bus. Worked as a laborer. At the Government Printing Office. I finally wound up becoming a elevator mechanic. I liked that. It's been eight years now. My work speak for me. I know what I do is great. And I do it to please myself.

When the Communists took over Vietnam, I began to think the war was a waste of time. I guess we were there for fun and glory. I didn't see us saving nobody. The Vietnamese didn't want us there. I could even think back to how they didn't want the French there. When I read where the Russians got our bases at Cam Ranh, I just figured the people who lived there, they ain't got no say. The poor Vietnamese. Somebody stuck it to them again.

Poor Vietnamese. So many times Americans would degrade them. At Cam Ranh Bay even. In paradise, man. That would be ridiculous. Havin' it so good, yet still treat 'em like trash. Especially these white guys, actin' like "I am the conqueror. I am supreme." Dirt, that's how they treat the Vietnamese, like dirt.

Let's say, riding down the road in the truck, I'll see 'em plow right through a bunch. It's fun to them. You see a Vietnamese might be walking down the street. This guy run up there and goose him. Stick his finger up the man's butt. Or smack him upside the head. Any type of derogatory thing to degrade them.

In the mess hall one day, this white dude wanted a whole bunch of chicken. The Vietnamese girl was doing what she was told. She say, "Two piece chicken. Two piece chicken." So this guy grabbed her by the neck and stuck her head in the mashed potatoes.

And like mama sans be on the base cleanin' our shoes. I give her a dollar. But this guy say, "You ain't do it good enough." Maybe smack her. Or throw her daughter down, pull her clothes up, try to have sex with her. She just thirteen or fourteen. She there tryin' to sweep the floor. The mother was just too scared to say somethin'.

And like they cleanin' up our showers while we takin' a shower. I see it's a woman, I'd keep my towel on me, right? This white guy didn't have nothin' on. He say, "Hey. Come here. Jump on this." He shake his dick at her. The Vietnamese, they be just noddin' their head, grinnin'. He say again, "Hey, Mama San, jump on this." Then he grabbed the little daughter. I say, "Hey, man. Why don't you leave the little girl alone? They just doin' their work." He say, "Aw, fuck it, man. We protectin' them. I'm over here savin' their life."

Me, myself, as a person, knowing from the experience that I had with whites back here in America, I could not go over there and degrade another human being. I see a little Vietnamese in trouble, I even bend over and help him out.

One time, it was a little Vietnamese boy was crying. I just went over there and played with him. Gave him some gum. You know, showing compassion toward him.

And I stopped his tears from crying.

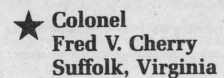

Colonel
Fred V. Cherry
Suffolk, Virginia

Fighter Pilot
35th Tactical Fighter Squadron
U.S. Air Force
Karot (Thailand) Air Force Base
October 1964–December 1964
Takhli (Thailand) Air Force Base
May 1965–July 1965
October 16, 1965–October 25, 1965
Various Prison Camps, Hanoi
October 25, 1965–February 12, 1973

All day long these aircraft would be flying at very low altitudes. Very slow. You could see the pilot, and we would wave to him.

There was this Navy auxiliary base near where I lived in Suffolk, Virginia. World War II had started, and the Navy was training pilots there.

I could see them do combat maneuvering, and I said that's adventure. I was still in elementary school, but I knew I wanted to fly.

Then I heard about the Tuskegee Airmen, the black pilots being trained for the 99th Pursuit Squadron. They went over to North Africa and Italy. I was keeping real close track in *The Afro-American* and the *Norfolk Journal & Guide*, the black newspapers. Yeah, they were doing a good job. Matter of fact, when I read that Lucky Lester shot down these three Nazi planes, I thought this was great. I said to myself, I'm going to be a fighter pilot just as soon as I get old enough.

My parents were just rural people. My father was a laborer, plus he farmed truck crops. Beans and peas and potatoes. We always owned our property. He worked places like the fertilizer factory and the railroads, puttin' in the rails and ties. My mother was a housewife that worked in the fields in the farming season. All they had was elementary school.

There were eight of us—four brothers and four sisters. But we were all kind of tough. I guess we picked it up in the family. I never saw a weakness in the family. My parents were always fair in doing things for people. And we went to church, and they taught us what the Bible says: "Do unto others as you would have them do unto you."

My family was really respected by whites in that area—as much respect as a black could hope to get from a white at that time.

We lived in an area where there might be a white home next to a black home. Ain't no problem there. But you go over to the white farmhouse to get some homemade butter, and you had to "Miss" and "Mister" them. You had to give the whites that master-type respect all the time. The man next door would be *Mister* Gregory. If it came out of your mouth any other way, they wouldn't allow you to have whatever you wanted. They would call my mother Leola, and my father John. Whites always called blacks by their first name. It was sort of understood you had your place.

I remember one day when my older brother, James, was riding with another friend on two bicycles. He was maybe fifteen. One of those two-lane country roads. There weren't many cars that drove down the highways back then. Well, this car pulls along, and it's two white teenagers. I saw 'em reach out and hit James in the back of the head. The bicycle and he went end over end. They were laughing, and they probably said, "Knock that nigger over on his bike."

I was angry, but my mother tried to smooth it over for us juniors. She said, "Well, James is all right. He's not hurt, so don't worry about it. You don't know who it was, so you can't mention it to their parents." Nothing came of it, but it stuck in my mind.

Being in a rural area, there weren't segregated swimming pools or recreation centers where you had to face that kind of racism. But the schools were all segregated. The whites had buses. We had no buses. So on the rainy days, the snowy days, the half-full buses would drive past us, and we would just go on walkin' that 3 miles each way.

But East Suffolk High School, where we went, was a very good school, because back in those times, in the all-black schools, the teachers really cared. They really cared. You would learn, or you would get whacked a little bit. And which I think is great.

My father passed away when I was eleven, and I went to live with my sister Beulah and her husband, Melvin Watts. My mother wasn't too particular in that you had to go to school, but my sister was. She pushed me. She thought I should be a doctor. I felt that also for a while. I majored in biology in college at Virginia Union. But I later decided that medicine isn't really what I wanted to do. I couldn't do my best in it. What I really wanted to do was fly airplanes.

In my second year of college I heard that if you qualified in all respects, you only had to have two years of college to go from civilian life straight into aviation cadet training. So I went to see this Navy recruiter in Portsmouth. I didn't know that the Navy didn't have any black aviators. The recruiter told me to fill out this application for enlisted service. I said, "No. I want to be a pilot." He said, "Oh." And he told me that the individual I would have to talk to was not in the office, and I could stop in some other day.

I went back three more times, and I was told this commander was never in. On the fourth time, I saw this door creeping close. I knew he was there and had been there every time before. I just sort of exploded. I kicked the door open. He thought I was coming across the desk. I said a few choice words to him. They were rather obscene. Then I told him I didn't want any part of his Navy.

Two years later, just before I graduated from college, I went to Langley Air Force Base in Norfolk. I took a whole battery of mental and physical tests for flight school. There were 20 of us, and I was the only black. And this white sergeant did something that in that day he certainly didn't have to do. He congratulated me on the highest overall score in the group. In October of 1951 I started flight school.

In Korea I flew 53 missions in the F-89G fighter-bomber, close air support and interdiction, hitting bridges, dams, railroads deep behind enemy lines. We were carrying 1,000-pound bombs, napalm, 5-inch rockets, and .50-caliber machine guns. I never encountered enemy aircraft, but I had to worry about ground fire. I was hit in the tail pipe once while carrying napalm, but I made it home. It was almost totally dark. I say we had a quarter-mile vision. And I was hit at 50 feet. That's low. That's low. But I climbed up, and the air got thin enough to put the fire out.

I had no problems with the orders to go to Vietnam. It was just like the people in South Vietnam wanna be free to make their own decisions, to have a democratic government. And the Commies were trying to take over. And being a serviceman, when the commander in chief says time to go, we head out.

I'm flying a F-105 by now. It was fast. Mach 2.5. Had good range. Dependable. Comfortable. Good weapons. Good navigational systems. But it was primarily a tactical bomber.

We could carry up to 16 750-pound bombs. On a normal flight, we'd have 10, and then 2.5-inch rockets, and a 20-millimeter cannon, which was a real jewel. It was a far cry from what I could load on a F-84 or F-100.

The F-4 Phantom was certainly a better aircraft for air-to-air combat. And sometimes they would give us coverage. But the F-105 could carry a bigger load, faster and farther. I really loved that airplane.

In 1964 we mainly hit the supplies going down the Ho Chi Minh Trail in Laos. But in 1965 it was sort of open bombing against the North. The initial targets were radar installations. Then we went after military barracks, and some bridges and roads. At the time they didn't have the SAMs, just plain old .57-caliber antiaircraft weapons with radar control. But they were pretty accurate.

I was leading the squadron that day, the twenty-fifth of October '65. The weather was bad. But they sent my wingman up and said you got a mission. The Ironhand.

That's the code name for the missile installations. So I rushed down and got briefed and picked up my maps. We had snake eyes, 500-pound target bombs. And CUBs. Cluster bomb utility. A pellet bomb. This would be my fiftieth mission in this war.

We refueled over Laos, the 19th Parallel. Then just east of Dien Bien Phu, we cut down to low altitude. I mean low. We call it the deck—50 to 100 feet. Just clearing the trees and sometimes below 'em to get under the radar net. I had to keep the wingman and everybody else higher than me. You gotta watch what's gonna be in the way of the wingman, 'cause he's not watching. He's watchin' the lead, and everybody's watchin' him. You flying for all four other guys.

We were on the deck 34 minutes at 500 knots when we reached the IP, the predetermined point, after which you don't make any deviations and just head for the target. And the maximum release altitude for the reference scan was 100 feet. To get the maximum effect for the bombing. Any higher, half of 'em be blowin' themselves up before they get to the ground.

About three minutes from the target, I could see 'em shootin' at me. Just rifle fire. Everybody carried a rifle down there. They just fired up in the air, and you run into it. Then I heard a thump. And I turned off the electrical stuff and hydraulics. I thought they hit something electrical.

I went right to the target, released my weapons, and started headin' out to the Tonkin Gulf, where the Navy could pick me up. The last thing I said to the flight was, "Let's get the F out of here."

Then smoke started to boil up from behind the instrument panel. Electrical smoke. I reached over to turn off the battery and the two generators. And before my hand got to the panel, the airplane exploded. Just blew up. The smoke was so dense, I couldn't see outside of the cockpit. I got a real jolt. Nothing like that thump. I couldn't see whether I was upright, upside down, or what. I just pulled the nose up a few degrees to give me the best ejection altitude. I ejected instantly. At 400 feet. And I prayed.

My lap belt didn't work automatically, so the parachute

didn't open automatically. At the speed I was going, that would have ripped my parachute apart, and I would hit the ground with no chute. The maximum speed to eject at so it won't be fatal is 575 miles an hour. I was doing almost 700. The fact that these gadgets didn't work is why I'm sittin' here now.

I looked around, and I was still in the seat. I reached down and pulled my ripcord. I saw the wingman. I looked down. And boom, boom, boom. I hit the ground.

The wingman radioed back, "Our lead got out. We saw him hit the ground, but I don't think he was conscious."

It looked like I was lying down on the ground, but I was sitting actually. It was 11:44 A.M. I was two minutes from the coast.

I fell right into the arms of a dozen militia. They all had guns. And about a dozen kids with hoes. Now I thought they might chop me up into little pieces with all those farm tools, but they just stood back and giggled. I could hear the bullets zinging past that short time I was coming down, but once I hit the ground, they stopped shooting.

They wanted me to put up both hands. And I could only get up one hand. I didn't realize that my left shoulder was all smashed and my left wrist was broken. It wasn't painful at the time 'cause the nerves were dead initially. Well, I said damn. I can't be moving around. I had my .38 butt showin'. That was what they feared most. So I sort of leaned into my battered arm and shoulder, and from above my head I pointed to my left side. About three times of that, they got the picture. So they move in very slowly, and the first thing they did was relieve me of my piece. Then they took my hunting knife, and they kinda relaxed. Then they took the parachute and my anti-G suit. And they wanted me to get out of my flight suit. It's on very tight. And this Vietnamese wasn't gon' just slide it down, he wanted to cut it someplace. So he brought this knife down. And I scooted back. The knife ended up stickin' in the ground, right between my legs, an inch from my genitals. I was able to calm 'em enough to show 'em how it all works. I took one zipper, and I opened it. They thought that was fun. So they played with the zippers for a minute or so. Up and down. *Zzzzzzzz*. Now the guy with the knife, he's gonna cut my boots off. Well, I didn't want to part with my boots. I started kicking and rolling around on the ground. After a minute, whoever was in charge told him to let me keep my boots.

Now they got me dressed the way they want me, and they are going to walk me 3 miles to this village. I didn't know my ankle was broken, too. I was dusty, hot, sweaty, and naturally, pissed off 'cause I was shot down. Didn't wanna be there. I'm thinkin' about two, three, four months. I'm not thinkin' 'bout years. I'm not even thinkin' six months.

I was the forty-third American captured in the North. The first black. And we are 40 miles east, northeast of Hanoi.

As we got closer and closer to the village, the gongs were gongin'. And that's callin' out the people. So more and more people start to line up along the rice paddies. They were comin' from everywhere. And the militia took me inside this hut in the village. And a medic came in and put something like Mercurochrome on the cuts I got on my face when the instrument panel shattered. And I sat and I sat. After a while, they took all of my paraphernalia, my pens and my pencils, my watch and my Air Force class ring. Then they tied my elbows back behind me again. And they put a black cape over my white T-shirt. My flight suit was still tied around my waist. And they started trekking me down the road again. I didn't have any idea at the time, but I was going to walk 5 more miles to this vehicle.

My shoulder and this ankle beginnin' to pain. And you know how somethin's frightenin' and your heart starts to pound. I never had that. I guess I was too ornery.

Sort of a crowd is followin' me now. And this Vietnamese keeps runnin' up the back of my ankles with this bicycle. I managed to get hold of the handlebars of his bicycle, and I shoved he and bicycle over the hedgerow into the rice paddy. Naturally, he was terribly angry. And he came like he was coming to get me. The honcho sends him back and wouldn't let him go on with us.

Near this time, two jets come over the mountain really low and slow. They're lookin' for me. I'm sure they're honing in on my beeper in my parachute, which is probably back at the village. And the militia shove me in the rice paddy. Luckily the jets didn't see us, 'cause they would've shot us all up. They would think that I'm not there because my parachute is someplace else.

And this guy jumps on me, straddling my back. And he puts his automatic weapon right behind my ear with my nose pretty much in the dirt. And I said to myself, you know, this man might even shoot me.

When we got to the vehicle, they had a cameraman there. And he wanted to take pictures of me walkin' towards him. I wouldn't do it. I'd frown up and fall on my knees and turn my back. Finally, they quit. They never took any pictures. And they got me in the jeep.

And I'm tired and sleepy. My elbows are still tied, so I can't lean back. I kept nudging this guard back there with me, tryin' to tell 'im to loosen the nylon cord. He keep saying, "No. No. No." I was ornery. I tried to push him out of the jeep with my shoulders. He was sort of hangin' off the side when he yells somethin' to the guards up front. They were just constantly talkin' and gigglin'. Then they told him to loosen my arms. The first place they tried to interrogate me appeared to be a secondary school. And they put me in this hut. I did what I was s'posed to do. Name, rank, serial number, date of birth. And I started talking about the Geneva Convention. And they said forget it. "You a criminal."

It was about 500 people out in this schoolyard chattin' Vietnamese. And the interrogator said they said, "Kill the Yankee." I said, "Well, kill me. You are going to kill me sooner or later." So we went round and round, and they got tired of it.

When they were taking me back to the jeep, a Vietnamese reached through a little circle of people around me and rubbed my hand, as if I'm s'posed to rub off on him. Well, all the bolts went forward on the rifles. I don't know if the militia thought he was trying to stab me or what. But he just scooted down and went through the crowd like you see a snake go through the grass, just the top of the grass moving. I think if he'd been in the open, they probably would've shot him.

The next place I end up was Hoa Lo Prison, which we

called the Hanoi Hilton. The first place Americans were brought for serious interrogation and torture. They played rough. And they took me to a room with stucco walls. We called it the Knotty Room. It was about ten o'clock, and I still hadn't eaten since I left the base.

They interrogatin' me all night. Asking me military questions. "Who was in your squadron?" They brought in my maps, which they found where the airplane crashed. They didn't have my point of departure. They didn't have my point of return. I knew what the headings were in my head. They said I killed 30 people. I told them I didn't hurt anybody. Then I made up stuff. I told them I was flying a RF-105. A reconnaissance plane for taking pictures. We don't have any such airplane. We had the capability, but they never made it operational.

They said, "You no have RF-105s."

I said, "We sure do. I had one."

"How does it work?"

"I have no idea. The pilot push the button. Leave it on to where you s'posed to be. Then turns it off. That's all the pilot knows. Okay?"

Some time later, I saw in one of their magazines a picture of the tail of a F-105, and it was called a RF-105. I thought it had to be mine. I don't think anybody else told them that lie.

They would kick the chair out from under me and bang my head on the table. I thought, Damn, that shit really hurts. Then, I'd just relax and think of something pleasant. I would be still flying air-to-air combat. Anything far away from this. But I was totally exhausted, and my head would go down to sleep. And they would just pull it back up and bang it down.

Just before daybreak they took me to this cell. It had the biggest rats you ever saw in your life. They would gnaw through the bottom of the wooden door. And I was sleeping on a concrete floor. No blanket. Just my flight suit. After a few days, they gave me a mosquito net. And that was God's gift to get that mosquito net.

Every morning they would take me to a place we called Heartbreak. These cells were their torture chambers. Built-in leg irons. And very high security.

At the time, James Stockdale and Duffy Hutton, Navy pilots, and Tom Curtis, an Air Force buddy, were in the camp. They were the first guys I made verbal communication with. They gave me the little bit of information they had acquired and told me to hang in there with the Code of Conduct.

I was taken to Cu Loc Prison—the Zoo—in southwest Hanoi on November 16. A Navy guy, Rodney Knutson, was in the cell next to me. In the morning and in the night one of us would tap one time and the other would answer with two taps. But I didn't see any Americans until the twenty-seventh, when they brought in Porter Halyburton, a Navy lieutenant jg, who got shot down five days before me. He looked like a scared rabbit, like I did.

Hally was a Southerner, who went to Sewanee Military Academy in Tennessee and Davidson College in North Carolina. The guards knew I was from the South, too. They figured under those pressures we can't possibly get along. A white man and a black man from the American South. And they got a long-term game to run.

At the time, Hally is a very handsome, young gent. Early twenties. Coal-black hair. And just what you expect a Frenchman would look like. I figured any white I saw in Vietnam other than our guys would be French. I thought he was a French spy put in my cell to bleed me of information.

He didn't trust me either.

He had a problem believing that I fly. And a major, too. He hadn't seen any black pilots in the Navy, and he didn't know anything about the Air Force. They had told him in the Navy that one reason blacks couldn't fly was 'cause they had a depth-perception problem.

For days we played games with each other. Feelin' each other out. We would ask each other a question. And we both would lie. He would change the name of the ship he came from. I didn't tell him much more than I told the Vietnamese, like I had flown out of South Vietnam. I figured he went back and told them the same lies I told him.

Finally, we got to the place where we could trust each other. It started when he told me about bathing. "When's the last time you bathed, washed up?"

I said, "Almost a month, I guess."

"Well, you should go at least every three or four days. I'll ask the guard."

Then he taught me the code. The first series of taps was in a line, and the next series in the column. Well, I learned it in reverse.

Hally said, "What in the hell is that?"

And I got vindictive. "That's what you told me."

"You learned it outta phase."

It didn't take long to learn it right. It's amazing how sharp the old mind gets when it doesn't have a lot to do.

Then he slipped out and kinda whispered it to Knutson next door.

Our cell door opened onto a porch. Then it was left down a hallway. We had peepholes. And if you caught the guard just right, you could slip out. But before long, they did something about the peepholes.

In December my ankle had swollen so big they let somebody come put a cast on it. They didn't x-ray it. But luckily it turned out okay. Only thing I haven't had trouble with since. My wrist had healed by itself, but I was in constant pain with my shoulder.

Early in February, when the bombing paused and President Johnson sent his fourteen-point peace plan to President Ho Chi Minh, they decided to schedule those of us still laying around injured for operations in case peace came and we'd be goin' home. On the ninth they operated on my shoulder and put me in a torso cast down to my hipline. But I didn't get a penicillin pill or a shot.

Ho Chi Minh gave President Johnson a very definite negative. The U.S. and its lackeys should withdraw all their troops from South Vietnam and allow the Vietnamese people to settle their own affairs. They said that from day one, and they said it when we left. And they got just that.

When they decided that we weren't going home, you were just left in the state that you were in. No medicine. No treatment. And I was in a bad state with this torso cast.

After a while, the incisions got infected. There are sores all over my body, and the pus is caking up. By early

March, I'm just phasin' in and out. I'm totally immobile.

Hally was feeding me. And he always made me welcome to any part of his food. If he thought I'd want the greens out of his soup, he'd give them to me. After I got really bad, they gave me sugar for energy. It was really something desired by all of us. Put it on the bread, and it would taste pretty good. Hally had the opportunity to eat the sugar himself, but he didn't.

I don't know why, but I would dream then about vanilla wafers and canned peaches. I just felt like it would be the best thing to taste in the world.

I couldn't stand up. Hally would take me to the wash area, hold me against the wall while he manipulated his towel, wet it, soap it, and wash my whole body. I was an invalid.

I would tell him when I had to go to the bucket. He'd put me on the edge of the bunk. Lean me back so I wouldn't pass out. And sturdy me over the bucket until I do what I had to do.

He'd take whatever clothes he had to make me a doughnut to sleep on. Naturally it got covered with the drainage he would have to wash out. And the room smelled like hell. Oh, terrible. And Hally had to keep the wounded side of me by the window to try to keep some of the smell out.

I was just lying there dying.

And in the delirium I was having illusions like you can't believe.

I just would leave my body.

I would go right through the wall.

One time, when I was coherent, I told Hally, "We have B-58s in the war now." I had been on a mission in a B-58 the night before. "They gave me an air medal, but I told them to give it to Jerry Hopper, another guy in the squadron. I told 'em I have enough."

Hally says, "That right?"

"Yes. The war'll be over soon."

Another time I left my body and went into town. Before then, when they moved you, it was in blindfolds. And if you could peek, you couldn't tell much 'cause it was at night. But the first time I was able to see anything in daylight in Hanoi, I recognized a stream, bridges, and other things I saw when I left my body.

Then my temperature really got high. I was just burning. I wasn't eating anything. My body was eating itself. And I found myself in this little, sorta greasy-spoon restaurant, we would call it. It was in South Vietnam. I was hungry, and this Vietnamese lady was frying pork chops on this vertical grill. I'm just waiting to get my order to eat. And this little fella comes in and says he's from somewhere just in the middle of North Vietnam. Says he was at a radar site, and he took care of the air conditioning. I told him I'm a prisoner and I have to go back to North Vietnam. And I said I'm having problems with my air conditioning. He said he'd see what he could do for me when he got back to the radar base.

Well, I wake up. Sorta come around. And I think I'm dying. I just can't stand the heat. I open my eyes, and I see right up on my chest two little men, 'bout a foot high. Big eyes and big heads. They are dark, but I can't make out their features. Their hands are almost normal size. And I see them working around my chest. To me, it's my air conditioning. Just every few seconds I say, "Please hurry." Then my temperature would break. And I would think, Thank God they did it in time.

And I'm scared the guards will see them and take them away. I can't raise up to look for them, so I call Hally. "Did you see anything off the end of the bunk?"

"Like what?"

"Well, do you see anything?"

"No."

"'Bout time for the guard, isn't it? You don't see anything look like little men?"

He looks again. "No. I don't see anything."

Hally didn't say, "Fred, have you gone crazy?" He was really cool. He accepted these little men and pretended they kept my air conditioning going.

Finally, on March 18, they took me to the hospital to take the cast off. I was down from 135 pounds to 80 pounds. When the guys in the camp saw 'em take me on a stretcher, they said, "He's gone. We'll never see Fred alive again."

When they took the cast off, a lot of skin came off with it. Then they washed me down with gasoline out of a beer bottle. That was 'bout the pits. I passed out from the fumes. I think my pulse stopped, because when I came to, they were slapping my arteries. Then they gave me a blood transfusion, fed me intravenously, and sent my butt right back to Hally.

The cast is off, but I'm still opened up. The flesh is draining away. The bed sores are opened up, 6, 7 inches up my back. Hally keeps my shoulder wrapped, but it's still smellin'.

On April 10, they finally operated. I was so weak they kept me there 22 days. They put me in a little damp room at the end of a hallway, away from everybody. The guard would bring me food twice a day, but he didn't particularly wanna feed me. I couldn't move my hands. I'm all hooked up. But these two teenage girls who cleaned the rooms would bring me fruit and candy. One would watch for the guard, while the other would take a whole banana and just stick it down my mouth. And when they gave me hard candy, they would try to tell me, don't let it get stuck in your throat.

After a while, I started to get a bad infection again. I mean really bad. It looks like gangrene is settin' in. So they decide to take me and John Pitchford—I think he got shot in the arm—to the hospital for an operation. It's the night of July 6, when they took everybody else to march down the streets of Hanoi.

This time there was no anesthetic. They just took a scalpel and cut away the dead flesh, scraped at the infection on the bones. I knew about what they should have to do, so I knew they were makin' it more painful than necessary, being very sadistic. I couldn't believe that a human being s'posed to be practicin' medicine was doing this.

Well, I knew they wanted me to cry out. Like a test of wills. We gon' break him.

Balls of perspiration was poppin' off me. Size of your fingertips. I was totally dehydrated. It was the worst straight pain I had yet known.

They had my face covered with a sheet. And they kept raising it to see if I'm going to beg for mercy, going to scream.

And each time they looked down at me, I would look

at them and smile.

They kept at it for three hours. And I kept thinkin', I can take it.

When they gave up, I was still smilin'.

Hally got back to the cell first. The public had gotten unruly during the march. They could hardly control them. They were kickin' the guys, throwin' rocks at them. Hally was all black and blue.

When the guard brought me to the door, Hally gasped, "Fred."

Blood was running everywhere, down to my feet. Hally caught me, and put me in my bunk. "Fred, what in the world did they do to you?" He thought I had been where he had been.

I cried, "Oh, Hally."

We both shed a tear or two.

"No, no. I went to the hospital."

Four days later, the guards came to get Hally. They just walk in and say, put on your long-sleeve prison pajamas, gather your stuff, and let's go.

Tears start to roll down my eyes. I'm just hoping nothing happens to him.

We cried.

And he was gone. It took about two minutes.

It was the most depressing evening of my life. I never hated to lose anybody so much in my entire life. We had become very good friends. He was responsible for my life.

Then they moved in John Pitchford and Art Cormier.

From August 4 to the end of the year, they would torture us once or twice a day. They wanted everything they could get about your personal life, your family. I would tell them anything, like I didn't have children. And they would make you redo it. You are tellin' so many lies, they know you are lying.

They would cup their hands and hit you over the ears. And the guard would come up behind you and kick the stool out. Or make you stand on your knees with your hands in the air. Or stand at attention with your nose to the wall, both hands in the air. In my case, one hand is all I can get up.

There was an officer we called Dum Dum, because he

really was kinda stupid. One day in August of 1967, he said, "You have a bad attitude, and you disobey camp regulations. You communicate with other criminals. You must be punished. You must have 'iron discipline.'" I said, Oh, shit. The torture is starting again.

I ended up in a place we called the Gatehouse with Larry Guarino and Don Burns. Except when you would eat—twice a day if you're lucky—and go wash, they kept you in manacles and leg irons.

Dum Dum would order the fan-belt treatment, beating with strips of rubber. Or you would be struck with bamboo. And you would fall around the floor because of the irons.

In November they took us to a building called the Barn. Burns was already there. He had lost 30 pounds. He was death warmed over. I was coughing up a big lump of somethin'. It was too dark in the damn cell to see what I was spittin' in the night bucket. We took a little white pot from where we bathed back to the cell, and I coughed into it.

I says, "Damn, it's blood."

Larry says, "We gon' have to tell the officer."

"No. No. I ask them for something, they gon' ask me for something. I ain't giving nothing." Not after three months of having my ass beaten.

"Well, we're going to because there's something wrong."

Thank God he did.

Some days later they x-rayed me at the hospital. After they brought me back, this officer came in. I knew something was wrong. This officer got so nice. But he just told me I had a problem. Not until early February do they tell me I have a bone that's in my lung, very close to my heart. I'm thinkin' it came off the rib cage from the beatings. I knew the shoulder area had fused together.

But they didn't open me up until the first of May. They removed my seventh rib to get the chips out. And when they put me back together, they did one thing I'm sure was intentional. They left some nondissolvable stitches in.

The Vietnamese guarding my hospital room would make me get up and mop the floor. But this lady who worked in the kitchen sorta chewed him out when she saw it. He wasn't the worst guard in the world, because he would close the door so nobody else would see her moppin' the floor instead of me. And she would bring me whole loaves of bread and put them in the drawer by the head stand. She knew nobody was gonna look in there, because they didn't want to touch anything I touched as sick as I always was.

They brought me back to the camp on May 27 and kept me in solitary. That stretch would run 53 weeks, the longest of 700 days of solitary that I would have.

Now they want me to make tapes, write statements denouncing the war, denouncing our government, and telling young GIs, especially black ones, they don't have any business in Vietnam fightin' for the American imperialists.

They want it from me more than anybody because I was the senior black officer. They wanted it bad. And by this time, our black guys are doing good work, hurtin' 'em down South.

Until the end of November they interrogated me four or five hours a day. Two of 'em, the good guy and the bad guy. The bad guy never gets to be the good guy. But the vice camp commander, he swings both ways. We called him Lump. He had a tumor on his forehead. The good guy was Stag. That's an acronym for Sharper Than the Average Gook. He was a very good interrogator. He read a lot of novels, and he knew black literature. He had read *Raisin in the Sun* and *Invisible Man*. He knew more about Malcolm X than I did. And we was versed in Stokely Carmichael's philosophy. Absolutely. Stokely was helping them with broadcasts from Hanoi.

In those brainwashing sessions, Stag would say, "Xu, we will change your base, your foundation."

They called each of us by a Vietnamese name. A *xu* is a little brass coin, like a penny. Maybe they gave me the name because of my color. Regardless, they made me feel that I was worth less than a penny.

I said, "You tryin' to brainwash me?"

And he would back off a little. They hated the word brainwash. Scared 'em.

Stag and Lump couldn't understand why I couldn't be on their side, on the side of another colored race. I told them, "I am not Vietnamese. My color doesn't have nothin' to do with it. We have problems in the U.S., but you can't solve them. Like you, I am a uniformed soldier. If I have you in the position you have me, I wouldn't expect you to do what you want me to."

I'm being as tactful as I can.

"A soldier's a soldier. Things go on that we have no control over. I'm still an officer in the United States services. I will respect that, and I would hope that you will respect that of me. I can't do what you ask."

They never got to home plate. Just like when they beat me, I always kept in mind I was representing 24 million black Americans. If they are going to kill me, they are going to have to kill me. I'm just not going to denounce my government or shame my people. All this time the wound don't heal up, because of these stitches. They looked like fishing cord to me. All black. But they're swearing there wasn't anything there. It would heal up.

They say, "No, no. These honorable stitches. Don't have to take out."

When I asked for a Band-Aid to cover the hole, Stag said, "We don't have. Many injured Vietnamese. We must use all medicine for Vietnamese."

I was hemorrhaging daily. And one time I woke up, and the stuff comin' out of the hole looked green. I am having a serious problem.

So when I go to interrogation, I ask for a pill. They said no. So I start quiverin' and shakin' on the stool. Stag starts to get excited, and he has a guard take me to my cell. Then they bring me out into the yard, so all the guys can see them give me medication. And when they pulled the needle of penicillin out of my arm, I was so infected, honest to goodness, that it felt like I was gettin' ready to explode. My body was so poisoned, I was about as sick as any time before.

The next day they took me to the hospital, took the stitches out, and cleaned up the hole. They knew exactly where the stitches were. And from that day, November 28 to the next February, 1969, they stopped puttin' the pressure on.

They put me back with Art Cormier in April. And for several days I was coughin' up blood clots in the mornin'.

I think it was because I was tryin' to exercise, primarily runnin' in place. And I had to cut that out.

One morning I spit into a piece of paper, because it felt like somethin' in my throat that wasn't normal.

I said, "Art, you won't believe this."

He said, "What you got?"

"Look at this."

It looked like a piece of regular fishing cord. Almost one year to the day they had operated, I had coughed up a piece of the stitching.

So we showed it to the guard, and he sent for the medic. Then they gave me some antibiotics.

I had been coughing up so much blood and mucus that the stitching was coming out that they hadn't removed.

I stayed with Art until the escape attempt May 10. Ed Atterbury and John Dramesi dyed themselves with a mix made from iodine pills, went through the roof and over the wall, shorting out the electrical shock on the barbed wire. But they were captured before morning. They brought them back blindfolded to the headquarters building in the camp. Then they were taken off to torture. Atterbury was never seen again.

By now we had secret committees for everything. We had the morale committee. We had an entertainment committee. Education committee. And, of course, we had the escape committee. And that was the one they really wanted to know about now.

So for months they really got hard on us. There was a shortage of water and toilet paper. They cut down your bath time to once every two weeks. No more cigarettes. And they nailed boards over the windows, so there was no fresh air. And they separated the senior officers, like me and Art and Bud Day, and worked us over with bamboo and rubber straps in the interrogation room. I don't think anyone got it nearly as bad as Bud and Dramesi.

It was no point in me thinkin' about escape at the Hanoi Hilton with only one good hand and one good leg. And I just forgot about gettin' over the wall. It was too high. I didn't have anything in my room to climb up on. And there was broken glass cemented to the top of the wall. Since they drove me in from forty miles, I knew all the checkpoints. You're not goin' anyplace. And at the Zoo, the senior officer would never approve anybody as injured and crippled as I was trying it. But I always thought about it.

And we always thought about rescue. We had a whole plan for aidin' any outside force that came to rescue us. We were organized into teams to go after the guards. We had plans to take over. We knew who would go to which doors first.

I learned about the Son Tay raid when they took us all to the Hanoi Hilton. The Green Berets got in there but found no Americans. That was in November of 1970. We put the story together from drawings the South Vietnamese prisoners made and left for us to find. They showed something like a C-130 transport, walls, guards, and bodies on the ground.

Not more than a dozen guys ever did anything that was aid to the enemy. Most of them were young troops, Army and Marine, who were captured in the South. But there were two senior officers who refused to take orders from us, made tapes for them to play on Radio Hanoi, and met with the antiwar people, the Jane Fonda and Ramsey Clark types.

Those two got good treatment. Good treatment. Extra food. Different food. Stuff to read. They could stay outside most of the day. They didn't lock 'em up until late in the evening. And they had fish bowls in their cell.

We were furious. And the Vietnamese knew it. They wouldn't let us get close to them. They would have been hurt very badly. Or worse.

I had less respect for those two than I did for our captors. Most of us did. We considered them traitors then. And I feel the same way today.

A few guys went through deep depressions and weren't cooperatin' with us as much as they should. But that is normal when you go through a deep depression. We just wouldn't let them quit. We would just keep bangin' on their walls and tell them if the guard hears, you are just as involved as us, so you might as well bang back. And it worked. They would start answering.

No matter how rough the tortures were, no matter how sick I became, I never once said to myself, I want to take my own life or quit. I would just pray to the Supreme

Being each morning for the best mind to get through the interrogations, and then give thanks each night for makin' it through the day. And you would meditate with your cellmate. Or tap the letter C from wall to wall through the camp. Then everyone would stop for silent prayer. C was the call for church.

Man, did we miss the movies. And when we finally got together, we have a movie committee, too. Bradley Smith, a Navy guy, could give you the best movie reviews you could ever hope for in your life. He would hardly miss a detail. Last almost as long as the movie. You could just close your eyes and see it.

John Pitchford was a racin' enthusiast. He knows every horse ever raced. He could do the same thing with a Kentucky Derby race Bradley did with a movie.

But I was fortunate to know one guy who talked sex from the time he got up until the time he was sleepin'. That's every day. And I really tuned it in. For the first several months, I was kind of pushin' it in the background. Then for months and months I was too far gone to think about it. And when you become more relaxed, natural things happen. If you didn't masturbate, you'd have wet dreams.

Man, in solitary, in the darkness, you would see everything you have ever done. You would fantasize anything you wanted. The mind goes like a computer. It picks up from everywhere, compensating for all the deprivations that you're goin' through.

Women? I had fantasy affairs with the ordinary women that I met in my lifetime. I had fantasy affairs with the most beautiful women in the world. Jewels of women. I did movie stars. I never would've been so successful out here.

I always wanted to race cars. I would race cars for hours on a race track. And I've never been on one in my life. And I would do air-to-air combat. And I would calculate and recalculate a bomb release. Lots of that.

And I would re-create the times I'd go picnicking with my children. Play ball with the boys. And come home and give everybody a ride through the area on a motor scooter. And I would imagine what size they are now.

In my dreams I always went somewhere and had to go right back, or go to the airport but the plane had left.

One time I was home. My daughter was walkin' down the country path. She was cryin'. And I never got to ask her why. I had to go back.

When I was shot down, the Air Force got my family out of Japan back to Virginia as soon as possible. Donald was twelve, Fred was ten, Debbie was eight, and Cynthia was six. Beulah sheltered them until they found a house near Langley, and they had all the facilities, Navy and Air Force, they needed within 15 minutes.

My wife got my first letter in December of 1969. My mother got to see it before she died of a stroke a few months later. She died believin' I was comin' home.

I got my first letter from home in May of 1970. From my sister. She had a helluva time gettin' forms from the Air Force to write to me or to send packages. 'Cause she wasn't the next of kin.

My wife was tellin' the kids that I was dead. I wasn't comin' home.

In November '72 I received a letter from my oldest son.

By then we knew the negotiations were going on in Paris. We could hear the B-52s. And we knew that they were going to solve it. When the bombing stopped, we knew they didn't have any more missiles. And that the agreements were going to be signed.

The sick and wounded, the guys who had been there the longest, were the first to fly out. But the Vietnamese sorta squeezed in the guys who had gone along with them. I guess that was more payoff for being traitors.

The first meal I wanted when I got to the Philippines was sausage and eggs.

I told the dietician, "One platter of scrambled eggs. One platter of sausage patties. Laid on two plates."

She said, "But, sir. It's five o'clock in the afternoon."

"I don't care."

She thought I had been to sleep and woke up thinking it was morning.

She brought the two plates. And I ate it. I ate it. I ate it.

Then I called Beulah.

She said, "You don't have a very nice situation to come back to."

I didn't ask any questions.

I said, "I guess I understand."

I didn't receive a single letter or package from my wife. And I'm not crazy. She's either dead, or she's taken off. I was really hopin' it was the way it was. I was hopin' it would be that way than she died.

"How are the kids?"

She said, "They're okay."

Then Beulah told me the boys had dropped out of high school and were in the Army.

I thought they would have been in school, but little did I know.

General Chappie James was handling the return of POWs. We were old friends, and he knew about my situation at home. So he sent a friend of ours, Colonel Clark Price, to escort me home.

Clark told me another man was involved. A child was born in October '69. A girl. The money was gone. My allotments. Salary. Everything. And the kids were in the Army.

I didn't even ask him about my coins. I got depressed; the boys weren't in school.

I wanted to be taken to Norfolk Naval Hospital in Portsmouth. That was closest to home. But Clark said Andrews Air Force Base near Washington, D.C., might be better, considering the situation I was returning to. I guess many people were afraid I might have been crazy enough to do somethin' violent. They didn't want to put me where the sparks might fly.

I asked to see Beulah and her husband. My sons made arrangements to get there. My daughters didn't come at first. They were living with my wife. Even after my name appeared in the newspapers that we were being released, she still told them I wasn't coming home. It was a mistake.

When she did come to Andrews, I told Clark I didn't want to see her.

Clark said, "I think you should."

"Okay."

I wouldn't see her with the door closed. My attorney told me not to put myself in a position where I could have the opportunity to cohabitate.

I asked her to be reasonable, to agree to an uncontested divorce so the stuff won't come out and embarrass the kids.

She said no, she didn't want a divorce. And she tried to fight it. I understand that, too. You been gettin' a nice fat check all these years, and all of a sudden, you ain't got it. Who's gonna take care of this and that?

There was no waiting period for the divorce. 'Cause I'd been separated seven and a half years.

I sued the Air Force because they were negligent in handling my money while I was away. About $150,000. And the U.S. Court of Claims upheld me. In the services we have volunteers and active-duty people who look after families split apart like mine was. They knew every letter that went one way or the other, so they knew she wasn't writing me. Something's gotta be wrong. They let her take the money out of my account to have the child in a civilian hospital. They didn't question that. The $450 a month allotment that was going to my savings bank? They gave her that, too. A form was signed on October 25, 1965, three days after I was shot down. It had to be forged. But the people handlin' the POW families were so into keepin' these families quiet, they'd do anything.

I hope my case sets a precedent. A serviceman who gets in a position like mine must be better looked after in the future.

They gave me an extensive battery of mental and physical tests at Andrews. They said the best thing they could give me was a little more forward movement in my arm.

I said, "No. What the hell. I've lived with it all these years and got used to it."

The only time it's aggravating is when I'm trying to do something like hang a picture. Or reach over my head. Now I can change a light bulb almost as fast with one hand as you can with two.

Physically, I can never recover totally. I still suffer muscle spasms. My eyes are not as good as they should be at this point in my life. That's because of all the periods of darkness. The years of darkness. And I don't hear too well out of my left ear. That was where the right hook usually got to first. But I still feel extremely fortunate.

They gave me the Air Force Cross, two Bronze Stars, and two Purple Hearts for resisting the enemy. I had already received the Distinguished Flying Cross and the Silver Star before for action in combat.

I had reached the rank of full colonel two months before my release.

In September of '81 I retired. Seventy percent disability. Thirty years.

I never dreamed about Vietnam. Not once since comin' back. But I still think about how we could have won the war. It should have been planned to hit the military targets early. It was only near the end that we started. And there would have been a lot less lives lost. And with proper leadership South Vietnam would've lasted a hell of a lot longer than it did. The war just went the way it did because the military was not allowed to win it. That's all.

I don't harbor no animosities against the Vietnamese people at all. North or South. Except as individuals. Isolated cases.

I guess I would still like to get my hands on Dum Dum. I'd like to have Dum Dum. I would know Dum Dum anyplace.

There were Vietnamese who were compassionate. The ones who fed me with bananas and pieces of candy in the hospital, taking a great risk to do that. And the doctor who acted like a doctor whatever the policy was in treating a prisoner. And the guard who caught me red-handed communicatin'. And he refused to turn me in because of my health being on the low side at the time. All he said was, "No, Xu. No. No."

After the release, I kept in touch with Hally. In 1977 he spent two weeks with me while he was doing research at the Pentagon for his master's degree. I gave him the key to my home in Silver Spring, Maryland. I gave him the key to a car.

We talked about how we looked at each other the first time we met. We talked about what we learned from each other. We remembered certain guys and tried to track down where they were. We rehashed the whole thing.

Naturally, I thanked him again for really, really saving my life. Other guys would've done the same thing, okay? But they didn't have the opportunity.

One daughter—the one who cried in my dream—lives with me now and goes to college. And back home in Suffolk there is a Colonel Fred Victor Cherry Scholarship Fund to help capable kids who run short of money get to college.

And I speak across the country for the Tuskegee Airmen's Association—black fighter pilots of the last three wars—telling young black people to study engineering, science, and technology.

Maybe one of those young black lads that hears me will walk across a field one day, look up at an airplane, like I did so long, long ago, and say, "I'm going to fly. I'm going to be a fighter pilot."

Chronology of Major Events in the Vietnam War

September 2, 1945   After the departure of Japanese occupation forces, Ho Chi Minh and the Communist-dominated Viet Minh Independence League established the Government of the Democratic Republic of Vietnam in Hanoi.

September 22, 1945   French troops returned to Vietnam.

December 19, 1946   The Viet Minh began an eight-year war against the French occupation with attacks in the North.

May 8, 1950   The U.S. announced it would provide military and economic aid to the French in Indochina, starting with a grant of $10 million.

June 27, 1950   President Truman announced the dispatch of a 35-member military mission to Vietnam, followed a month later by an economic aid mission.

December 23, 1950   The U.S., France, Vietnam, Cambodia and Laos signed an agreement which granted U.S. aid and recognized their common interest in defending the principles of freedom.

May 7, 1954	The survivors of the French garrison at Dien Bien Phu surrendered to the Viet Minh.
July 1954	The Geneva Agreements were signed, partitioning Vietnam along the 17th Parallel and establishing an International Control Commission to supervise compliance.
October 11, 1954	The Viet Minh took formal control over North Vietnam.
October 24, 1954	President Eisenhower advised Premier Ngo Dinh Diem that the U.S. would provide assistance directly to South Vietnam rather than channeling it through the French.
May 10, 1955	South Vietnam made a formal request for U.S. military advisors.
July 20, 1955	South Vietnam refused to participate in Vietnam-wide elections as called for in the Geneva Agreements on the grounds that elections would not be free in the North.
April 28, 1956	A U.S. military advisory group replaced French training of the South Vietnamese Army.
January 3, 1957	The International Control Commission declared that neither North Vietnam nor South Vietnam had complied with the Geneva Agreements.
June 1957	The last French military training mission left South Vietnam.
July 8, 1959	Two U.S. military advisors were killed during a Communist attack at Bien Hoa.
May 30, 1960	A U.S. Special Forces team arrived to assist in training.
December 31, 1960	Nine hundred American troops were in Vietnam.
January 29, 1961	Radio Hanoi proclaimed formation of the National Front for Liberation in South Vietnam.
March 19, 1961	The National Front announced an offensive to prevent presidential elections.
May 11, 1961	President Kennedy dispatched 400 Special Forces soldiers and 100 additional military

	advisors, and authorized a campaign of clandestine warfare against North Vietnam to be carried out by South Vietnamese personnel.
October 18, 1961	A state of emergency was declared in South Vietnam by President Diem.
November 1961	The U.S. enlarged the military advisory mission and assigned combat support missions to South Vietnam.
December 31, 1961	U.S. forces in Vietnam totaled 3,200.
February 8, 1962	The U.S. established the Military Assistance Command in Saigon. Meanwhile, U.S. Special Forces were training Montagnards for combat against Viet Cong guerrillas.
December 29, 1962	South Vietnam proclaimed 39 percent of its population living in fortified "strategic hamlets."
December 31, 1962	U.S. forces in Vietnam totaled 11,300.
May 8, 1963	Twelve people were killed in Hue in rioting during a celebration of Buddha's birthday. Rioting and anti-government demonstrations spread elsewhere in the following weeks.
September 2, 1963	President Kennedy criticized the Saigon government for being out of touch with the people and said that the U.S. would play only a supportive role.
November 1, 1963	A military coup with tacit U.S. approval overthrew President Diem. Diem was assassinated with his brother, Ngo Dinh Nhu.
November 4, 1963	The U.S. recognized the new government in Saigon.
December 31, 1963	U.S. forces in Vietnam totaled 16,300.
February 4, 1964	The Viet Cong launched an offensive in Tay Ninh province.
June 20, 1964	General William C. Westmoreland took command of MACV.
August 1964	North Vietnamese torpedo boats attacked the U.S. destroyers *Maddox* and *Turner Joy*, prompting the U.S. Congress to adopt the

Tonkin Gulf Resolution endorsing measures needed to repel attacks on American forces.

December 31, 1964 — The first North Vietnamese Army regulars appeared in South Vietnam. U.S. forces in Vietnam totaled 23,300.

February 7, 1965 — The Viet Cong attacked the U.S. base at Pleiku, killing eight Americans.

March 2, 1965 — "Operation Rolling Thunder," a sustained American aerial bombardment of North Vietnam, was launched.

March 8, 1965 — The first U.S. Marine battalion arrived at Danang.

March 19, 1965 — The first full U.S. Army battalion arrived.

April 7, 1965 — President Johnson proposed negotiations to end the war and offered $1 billion in aid to Southeast Asia, but Hanoi denounced the plan.

July 28, 1965 — President Johnson announced his decision to greatly increase U.S. combat forces in Vietnam.

October 1965 — U.S. troops launched the month-long Ia Drang campaign, which was the first major confrontation between U.S. and North Vietnamese forces.

December 31, 1965 — U.S. forces in Vietnam totaled 185,300.

January 31, 1966 — Bombing of North Vietnam resumed after a 37-day pause.

April 12, 1966 — B-52s from Guam bombed North Vietnam for the first time.

October 24, 1966 — President Johnson met Premier Ky and leaders of five other nations involved in the war and pledged a 4-point "Declaration of Peace."

December 31, 1966 — U.S. forces in Vietnam totaled 185,300.

August 3, 1967 — President Johnson announced an escalation of troops and requested a 10 percent income tax surcharge to finance the war.

September 3, 1967 — General Nguyen Van Thieu was elected president of South Vietnam with 35 percent of the vote.

December 31, 1967	U.S. forces in Vietnam totaled 465,600 and those killed in combat totaled 9,378 for the year.
January 30, 1968	The month-long Tet Offensive erupted throughout South Vietnam, raising questions about the capacity of U.S. military forces to end the war.
February 24, 1968	The royal palace at Hue was recaptured by Marines and South Vietnamese troops after 25 days of struggle.
March 16, 1968	The My Lai massacre took place, killing at least 450 unarmed South Vietnamese.
March 31, 1968	President Johnson ordered a partial halt in the bombing of the North and announced that he would not seek reelection.
April 6, 1968	Relief forces arrived at Khe Sanh, ending 77-day siege of the Marine combat base.
May 13, 1968	Delegates from the U.S. and North Vietnam held their first formal peace meeting in Paris.
October 31, 1968	President Johnson announced a cessation of all bombing of North Vietnam.
November 1, 1968	Hanoi announced that the Paris peace talks would be expanded to include South Vietnam and the National Liberation Front, but Thieu refused to participate.
December 31, 1968	U.S. forces in Vietnam totaled 536,000 and those killed in combat totaled 14,592 for the year.
March 1969	President Nixon secretly authorized bombing raids over Cambodia.
May 12, 1969	Communists launched some 200 attacks against military and civilian targets.
June 8, 1969	President Nixon announced the first U.S. troop withdrawal.
October 4, 1969	According to the Gallup Poll, 58 percent of the American public believed the war was a mistake.
December 31, 1969	U.S. forces in Vietnam totaled 475,000 and those killed in combat totaled 9,414 for the year.

March 27, 1970	South Vietnamese forces, supported by U.S. helicopters, attacked Communist camps across the Cambodian border.
May 1970	Demonstrations opposing the Cambodian bombing took place on U.S. college campuses. The protest intensified after National Guardsmen killed four students at Kent State University.
December 1970	The U.S. Congress repealed the Tonkin Gulf Resolution and approved an amendment barring U.S. military personnel from Cambodia.
December 31, 1970	U.S. forces in Vietnam totaled 334,600.
February 8, 1971	South Vietnamese forces invaded Laos to interdict North Vietnamese supply lines.
June 13, 1971	The *New York Times* began releasing the "Pentagon Papers," a study of U.S. involvement in Indochina.
December 1971	U.S. planes staged heavy bombing raids over the North.
December 31, 1971	U.S. forces in Vietnam totaled 156,800.
January 25, 1972	President Nixon revealed that Henry Kissinger, his national security advisor, had been conducting secret Paris peace talks since August 1969.
March 30, 1972	North Vietnamese forces launched an offensive against South Vietnamese bases throughout the country.
April 16, 1972	B-52s resumed bombing raids around Hanoi and Haiphong.
May 8, 1972	President Nixon ordered the mining of Haiphong and other North Vietnamese harbors.
August 12, 1972	The last American ground troops left South Vietnam; airmen and support personnel remained.
October 26, 1972	Kissinger announced that "peace is at hand."
November 7, 1972	President Nixon was reelected. His opponent, Senator George McGovern, had offered a plan to end all bombing and withdrawal of all forces.

December 18, 1972	President Nixon ordered resumption of full bombing and mining of North Vietnam.
December 31, 1972	U.S. forces in Vietnam totaled 24,200.
January 23, 1973	Secretary of State Kissinger and North Vietnamese negotiator Le Duc Tho initiated an agreement to end the war and provide for the release of POWs.
January 27, 1973	A cease-fire began.
April 1, 1973	The last American POW arrived at Clark Air Force Base.
January 4, 1974	President Thieu announced that the war in South Vietnam had resumed.
April 17, 1975	Phnom Penh fell to Communist insurgents.
April 30, 1975	North Vietnamese troops entered Saigon while the remaining Americans were evacuated.
March 26, 1976	Kissinger announced that the U.S. was prepared to normalize relations with Hanoi.

 **Glossary**

AIT advanced infantry training, which usually follows basic training for enlisted personnel.

AK an AK-47.

AK-47 a Soviet-made assault rifle, copied by the Chinese and used by the Communist forces in Vietnam.

Amtrac amphibious armored vehicle used by Marines to transport troops and supplies.

APC armored personnel carrier.

article 15 non-judical punishment, meted out by an officer to enlisted personnel.

ARVN the Army of the Republic of Vietnam or the South Vietnamese Army.

AWOL absent without leave.

B-40 rocket-propelled grenade launcher used by Communist forces.

BAR Browning automatic rifle.

BCD bad conduct discharge.

BK amputee below-the-knee amputation of the leg.

Charlie the Viet Cong, short for the phonetic representation Victor Charlie.

CIB combat infantryman's badge, representing actual time in combat.

CID criminal investigation division.

chieu hoi surrender program, aimed at Communist soldiers.

Cobra the AH-1G attack helicopter.

connex a large metal box used for shipping and storage.

CP command post.

cyclo a motorized three-wheel passenger conveyance.

di di mau move quickly.

DMZ demilitarized zone separating North and South Vietnam at the 17th Parallel.

eagle flights large air assault of helicopters.

EM enlisted man.

GED general education diploma, equivalent of a high school education.

JAG judge advocate general, the legal department of the armed services.

KIA killed in action.

KP kitchen police.

LURP long range reconnaissance patrol.

LZ landing zone.

M-16 American-made assault rifle.

M-60 American-made machine gun.

Mach the speed of sound.

mama san female Vietnamese, usually older, child-bearing woman.

medcap Medical Civic Action Program.

medevac medical evacuation by helicopter.

MP military police.

mpc military pay certificates, used in lieu of American green currency in war zones to discourage black marketeering.

NCO non-commissioned officer.

Nung Chinese tribal troops found in the highlands of North Vietnam.

NVA the North Vietnamese Army.

Phoenix Program U.S. program aimed at Communist subversion.

platoon   approximately 45 men belonging to a company.
profile   a description of medical problems during military service.
purple out-zone   emergency evacuation.
quad-60   four .60 caliber machine guns mounted as one unit.
rabbits   white American soldiers, according to black vernacular.
RPG   rocket propelled grenade.
ROK   the Army of the Republic of Korea or the South Korean Army.
SAM   Soviet-made surface-to-air missile.
SEAL   highly trained Navy special warfare team members.
search and destroy   offensive operations designed to destroy enemy forces without maintaining holding actions.
slicks   Huey helicopters used to lift troops or cargo.
Tet   the Chinese and Vietnamese lunar new year.
track   GI slang expression for an APC.
USAID   United States Agency for International Development.
USO   United Service Organizations.
VC   the Viet Cong or members of the Communist insurgency in South Vietnam, the National Liberation Front.
white mice   South Vietnamese police.
the World   the United States; home.